CONSTITUTIONAL DEVELOPMENTS IN THE POST-COLONIAL STATE OF SIERRA-LEONE 1961-1984

Sheikh Batu Daramy

African Studies
Volume 30

The Edwin Mellen Press
Lewiston/Queenston/Lampeter

Library of Congress Cataloging-in-Publication Data

Daramy, Sheikh Batu, 1924-
    Constitutional developments in the post-colonial state of Sierra
-Leone, 1961-1984 / Sheikh Batu Daramy.
        p.   cm. -- (African studies ;   30)
    Includes bibliographical references and index.
    ISBN 0-7734-9290-9
    1. Sierra Leone--Politics and government--1961- 2. Sierra Leone-
-Constitutional history. I. Title. II. Series: African studies
(Lewiston,N.Y.) ; 30.
JQ3121.A2D37 1993
966.4'04--dc20   93-14707
                                                                      CIP

This is volume 30 in the continuing series
African Studies
Volume 30 ISBN 0-7734-9290-9
AS Series ISBN 0-88946-175-9

JQ
3121
.A2
D37
1993

A CIP catalog record for this book
is available from the British Library.

The Edwin Mellen Press   The Edwin Mellen Press
       Box 450   Box 67
   Lewiston, New York   Queenston, Ontario
      USA 14092   CANADA L0S 1L0

                    Edwin Mellen Press, Ltd.
                    Lampeter, Dyfed, Wales
                 UNITED KINGDOM SA48 7DY

              Printed in the United States of America

Dedicated

to

Hadja Hawa Daramy

For freedom, we know, is a thing we have to conquer afresh for ourselves, everyday, like love; and we are always losing freedom, just as we are always losing love, because, after each victory, we think we can now settle down and enjoy it without further struggle....

The battle of freedom is never done, and the field never quiet.

Henry W. Nevinson,
Essays in Freedom, p. xvi.

The great question is to discover not what governments prescribe, but what they ought to prescribe; for no prescription is valid against the conscience of mankind.

Lord Acton,
History of Freedom, p. 24.

Those who would deny freedom to others deserve it not for themselves, and under a just God, cannot long retain it.

Abraham Lincoln 1859.

Birth is never easy, and those who are the midwives in its attendance are never the inflictors of the pain which have accompanied their labour. Their work is to help bring forth that which is new. The pain is caused by the process through which the new comes into being. Such is the law of nature and such is the law of history.

Dr. James E. Cheek
President
Howard University

Address delivered at Howard University's 102nd Convocation

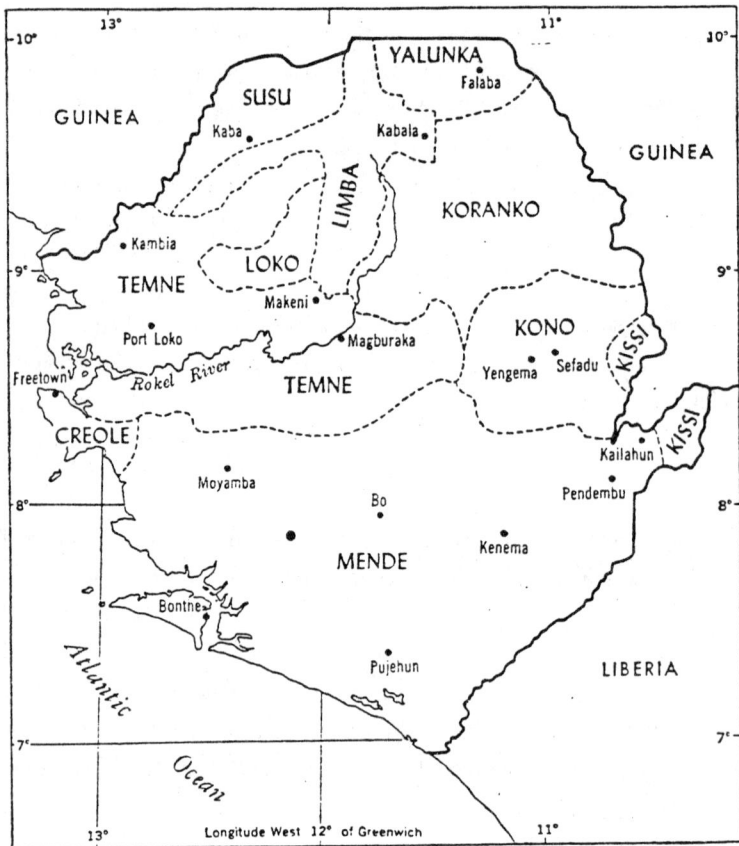

Map of Sierra Leone

TABLE OF CONTENTS

Part III - Forever and Ever

Preface

The Republic of Sierra Leone is in West Africa. Africa was only part of a grand conspiracy by the European nations to conquer and to subjugate non- European races, for the systematic exploitation of their vassals. Imperialism was the epitome of that grand conspiracy. What began as a general scramble for colonies, was institutionalised at the Berlin Conference in 1884. From then onwards, imperialism and colonialism became global phenomena with uniform and concerted objectives which permeated the economic, social and cultural fabric of the colonies and their peoples. They sapped the marrow from the bones of the vanquished until the latter revolted, as they could bear the yoke no longer.

Before the advent of foreigners, there were well flourishing empires in Africa. European invaders exported 40 to 50 million[1] Africans from their homelands, destroyed or fragmented empires in Africa. They established colonies for the exports of their surplus manufactured goods, and exported the raw materials of the colonies to the factories of Europe, while the art treasures of the colonies were used to establish and expand the British Museum, the Louvre in Paris, and other museums in Europe. While Europe prospered, the colonies stagnated and their economies decayed progressively.

Before the Second World War, only three countries in Africa were independent, namely, Abyssinia (now Ethiopia), Egypt and Liberia. In thirty-nine years after the capitulation of Japan, Italy and Germany, only one colony remains in Africa – Namibia. It is hoped that the centuries of African exploitation by Europeans has been halted, at least in its vicious forms. It might be asked legitimately therefore, what progress, political, economic, and social have the liberated Africans made, and more urgently, Quo vadis Africa? Have the African workers and peasants benefited from government 'of the people, by the people, and for the people?'

One of the arguments advanced by imperialists against independence was, that since the mass of the people were illiterate, if they were granted independence, only a handful of educated middle-class Africans would benefit from it. Since they had no examples to go by, because Africans had been deprived of their freedoms for centuries, and human memory is so short, they must have based their arguments on European experience. In Europe, without exception, the lords of the manor exploited the serfs who were virtually slaves. The industrial revolution intensified this exploitation by reducing the farm workers who had been drawn into the machine orbit, into proletariats, or factory workers. In summary, while the bourgeoisie fought the lord of the manor, the proletariats fought the bourgeoisie.

The history of working-class movement in Africa and elsewhere, shows that it was the African elite who organized the workers into trade unions, to improve the conditions of employment of their brothers in the European factories, mines, plantations, firms, in the colonies. In Sierra Leone, men like Siaka Stevens, Marcus Grant, George Thomas, H. N. Georgestone, Komba Kono, were actively involved. In Ghana, John Tetegah, was the main figure; in Tanganyika (now Tanzania) Rashidi Kawawa (now Vice-President); in Kenya-Tom Mboya was the leading unionist. These were dedicated trade unionists who toiled day and night in the jungles of Africa against the employers and the governments, in order to improve the working conditions of their brothers and sisters.

They were not the only freedom fighters, but they were also politically involved and were always in the firing line. In the early stages of the labour struggle, they were hounded from their homes by the colonial police force for daring to challenge the status quo of imperialism. Outstanding though they were, there were other Africans who fought gallant battles against imperialism. The African middle-class elite, (politicians, lawyers, doctors, businessmen, civil servants and traders) all joined in the nationalist struggle. Most of them formed political parties, while others were indomitable and uncompromising pamphleteers who were constantly at the heels of the wolves. They criticised forced labour, low wages, unsanitary conditions in the work places, child labour, low levels of education. As in every country, it is always the middle-class who lead the lower-class to revolt against despotism. They were dedicated men and women who saw no immediate results in their tasks, yet fought on relentlessly, until the battle was won. In the words of Amilcar Cabral,

> On one side the petite-bourgeoisie is the victim of frequent if not daily humiliation by the foreigner, and on the other side it is aware of the injustice to which the masses are subjected and of their resistance and spirit of rebellion. Hence, arises the apparent paradox of colonial domination; it is from the indigenous petite-bourgeoisie, a social class which grows from colonialism itself, that arise the first important steps towards mobilizing and organizing the masses for the struggle against the colonial power.

Now then by the nature of things, because of their leadership role against colonialism, they negotiated the terms of independence on behalf of the masses. The mantle of government was therefore, taken over by them.

After centuries of colonial rule, the people of Africa intensified their struggle against foreign domination during and immediately after the Second World War. The imperialists who seemed to have an inexhaustible store of excuses for not granting independence to their subjects countered, that, good government is better than self-government. The reply was, that it is better for people to exploit and repress themselves, than for foreigners to deprive them of their inalienable right to self-determination.

Valid though these nationalist sentiments might be, the Second World War brought dramatic improvements in colonial policy. But for their unmitigating and supercilious arrogance, they might have delayed the complete capitulation of their empires. For instance, General de Gaulle was able by his personality and charisma, to delay complete self-government in the French African Empire, with the exception of Guinea. That he was able to brow-beat Leopold Senghor and Houphouet Boigny, two outstanding personalities and former cabinet ministers in the French Government, underscores this point.

Have the misgivings and scepticisms for improvements in the future disappeared? Are the Africans still of the view that self-government is better than the Europeans' so-called good government?

First, colonial governments were not benevolent. Second, sooner or later Africans would have had to govern themselves, for good or evil. Government is a political experiment which cannot be practised on paper or in the universities. The latter can only theorise. The art would have to be practised. By trial and error, Africans will evolve democratic forms of government along the patterns of Westminster.

It has been a long up-hill haul. The euphoria of freedom has vanished from the continent. Not one after the other, but at times in rapid succession or simultaneously, despots of a vicious kind have emerged like mushroom. The wolves have shed their sheep's clothing, laying bare the venom of their fangs, ready to pulverise any one who attempts to challenge their authority. That there is any difference between African despots and their colonial predecessors, it is hard to say. That is to say, in so far as it is odious to compare two evils. The pathetic and inevitable tragedy about African despots, is that, they cannot escape the wrath of Africa; whereas, the imperialist Europeans, left no legal issues to account for the iniquities of their fathers.

Because of his eccentricities, it was fashionable to stigmatise Idi Amin Dada of Uganda as the most capricious despot in Africa, or to stigmatise Bokassa as a scare-crow, and jester. There is a plethora of despots in Africa, some of whom would put Idi Amin to shame and make him appear like an angel. President Dr. Siaka Stevens of Sierra Leone in West Africa, is without peer.

When Sierra Leone became independent in 1961, there were two political parties, namely, The Sierra Leone Peoples Party (SLPP) and The All Peoples Congress Party (APC) in Parliament. The former formed the Government, while the latter became the Opposition, led by Sir Milton Margai and Siaka Stevens, respectively. On the death of Sir Milton, his brother Albert Margai, became Prime Minister. When the SLPP proposed a one-party system, Dr. Raymon Sarif Easmon, a medical practitioner, wrote articles against the proposal. I arranged a meeting between him and Sir

Albert, chaired by Reverend Professor Harry Sawyer, then Acting Vice-Chancellor of the University of Sierra Leone, to reach some rapprochement. They agreed a cooling-off period, until the Sierra Leone Peoples Party eventually abandoned the one-party proposal.

Yet, as soon as Siaka Stevens became Prime Minister, he broke agreements reached with the SLPP Opposition, declared a state of emergency and unleashed a reign of terror unknown in the annals of modern Sierra Leone. He arrested Opposition Members of Parliament and persons associated with the Sierra Leone Peoples Party, directly or indirectly, and detained them without trial; charged seventeen of them (including me), with treason, treason felony and misprision of treason, the first treason trial in the history of Sierra Leone. He declared a republic immorally, and introduced the one-party system by a fraudulent referendum which was rigged.

This book is written by a victim of Siaka Stevens' reign of terror. I was one of the 17 persons who were arrested on the 28th of May 1968, and detained at Pademba Road Prison without charge, minutes after his notorious 'subversive elements' broadcast. Three weeks later, following a writ of *habeas corpus* by one of the detainees, Berthan Macaulay Q. C., and former Attorney General, we were charged with treason, treason felony and misprision of treason. Ten of us were convicted of treason and sentenced to be hanged, while two (including the author) were convicted of treason felony, and sentenced to 7 years' imprisonment, with hard labour. For doing what, I have always asked myself? We appealed, won, were re-arrested, and re-detained. Seven of us were released six months later in October 1971, after 3½ years in detention and gaol, while the rest were released later. Although we were political prisoners we were treated worse than common criminals, in compliance with "orders from above", as we were constantly told by the Director of Prison.

The treason trial was prosecuted by Cyril Rogers-Wright, described by Gershon Collier former Sierra Leone Ambassador to the United Nations and former Chief Justice of Sierra Leone, as "a notorious criminal lawyer (later disbarred in a case presided over by the then Chief Justice Bairamian) who also specialised in flamboyant and dishonest practices to gain court victories."[2]

The late Cyril Rogers-Wright was given the task of prosecuting us by Siaka Stevens, usurping the functions of the Solicitor General (as the Attorney General was one of the accused in the treason trial) who, together with his officers, took orders from him. The distressing irony about this immoral and unconventional practice was the fact that, as the leader of the All Peoples Congress Party, Siaka Stevens had in 1961 published a document in London entitled "Sierra Leone's forthcoming Independence-Ponder", on behalf of the APC Working Committee, stating, *inter alia*, that:

> Worse still, the inclusion in the Coalition of an individual who was twice suspended from practice as a lawyer for dishonest practices, and was on the third occasion debarred altogether, has made many people wonder whether this is the standard of honesty and integrity which is to be set for independence....

The above is an extract from the quotation culled from *Freedom* Vol. 1 No. 38 of July, 1969. The complete quotation is at Part 1 Chapter 6 (b) herein.

The lawyer referred to was Cyril Rogers-Wright. After he was disbarred by Chief Justice Bairamian, Cyril Rogers-Wright appealed to the West African Court of Appeal, but lost. He pursued his case to the Judicial Committee of the Privy Council in London, and again lost. Later, he was also disbarred by his Inns of Court in London. When he started prosecuting us, Berthan Macaulay Q. C., former Attorney General, threatened to challenge his *locus standi* in a court of law. Mr. Siaka Stevens hurriedly bulldozed Parliament into passing a law allowing Cyril Rogers-Wright to practise law again in the Supreme Court of Sierra Leone. And so, a member of the Commonwealth overruled, not only the Inns of Court, which conferred the Barrister's Degree on him, but a Committee of the House of Lords. One can only conclude that Stevens' plan was to secure our convictions by hook or by crook, and Cyril Rogers-Wright was the most qualified architect of such diabolical scheme. And so, Cyril Rogers-Wright became the All Peoples Congress Party prosecutor at large. We shall give additional evidence later to show that Siaka Stevens was determined to secure our convictions at all cost.

These incidents occurred only 30 days after he became Prime Minister of Sierra Leone. What "standard of honesty and integrity" to quote Siaka Stevens, was Siaka Stevens now setting after independence? Furthermore, that Cyril Rogers-Wright, a legally discredited lawyer who had been disbarred by the House of Lords and his name struck off his Inns of Court, could have been legislated into practicing law in Sierra Leone without the usual hue and cry of corruption and immorality for which the Sierra Leone elite are renown, is clearly beyond explanation. All these things and more have happened since Siaka Stevens became Prime Minister of Sierra Leone. We shall continue the summary of the catalogue of the All Peoples Congress Party records as led by Siaka Stevens.

Brigadier Andrew Juxon-Smith was charged with treason, was convicted and sentenced to 7 years imprisonment. Brigadier John Bangura who trained the APC guerrillas in Guinea, was with four senior army officers, charged with treason. He, Colonel Farrah Jawara, and Captain Korlu Gbonda were convicted and executed. Brigadier David Lansana, Dr. Mohamed Forna, a former medical practitioner and medical colonel of Siaka Stevens' guerrilla army in training in Guinea, former Minister of Finance in the APC Government; Ibrahim Taqui (his former Minister of Information and Broadcasting) were similarly charged with treason. They, and 6 others were executed. Mr. Siaka Stevens detained Dr. John Karefa-Smart (MD), former Deputy Director of the World Health Organisation; detained Dr. Raymon Sarif Easmon (MD), one of Africa's most brilliant politico-medical practitioners who is also renown for his independent, indomitable and uncompromising fight for democracy. He belongs to a generation that is ill-equipped to appreciate that criticism does not imply hostility, and that the right to dissent is an essential ingredient of a democratic system.

Since the All Peoples Congress Party came to power in Sierra Leone, there has been a perpetual state of emergency. Hundreds of people have been executed, assassinated in cold blood, detained illegally without trial. Some of the executions have been as a result of court proceedings which most people allege were interfered with and orchestrated by Siaka Stevens. For example, Dr. Easmon was arrested following a publication that he had learned that President Siaka Stevens was about to pervert the Appeal Court in the first treason trial to reject our appeals. He had an interview with the President protesting such action, if it were true. The President denied the allegations, in characteristic style. He then advised him to publish a denial of the allegations, to allay the suspicions of the populace. The President refused. Thereupon, he published the interview he had had with the President. He was immediately arrested and detained.

The tragedy in Sierra Leone is that some intellectuals are alleged to be misleading Siaka Stevens by giving him wrong legal advice. For instance, as a layman, he must have sought legal advice, before embarking on the republican and one-party constitutions, or legislating to reinstate a disbarred lawyer. Civil servants are brought into the picture at the execution stage.

The Honourable Salia Jusu Sheriff, the then leader of the Opposition Sierra Leone Peoples Party, was disillusioned with Sierra Leone's intellectuals. As reported in an issue of West Africa:

> Mr. Jusu Sheriff spoke indignantly about the Speaker's ruling that he was not the official leader of the Opposition and about attempts to make his followers sit on the government benches. He also said; 'I have become more and more disillusioned with people with an intellectual background....I cannot see how they sit down in Parliament and support the Speaker in these sort of rulings.' Lawyers seemed nowadays to act only for money. Academics were doing nothing and the University had become only 'special source of ambassadors.'[3]

The one-party fraud is becoming infectious as it assumes epidemic proportions in the continent of Africa. Its protagonists weave all sorts of spurious arguments that make colonial double-standards look like scientific theories.

The change of government in Sierra Leone led to incalculable harm to the people and the prestige of Sierra Leone abroad. It has taught us all a lesson. It is hoped that posterity would learn from this lesson. Change for the sake of change, should not be the criterion in political evolution. Change is desirable, only if it is necessary, as it is long over-due for Siaka Stevens and his All Peoples Congress Party to resign, since it is quite clear that they are incapable of governing a country. These charges will be examined in detail in this book.

President Siaka Stevens and his SPC cohorts inherited from Sir Albert Margai and his SLPP stalwarts, a country, rooted in the best traditions of the fear of God, respect for the rule of law, and all the fundamental rights of the citizens as entrenched in the Constitution. By hook or by crook, Stevens and the APC and their clandestine advisers the vicars of Bray, et al, systematically eroded all these freedoms, and today, people live in fear of their shadows, not knowing how soon they would be picked up by the Internal Security Unit. These violations and more, will be examined in this book to show how Siaka Stevens endeavoured to pervert the courts by creating a psychological atmosphere in the community that we were subversive elements. It is hoped that the experience of Sierra Leone over the past sixteen years, of APC misrule, would disillusion Africans elsewhere and remind us all that when we pointed our fingers at Idi Amin, four of our fingers were pointing at us.

It is the constitutional right of the electorate to vote for the party of their choice. After 6 years of SLPP rule, the people of Sierra Leone were entitled to a change of government, so long as the process of change was by democratic means and the people were satisfied that a change was necessary. Once there had been a change of government, the government should be allowed to govern, while the opposition permitted to oppose in a constitutional manner. When, however, a change of government is accompanied by harassment of the opposition and, what is more, flagrant perversion of the judicial system, then democracy is in peril. That was what happened in Sierra Leone when the SPC Government seized power from the mouth of guns.

It has been a concatenation of unfortunate circumstances which have brought Sierra Leone to the brink of disaster. It is hoped that when Sierra Leone regains its freedom, it would be less gullible to the capricious intrigues of ill-disposed politicians, and self-appointed advisers.

Some notes have been added to the Postscript stating that when President Siaka Probyn Stevens handed over to Dr. Joseph Saidu Momoh on the 28th November, 1985, Sierra Leoneans were jubilant that a regime of unprecedented barbarism had come to an end, with the immediate return of freedom of the press.

Preface Notes

1.   King, Victor E.:   *The Unified Party System in Emerging Africa*, pamphlet published in Sierra Leone in the mid-1960's.

2.   Collier Gershon: *Sierra Leone. An experiment in democracy in an African Nation*, New York University Press, New York, 1970.

3.   *West Africa, May 22nd., 1978*. Published by the Proprietors, West Africa Publishing Company, Ltd., 653 Holborn Viaduct, London EC 1A2FD.

Acknowledgements

After 30 years service, I was retired from the Sierra Leone Civil Service in February, 1973.

I went to the United States of America. Through the help of our life long friends, Professor and Mrs. Harrison Tucker and our mutual friend, Mr. York Van Nixon, I got a job in the Budget Office, Howard University, Washington, D.C. as Budget Analyst, in September, 1973.

Hadja Hawa and I associate our family with thousands of Africans who have been granted refuge from political persecution in Africa, in expressing our sincere appreciation to the United States Government for their magnanimous hospitality. We also thank Howard University for providing me with suitable employment, particularly, Colonel Robert Wilson, the Personnel Director, of Howard University and his secretary, Mrs. Mildred Peters; Mrs. Dorothy Bayen, the Budget Director, and her successors, Mrs. Julia Feemster and Mr. George E. Miller.

The academic atmosphere in which I worked for 13 years, particularly, the lectures I attended in the Graduate School, The African Studies and Research Program, Howard University as a graduate student, have been most valuable to me in writing this book, for which I thank the Professors, particularly Professor Sulayman Nyang, for his valuable corrections to this book and for helping in its publication, and their supporting staff headed by Mrs. Ann Brown.

Sweet (indeed) are the uses of adversity which like a toad venomous, Wears yet a precious jewel in its head.

William Shakespeare

As deputy-clerk (in the dock) to Mrs. Margaret Macaulay, for Mr. Berthan Macaulay Q.C., a fellow prisoner in the dock during the treason trial, I had to listen carefully to his fertile legal submissions and arguments. In his cell, he went to great pains to explain some legal points and decided cases to me. I have tried to record what I understood. Therefore, I and not he, am accountable for any legal interpretations which I might have made in this book.

My father, Sergeant Foday Sarakulay was a very devout Muslim, and so was mama Wango. They brought us all in that noble and life-sustaining tradition. While I was at Pademba Road Prison, I realized to the fullest, the unqualified need for God in our lives. Kandeh Bureh, who acted several times as Prime Minister, is one of the finest human beings it has been my privilege to associate with. He took me in hand, and in 12 months, I became a far more, studious, ardent and practicing Muslim than I ever was in my 44 years.

Dr. Raymon Sarif Easmon, another great African who stood up against the colonial raj and was terminated from the service, challenged the Sierra Leone Peoples Party for daring to propose the introduction of one-party system, attacked President Siaka Stevens for reneging on his stand against the one-party, and for alleged attempts to pervert the Appeal Court Judges in our treason trial, for which he was detained at Pademba Road Prison by the said President Siaka Stevens. Dr. Easmon remains the leading bulwark against despotism in Sierra Leone and a brilliant role model on the continent of Africa. He is an indefatigable and uncompromising advocate of the multi-party system of government and therefore, a relentless and fearless fighter against the one-party system that seems to have permeated the African polity. I record my gratitude to him and Paramount Chief Julius Gulama for helping me to get a scholarship to the London School of Economics and Political Science.

I wish to record my appreciation to Africa Confidential and West Africa for the profuse quotations I made from their invaluable reports, and to the publishers of the journals and other authors that I have quoted. Finally, I am extremely grateful to Mrs. Shirley Adams, Mrs. Laura Anderson, and Miss Kathleen Bullen for typing this book and for their charming patience with a young writer.

Hadja Hawa continues to inspire us with her devotion to Allah. Nfatorma, Sheriff, Natorma, Sheikh, Jr., Ibrahim, Mariama, Mahawa have adjusted admirably in America. Mrs. Olabisi Daramy has added her quota to our resettlement. Although she is away in London, Kumba has always been a constant reminder that she and Bob care. But for the patience and understanding of my wife and our children during our sojourn in the USA, I would not have completed this book.

May Allah Bless you all
Sheikh Batu Daramy Ph.D.

PART I

NOW OR NEVER

INTRODUCTION

SITUATION

The Republic of Sierra Leone is situated on the West Coast of African, between the Republics of Guinea and Liberia. It is 10 degrees north of the Equator, and is 27,925 square miles, (72,325 sq. km.) with a population of 4 million, comprising of 18 tribes, namely, Bullon, Creole, Fullah, Kissi, Kono, Krim, Kuranko, Limba, Loko, Kroo, Maninka, Mende, Sarakulay, Sherbro, Susu, Temne, Vaii, Yalunka.

CLIMATE

There are two seasons in Sierra Leone; the rainy and dry seasons. The rainy season lasts from June to October, and the dry season from November to May. In the latter part of December and January, a cold, dry dust-ladden wind blows southwards from the Sahara Desert in the north over Sierra Leone, to the Atlantic Ocean. It is known as the harmattan.

EARLY EXPLORERS

Pedro da Cintra, a Portuguese navigator and his sailors were the first Europeans who visited Sierra Leone in 1474. He it was, who called it Sierra Lyona (Sierra Leone) or Lion Mountains.

Then followed the slave trade, beginning with John Hawkins in 1562. When Britain declared the slave trade illegal, the Act of Parliament provided that slaves who set foot on British soil, became free. Within a couple of years, hundreds of slaves found their way to England. The number increased year by year, and the English people were alarmed by the influx of Africans and African-Americans into the British Isles. Some of them were subjected to inhuman and brutal treatment. A classic example was the case of Jonathan Strong who was beaten so badly by his English master Granville Sharp, that he damaged his eye.

A lawsuit was filed against him. This case aroused the conscience of some English people who felt that, since Africans were not wanted in England, they should be sent away to a place where they could live like human beings. This movement was led by William Wilberforce. Through the efforts of Wilberforce, the first Africans and African-Americans and 70 white women, about 400 in all, set sail for West Africa.

BRITISH COLONY

In 1787, the first settlers were sent from England - 290 blackmen, 41 blackwomen, and 11 black children; together with 70 white women and 6 white children who were indigents rounded up from the streets of London....[1]

The ships arrived at the site which became known as "Freetown", a town for freed men, and in later years, became the capital of Sierra Leone. In 1808, the peninsula on which Freetown was located, became a Crown Colony. In 1866, a new constitution was drawn up unifying Sierra Leone, Gold Coast, Gambia and Nigeria with Freetown as Headquarters. In 1874, Gold Coast and Nigeria were separated from this unified control, and in 1889 the Gambia was separated from Sierra Leone.

The British Government's 'right' to colonise Sierra Leone after the Berlin Conference in 1884, which partitioned Africa among the European powers, was 'legalised' in the Foreign Jurisdiction Act of 1890. It authorised the British Crown to exercise "any jurisdiction claimed in a foreign country as if by right of cession or conquest." Britain extended its hegemony over the hinterland of the country and declared it a Protectorate in 1896, while the peninsula was called the Colony.

POLITICAL PARTIES

In April 1951, the Peoples Educational Protectorate Union which was formed to accelerate the educational advancement of Protectorate peoples, was re-christened, the Sierra Leone Peoples Party, a political organisation, to reflect the spirit of the times. It was led by a former medical officer, Dr. Milton Margai, a Mende.

The National Council of the Colony of Sierra Leone, was formed under the leadership of another medical practitioner, Dr. H.C. Bankole-Bright, as a counter-weight to the Protectorate Peoples' Party. This Party was the crowning point of the Creole struggle. In his book, Gershon Collier wrote:

> Not surprisingly, the Colony leaders strongly opposed the 1947 constitutional proposals. They saw in them a blatant attempt on the part of the British authorities to impose Protectorate leadership, since the new constitution gave so many more seats to the Protectorate and ensured for it a built-in majority....
>
> The Creoles of the Colony vehemently argued that 'illiterates' should not be allowed to be members of the same legislature as Colony members and use the majority thus acquired to legislate for them. In a spirited despatch to the Secretary of State for the Colonies, following a public meeting in Freetown in 1948, the Creoles disparaged the people of the Protectorate as 'foreigners' and stated gingerly that
>
>> 'a legislative Council in the Colony with a majority of foreigners, as British Protected Persons are in the Commonwealth, is contrary to the conception of British citizens. British citizens have the right that they shall be governed only by such persons as are of the same status as themselves. By the suggested set-up of Protectorate majority, persons who are not British subjects would be empowered to make legislation that may seriously affect the rights of British subjects.'
>
> ...The Protectorate leaders had also scathingly described the Colony Creoles as...
>
>> 'a handful of foreigners...that our forefathers had given shelter... who have no will to cooperate with us and imagine themselves to be our superiors because they are aping the Western mode of living and have never breathed the true spirit of independence.'[2]

From the onset, therefore, the SLPP and the NCCSL were diametrically opposed to each other. While the SLPP advocated outright independence based on one man one vote, the NCCSL maintained that independence should be granted to them, because they were more educated and therefore, more civilised than the Protectorate people, the bulk of whom, were illiterate tribesmen. As in the case of South Africa, they asked the British Government to grant them independence to govern the Protectorate people, or else that the colony should remain as a Colony and separated from the Protectorate. In the words of their leader, Dr. Bankole Bright, the peoples of the Protectorate and the Colony are like two mountains that can never meet.

The National Council of the Colony of Sierra Leone sent a delegation to Great Britain to petition Her Majesty the Queen, opposing independence for Sierra Leone. It comprised of Dr. Buck, a medical practitioner who had spent most of his life-time in England, and J.M. Rose, a journalist. Their petition was rejected by the British Government. Mr. J.M. Rose dropped anchor in London ever since.

There was a plethora of political parties during this decade. Early in 1950, the Kono people became dissatisfied with the poverty and relative underdeveloped state of their District, which produced the greater share of the country's revenue from diamonds. They formed the Kono Progressive Movement under the leadership of Paramount Chief Tamba Songu-Mbrewah, and merged with the Sierra Leone Progressive Independence Movement which was formed by Dr. Edward Blyden III, extramural lecturer at Fourah Bay College. Mr. I.T.A. Wallace-Johnson, one of the pioneers of nationalism in West Africa, formed the Radical Democratic Party.

In 1955, Cyril Rogers-Wright, a Creole lawyer, formed the United Progressive Party. Mr. Albert Margai, the first Protectorate lawyer, and Siaka Stevens, former General Secretary of the United Mine Workers Union, broke away from the Sierra Leone Peoples Party in 1957, and formed the Peoples National Party, which was ridiculed by the SLPP as, "pikin na pikin", (Creole-a child is a child).

CONSTITUTIONAL CONFERENCE

Dr. Milton Margai unified all the political parties in 1960 into the United National Front for the constitutional conference in London. Another problem arose during the negotiations in London when Siaka Stevens refused to sign the Sierra Leone Independence Constitution Instrument, because he alleged that it contained a clause allowing the British Government to maintain a naval base in Sierra Leone, and that there should be general elections before independence. Such a clause never in fact appeared in the final Order-in- Council, and no general elections were held before independence. On his arrival home, Siaka Stevens formed the All Peoples Congress Party. So that on independence on the 27th, April 1961, the SLPP formed the Government while the APC formed the Opposition in Parliament.

GENERAL ELECTIONS 1962

The SLPP won the 1962 General Elections by a land-slide majority, and the APC continued in Opposition with 16 members in a Parliament of 54 members. As time went on 3 APC members joined the SLPP. They were alleged to have been poached by the SLPP, thereby reducing the Opposition APC to 13 members.

General Elections were held in Sierra Leone in March, 1967. The Sierra Leone Peoples Party and the All Peoples Congress Party were dead heat at 32 each, of the Ordinary Members elected. The Governor-General invited the leaders of both Parties and suggested the formation of a coalition government in view of the tribalistic division which the elections results revealed. Before the meeting was held, the Governor-General appointed Siaka Stevens as Prime Minister. Details of the military interventions which followed are at Part 1 Chapter 5. The officers who staged the first coup d'etat, formed the National Reformation Council on the 23rd, March, 1967. They were overthrown by the junior army officers in April, 1968, and supervised the appointment of Siaka Stevens as Prime Minister.

HYPOTHESIS

The hypothesis of this book is, that, the policy of the All Peoples Congress Party Government, has been a betrayal of democratic government.

CONCEPTUAL FOCUS

The conceptual focus is democracy. President Siaka Stevens and his All Peoples Congress Party (APC) betrayed the confidence of Sierra Leoneans who voted for the APC in the 1967 general elections, by the undemocratic form of government which that Party has resorted to since assuming the reins of power in 1968. The main conceptual thrust therefore, is the indescribable manner in which democratic principles enshrined in the Independence Constitution have been flouted with reckless abandon. This glaring abuse of democracy would appear to be the general pattern in post-colonial Africa. We shall therefore, review briefly the concept democracy as the foundation of the charges against Siaka Stevens and his All Peoples Congress Party Government.

When the present leaders of Africa attended higher institutions of learning in Europe and America, in their political science studies, they learned about democracy, not that it was some strange political concept to them, but since they had been deprived of the fundamental foundations of their cultures by the imperialist countries, which had imposed their own systems of government on the African continent, they perforce had no choice but to begin afresh to learn what in fact was also at one time the underpinning of their African cultures.

Place and time would not permit a digression on the concept and practice of democracy in Africa before the advent of the Europeans with their pretensions to democracy which they abandoned as soon as they arrived in the colonies. Suffice it to say that it is infantile to ignore, as some Western political scientists do even today, highblown civilisations like Mali, Songhai, Ghana, Kanem Bornu that flourished to the heights to which they reached from the 14th century onwards. In this connection, John Strachey reminds us:

> Let us never forget that we are here concerned with the descendants of one of the major civilisations, the major

empires of the world. We all know, of course, that while we in Western Europe were sunk in our dark ages, the Caliphate of Baghdad was the centre of a civilisation stretching from the Euphrates to the Zambesi, to the Pyrenees.[3]

Since independence however, the rapidity with which African countries have deteriorated to the one-party dictatorships under various pretexts has been staggering. What is sad about this falsification of democracy, whatever name it assumes, is the blatant fabrications that have been woven to justify the one-party or single-party systems. Furthermore, it has become fashionable among Africans to attach all kinds of metaphysical interpretations to democracy, which would tend to lend some academic support to the new definitions of democracy. The leading parts which some of them played in the nationalist struggle, seem to be the credential to African expertise. For example:

> The immortality of Sekou Toure still depends on his great act of defiance in 1958, when, despite all pressures to the contrary, he encouraged his people to vote a massive "no" in the referendum of de Gaulle which would have set up a Franco-African community conferring a state of semi-independence on the participating countries. Sekou Toure's resistance, although carried out alone, cracked the image of the community idea and ensured that full independence followed for all of what was then French Africa as surely as night follows day.[4]

Regrettably however, once in power, power tended to corrupt them absolutely. Overnight, some of them became new messiahs with incontestable right to tell the people of Africa what the customs of their ancestors were. Again, when some of them introduced the one-party or single-party system of government their admirers could not readily unveil the myth of the so-called 'one-party democracy' - a palpable contradiction.

Centuries of colonial exploitation had made the Africans repulsive of any other forms of dictatorship, particularly from their kith and kin. And so when some of these leaders began creating impregnable walls around themselves through the one-party systems, and by false pretenses, even the peasants became completely disillusioned, disheartened and frustrated. When therefore, the government began to introduce collectivisation, however well meaning the authorities might have been, the suspicions which they had aroused in the minds of the people, made them disinterested in the 'new methods.'

To further complicate the situation, the party stalwarts who were sent to implement some of these new policies were more concerned about making themselves the new administrators of Africa, that they antagonised the peasants and more particularly, they fell foul of the seasoned civil servants who because of their training and experience, knew more about the idiosyncrasies of their people than the party men. The latter were preoccupied with establishing the one-party by reciting the most atrocious gibberish. All else was subordinated to the whims and caprices of party zealots with primary school education, to explain controversial political doctrines to civil servants who were graduates in political science.

And so the peasants revolt, and the civil servants become disenchanted and indifferent to the new methods. Some of them might be genuinely sympathetic to the new order. But they refused to be bulldozed into interpreting half-baked ideological cliches. At party headquarters, reports are made that the chiefs are sabotaging the efforts of the party in the country, with the aid and support of the civil servants who do not want to change with the times. Decrees are hastily passed through cabinet abolishing the post of paramount chief, and bringing the civil service under the control of the party, as was done by Sekou Toure in Guinea.

Chieftaincy is a sacred institution through which the Europeans ruled Africa. In Nigeria, where it was perfected by Lord Luggard, it was called Indirect Rule. That is to say, rule through the traditional chiefs. This practice soon became the pattern in other British colonies. Some countries retained the position of chiefs in the independence constitution, as in Sierra Leone. In Guinea, Sekou Toure abolished paramount chieftaincy. That was when his troubles began, and never ceased until his death. The chiefs were and still are the embodiment of the African customary practices which are at par with other customs and cultures. To derogate them in place of an alien culture is to perpetuate European culture, even with its contradictions.

Second, the new policy of bringing the civil service under the control of the political party, which is made of people who have no training in administration, and whose only value is their loyalty to the political party, is to say the least the saddest error which Sekou Toure made in Guinea. Siaka Stevens is now regretting the one-party dictatorship which he has foisted on the people through his Internal (In) Security Unit. During the independence movement to expel the imperialists, civil servants and all were coopted secretly into the nationalist movement. But once the battle had been won, it was of the utmost importance, that the civil service should have been allowed to develop along the traditional line of independence of the political parties, although as individuals they were free to join parties of their choice.

The disregard and in some cases active disruption of well tried administrative practices elsewhere led to the ludicrous redefinitions of democracy by persons who have not taken the pains to study it, or who having done so, but for personal reasons, now choose to misinterpret it. Since the variable factors listed below constituted the numerous ways in which democracy was perverted in Sierra Leone, we shall devote a few pages to an analytical discussion of this concept.

DEFINITION OF DEMOCRACY

In his book, *The Democratic Theory*, Giovanni Sartori of the University of Florence, objects to a definition, because (a) "It is dangerous to define, *Omnis definitio est periculosa*," as definitions tend to freeze language, and (b) scholars disagree on definitions.[5] He then went on to give the historical development of democracy from the Greek city state. Democracy is derived from two Greek words, *demos*, and *kratos*, meaning, people and rule, respectively. That is, rule by the people.

In ancient Greece, all the people met and by a method of majority rule decided to govern the state directly. This was known as direct democracy. Where they elected people to do the job of governing on their behalf, it was known as representative democracy. It must be noted that direct democracy as defined above was possible because the city state was not larger than 10,000 inhabitants. Representative democracy was substituted for direct democracy as the state grew bigger and bigger. Women and slaves were barred from political participation. Elections must be free, other-wise the electors are not responsible to the electorate, and hence no representative democracy exists in such a state. In other words, as Giovanni Sartori puts it, the *demos* must precede *kratos*.[6]

We have come a long way from direct to representative democracy. By the latter, expediency dictates that we elect some members of the *demos* to govern us. It is in this sense that Sartori differentiates between ideals and practice. It is wrong, he says, for us to expect democracy to correspond to its prescriptive requisites.

> Since a prescriptive definition is not an existential definition, it is true *ex hypothesi* that what is prescribed does not exist.[7]

The perfectionist's error equates prescription to reality. What *ought* to be is not the same as what *is*. For instance, "a governed democracy is still a democracy."[8] Quoting H.D. Laswell, he adds

> Government is always government by the few....since a society may be democratic and express itself through a small leadership. The key question turns on accountability.[9]

Leadership in a democracy refers to a minority, an inner circle. Democracy is therefore, leadership by a few and the many follow. Herodotus emphasized this point and the legal aspect as Roland Pennock quotes him as defining democracy as

> a society in which 'equality before the law' prevails and where the holder of political office 'is answerable for what he does.'[10]

In the *Logic of Democracy*, Thomas Landon Thorson laid down criteria governing a democracy. These include, political parties that are freely elected at ascertainable intervals, adult suffrage and free elections, majority party to form a government and minorities should be free to associate into an opposition party. So that plurality of parties is essential to democracy.[11]

From the foregoing definitions of democracy it is clear that the central characteristics of this concept are liberty (i.e. freedom), and equality.

AFRICAN DEMOCRACY

It was fashionable for Western academics to stigmatise Africa as being so backward, primitive and illiterate that even W.G.F. Hegel wrote that, "Africa is no historical part of the world; it has no movement and development to exhibit."[12] Sir Hugh Trevor-Roper, the Regius Professor of Modern History at Oxford University echoed this falsehood in the second half of the 20th century that

> Maybe in the future there will be some African history, but at the moment there is none.... There is only the history of Europeans in Africa.... The rest is darkness, and darkness is not a subject of history.[13]

Now according to archaeological and anthropological evidence,

> recent discoveries show that the priest of the African state of Meroe invented an alphabet toward the third century B.C....other wholly African- invented scripts such as the recently unveiled Mandingo, indicate the extent of our previous ignorance,....Books on all subjects were available, written in both Mandingo and Arabic;....[14]

These self-same archaeological and anthropological findings show that

> Indians in the West Indies told Columbus that they had obtained gold from black men who had come from across the sea. Amerigo Vespucci claims to have witnessed the return of these sailors to Africa when he was in mid-ocean.[15]

There were black settlements in the New World in the fifteenth and sixteenth centuries long before the Pilgrim Fathers set sail from Plymouth in 1620. Dr. Chancellor Williams also writes that

> an ancient system of democracy (existing before Greece) evolved from a continent-wide constitution that governed the whole African people as a single race. This all-important finding was arrived at by comparative studies of African customary laws in every region of the continent. The Europeans were confronted with a real social democracy that existed long before the terms "socialism" and "democracy" were invented in the West.[16]

It was therefore, startling to him, as he sat at the lecture at Oxford, on the History of Colonialism in Africa, to hear Dr. Madden

> lecture how difficult - and even impossible - it was to rule Africans in view of their "wild and most primitive system of democracy."

When Lord Luggard introduced Indirect Rule in Northern Nigeria this "primitive African democracy had to be destroyed"....[17]

"Government of the people, by the people, for the people," was Abraham Lincoln's definition of democracy, which is not foreign to Africa. According to Chancellor Williams,

> traditional political system...was already highly - and efficiently organized before any Europeans came - organized with each village and town under a chief (called *mani*), each district under a *mani*, and each of the six major provinces that made up the kingdom was under the administration of a governor, also bearing the title of mani. (Italics supplied)[18]

Before the impact of Europeans, there were factions, which were similar to multiparty political systems but which centered around leading warrior families. When a king died, if he was a popular and progressive ruler, his eldest son became the leading contender for his post. There were no entrenched hereditary successions, as in Europe.

A meeting of the elders was held to arrange for an election, which was conducted by "open voting" and not by "secret ballot" which was introduced by Europeans with all its attendant corruption. Other prominent warrior families invariably contested the election. At the election, the people voted openly by grouping behind their respective candidates. The elders acted as returning officers and adjudicated disputes. The candidate who had the largest number of supporters became the next king.

During the heat of the nationalist movement, prominent Africans spoke and wrote extensively on the subject of democracy. For example, Dr. Nnamdi Azikiwe, former governor-general of Nigeria wrote that

> Democracy is government by discussion, based on the consent of the governed, whose will is collectively expressed by the majority of the duly accredited representatives of an electorate

that is based on a universal adult suffrage, and votes by secret ballot at periodic elections.[19]

What was "open voting" in traditional Africa, now became secret.

Chief Obafemi Awolowo, former leader of the opposition party in the parliament of Nigeria, is another prominent African who speaks and writes extensively on this subject.

> In a democracy, the government must rule with the consent of the governed. The governed are inalienably entitled at periodic intervals to give this consent to the same or a different set of people who form the government. The expression of such consent must be free and unfettered, and must on no account be stultified or rigged. Furthermore, the consent must never be obtained by duress, threat or intimidation, undue influence or fraud.[20]

It must be noted how Awolowo emphasizes freedom of association, "without duress", which is the chief pillar of democracy.

Therefore, the so-called Western liberal democracy, with its built in massive corruption orchestrated by giant vested monopolistic combines that would buy out time and men to return their candidates, has been exported to Africa. For example, when Sekou Toure began to intensify his opposition to French rule in Guinea, the French put up a rival candidate against him, Yacine Diallo.

> Moreover, the administrations' support of its favored candidate, Yacine Diallo (carried in the election of 1951 to the extent of rigging the ballot boxes), aroused strong resentment among the 80,000 new voters who were added by changes in the franchise laws.[21] (Parenthesis supplied)

In the bye-election following Diallo's death, there was "violence when Sekou Toure was defeated in the election...under circumstances which strongly implicated the administration in falsification of the counts."[22] Given the inherent propensity of the African to elect his representatives, the introduction of Westminster type democracy which, by and large, is similar to the African model, presented no problems.

THE COLONIAL HERITAGE

Despite the Magna Carta and the Bill of Rights, Great Britain has no written constitution. Yet from the wealth of experience which she had amassed by governing her colonies, she bequeathed written constitutions to these dependencies before independence. By and large, the "Fundamental Rights and Freedoms of the Individual" clauses of these constitutions, contain the definition of democracy, namely,

> Protection of rights to life,...from arbitrary arrest or detention,...of freedom of movement,...from slavery and forced labour,...from inhuman treatment,...from deprivation of property,...for privacy of home and other property,...to secure protection of law,. of freedom of conscience...of expression,...of assembly and association,...from discrimination on the grounds of race,...[23]

These provisions are *ipssissima verba*, the provisions in the Independence Constitutions of the British colonies. In order to ensure that the individual's legal rights are not abused by the corruption of judges, their employment was entrenched in the constitution. For example Section 77. (1) of the Sierra Leone Constitution (Independence, 1961) provides that the chairman of the tribunal appointed to investigate the conduct of a judge shall be appointed from the Commonwealth. In this way judges are protected from executive interference by threats of immediate dismissal or victimisation of one sort or the other.

So long as there is reciprocity, in the sense that similar provisions are made by all members of the Commonwealth, this clause is innocuous. In colonial days, the West African Court of Appeal was highly respected by all members, because of its independence. As soon as Kwame Nkrumah abolished it, the flood-gates were opened for all sorts of executive abuse of the judiciary.

We shall now analyse the important ingredients of democracy, viz., liberty (freedom) and equality, the underpinnings of democratic government which is on trial in Africa today.

THE FUNDAMENTAL CRITERIA OF DEMOCRACY

The fundamental criteria of democracy are, (a) liberty (freedom) and (b) equality. Liberty means, freedom to do a host of things, so long as one does not transgress the laws which apply equally to everybody in the state without discrimination.

(a) LIBERTY (FREEDOM)

A free man is defined in Leviathan as

he that in those things, which by his strength and wit he is able to do, is not hindered to do what he has a will to do.[24]

An English writer puts it this way, that a free

man can be rational and not to be free is to be frustrated, impotent, futile....not to be responsible....responsive, not to be human. Freedom is a good, if anything is.[25]

Lack of freedom is like being in chains physically and psychologically. According to Giovanni Sartorie, "without liberty, democracy has no meaning."[26] As Rousseau said, "one should pursue equality... 'because liberty cannot exist without it.'"[27] The late Professor Harold Joseph Laski underscored this point, that liberty means nothing in the absence of equality. And where liberty and equality coexist with wealth and poverty, the government is biased in favour of the rich.[28] In this connection, Laski equates democracy with socialism.

Socialists seek an egalitarian society which caters for the needs of the poor. As Antole France is quoted by Pennock as castigating the Western rule of law which protects "alike for prince and pauper the right to sleep under bridges."[29]

Liberty as a democratic process means freedom of association, freedom to form political parties and therefore, a negation of one-party system. As Kelsen is quoted by Sartori as saying, "Modern democracy is founded entirely on political parties;...."[30] Kelsen then calls democracy as a "party-cracy-*partitocrazia*." A democracy has, therefore, been defined as "A multi-party system in which the majority which governs respects the rights of minorities."[31] The minorities might constitute one or more political parties in parliament forming the opposition. Here he quotes Allen Smith, that

> Liberty for the individual means nothing if it does not imply the right to pursue a course of conduct and to hold and advocate views which do not have the approval of the majority.[32]

The existence of parties and respect for the opposition are the underpinnings of democracy. The determining factor here is "one man, one vote." As Walter Lippman once said

> deride the talk as much as you like; it is the civilized substitute for street brawls, gangs, conspiracies, assassinations, private armies. No other substitute has yet been found.[33]

Dr. Pennock adds that

> The fact that democracy provides a peaceful means for bringing about change, including the inevitable change of leaders, is one of its important accomplishments.[34]

(b) EQUALITY

The case for equality is that justice demands that all men are equal before the law; that the priest and the pauper, the beggar and the clerk, all have equal rights which the law seeks to protect. If both elect to go to Koinadugu and pick tomatoes, then the principle of "equal pay for equal work" should apply to them. It means that similar cases should be treated alike. Equality as spelled out in written constitutions means, equality before the law, without any preconceived sophistries.

In *The Moral Foundation of Democracy*, John H. Hallowell concludes that reality is a fact of life and since all men are capable of recognising it, all men are equal. He goes on,

> It is in the light of this law that all men are created equal not in wealth, in talents, in physical strength or learning but equal in the capacity to distinguish justice and injustice, right from wrong.[35]

Jefferson's Gettysburg address that "All men are created equal" was delivered on July 4, 1776 at the crowning point of the American War of

Independence, which the British called the American Revolution. It was succinctly interpreted by the French Declaration of the Rights of Man and Citizens in 1789, that "We are born and remain free and equal in rights." According to Geoffrey Marshall

> equality under the law....In its narrowest sense it may mean that the existing machinery of law and all government facilities should be equally available to all citizens. At its widest it may imply that governments should make laws to compel every person and institution in the community to behave impartially in all their relations with others. *Tensions between equality and liberty begin at this point.* (Emphasis supplied)[36]

"Equality does not mean identity of treatment,"[37] says Harold Joseph Laski of London School of Economics. It means that adequate opportunity is open to all without discrimination.[38] Implicit in this is the requirement that all children should be fed before going to school. In the words of Laski

> A state divided into a small number of rich and a large number of poor will always develop a government manipulated by the rich to protect the amenities represented by their property. (Therefore) either the State must dominate property, or property will dominate the State.[39] (Parenthesis mine)

This was prophesied by Karl Marx.

The fundamental basis of a democratic state is one in which there is freedom and equality before the law. Any interference with the fundamental freedoms of the individual as contained, for example, in the 1961 Independence Constitution of Sierra Leone, is a denial of a democratic system. In a democratic state, there is freedom of association to belong to a political party of ones choice. This is the criterion of participatory democracy. Where however, as is common practice on the African continent, the government prevents its citizens from forming opposition political parties and in the final analysis, imposes a one-party system on its citizenry, there can be no democracy in such a state.

We shall now briefly list the undemocratic methods employed by the All Peoples Congress Party in Sierra Leone under the leadership of President Siaka Stevens from 1968.

VARIABLE FACTORS

The variable factors which we shall rely upon to substantiate our indictment that the All Peoples Congress Party (APC) government in Sierra Leone (i.e., the first opposition party government) is a collosal failure, are (excluding economic policy):

(1) A reign of terror;

(2) Abuse of the executive powers of government; malicious use of the Treason and State Offences Act, 1963; and the reckless use of the Public Order Act, to molest, harass, intimidate, illegally detain opposition members, i.e., without warrant signed by a Police Magistrate or a Judge of the Supreme Court;

(3) Perversion of legislative powers of government;

(4) Interference with the judicial processes;

(5) Illegal abolition of Independence Constitution Act, 1961; Illegal introduction of Republican Constitution No. 6 of 1971 Act;

(6) Rigged referendum as preliminary step to the introduction of a one-party government;

(7) 1978 Republican One-Party Constitution is illegal, because of (6) above- a conclusion based on a wrong premise, must be wrong;

(8) Breach of international law and illegal indictment of Brigadier David Lansana.

A brief summary of the variable factors is as follows:

(1) A reign of terror

The All Peoples Congress Government unleashed a reign of terror within 30 days of their assumption of the reins of government and arrested many opposition party members, and persons associated with them, directly or indirectly, without warrants and detained them unlawfully for weeks and months, in some cases, without trial, contrary to Section 13 (2) of the Independence Constitution of Sierra Leone, Act, which reads as follows:

> Any person who is arrested, or detained shall be informed as soon as reasonably practicable, in language which he understands, of the reasons for his arrest or detention.

(2)   Abuse of the executive powers of government

The All Peoples Congress Party Government perverted the Treason and State Offences Act of 1963, by recklessly and maliciously charging persons with treason, treason felony and misprision of treason, punishable by death in the case of treason; 6 treason trials were instituted in 10 years of the APC Government, the first beginning within three weeks of their assumption of power.

(3)   Perversion of legislative powers of government

The All Peoples Congress Party Government abused the executive powers of government and legislative powers of an APC dominated parliament by the enactment of legislation, allowing Cyril Rogers-Wright who had been disbarred by the Supreme Court of Sierra Leone, to practise law again in Sierra Leone. The decision against Rogers-Wright was upheld by the West African Court of Appeal, and the latter's decision also upheld by the Judicial Committee of the Privy Council, in London, and his name subsequently struck off the Roll of his Inns of Court in London. Mr. Siaka Stevens had, in an open letter to British Members of Parliament, described the said Rogers-Wright as "dishonest". Yet, as Prime Minister 8 years later, Siaka Stevens engineered and directed his appointment to prosecute persons charged with treason, that carries capital punishment, treason felony and misprision of treason, with full knowledge of the fact that he was dishonest in the legal profession. At the time that he wrote the letter referred to above, he was a member of the National Front, a coalition of all political parties which negotiated the terms of the Independence Constitution of Sierra Leone in 1960 with the British Government in London.

(4)   Interference with the judicial processes

President Siaka Stevens arrested and detained Dr. Raymond Sarif Easmon, a medical practitioner, for publishing an article in which he said he had interviewed the President about allegations that he planned to pervert, or was in fact in the process of perverting the Judges of the Court of Appeal to reject the appeals of 12 persons convicted of treason, or treason felony, or misprision of treason. The President refused to disclaim the rumour as requested by Dr. Raymond Sarif Easmon, to allay the fears of the populace.

Thereupon, Dr. Raymond Sarif Easmon published the interview, and he was detained at Pademba Road Prison. In 1984, Sir Banja Tejansie former Acting Governor-General, and who appointed Siaka Stevens as Prime Minister, gave an interview with *West Africa* in which he alleged that Siaka Stevens "got Luke to do all the dirty work for him." The Honourable Justice Luke was then the Speaker of Parliament. Siaka Stevens' reply to this allegation in *West Africa* of May 1, 1984, was that, "the only thing I have to say is that the wicked flee when no man pursueth." Posterity shall be the judge of who is wicked.

(5)   Illegal abolition of Independence Constitution Act, 1961; Illegal introduction of Republican Constitution No. 6 of 1971 Act.

The All Peoples Congress Party Government abolished the Independence Constitution of 1961, and substituted therefore, the Sierra Leone Peoples Party Act which the Party had abandoned, thereby introducing the Republican Constitution No. 6 of 1971 Act, with an executive president against popular opposition of Sierra Leoneans and three cabinet ministers of the All Peoples Congress Party, who resigned from the Party in protest. Appeals to the Judicial Committee of the Privy Council were abolished.

(6)   Rigged referendum as preliminary step to the introduction of a one-party government.

The history of the All Peoples Congress Party is littered with deceptions. In the "Forward" to the "1967 General Elections All People's Congress Party Manifesto", Siaka Stevens, the Secretary-General of the Party warned the electorate, inter alia,

> If you vote for the SLPP you are encouraging the introduction of a One-Party System of Government in Sierra Leone and the ruthless silencing of all critics of Government policy.[40]

This point was stressed by the Party under Section *(A) Constitution* of the Manifesto, that, "We pledge ourselves to respect freedom of assembly and association and to put no hindrance in the way of any citizen wishing to join any political party of his choice."[41]

No denunciation of a one-party system could be clearer than the declarations on the eve of the 1967 General Elections. Five years after the APC had been in power, they continued to renege on their promises during the 1973 General Elections. In their Manifesto for the elections, they began to insinuate their interest in the one-party surreptitiously, as follows:

> We have maintained parliamentary democracy with an official opposition. We have even increased the emoluments of the leader of the opposition. Even though the performance of his duties has shown no corresponding increase.
>
> This does not mean that we have not been following with interest the many advantages gained by our sister states who have adopted a One-Party System of Government. We have already provoked public discussion of this issue.[42]

In this paradoxical quotation, the APC acknowledged the difference between a "parliamentary democracy" and a "One-Party System of Government"; although the comparison between the latter and the "emoluments of the leader of the opposition" is nebulous.

The All Peoples Congress Party rigged the referendum in 1978 in contravention of the Electoral Provisions Act No. 14 of 1962, as a stepping stone to the introduction of the One-Party Republican Constitution Act, No. 12 of 1978.

(7)   1978 Republican One-Party Constitution is illegal, because of (6) above - a conclusion based on a wrong premise, must be wrong.

The 1978 Republican Party Constitution was conceived illegally by a fraudulent referendum and therefore, is itself, illegal. By this Act, the All Peoples Congress Party became the only political party in Sierra Leone, and the APC was allowed to have a par a-military force.

(8)   Breach of international law and illegal indictment of Brigadier David Lansana.

The All Peoples Congress Party breached international law when, by fraudulent misrepresentation, they secured the extradition of Brigadier David Lansana to be indicted for alleged false imprisonment of the Governor-General, for which he was imprisoned for 5 years. The APC

Government then indicted him illegally for treason, treason felony and misprision of treason, which are political offences and for which the Liberian Government would not have extradited Brigadier David Lansana if the APC Government's application had not been falsified.

LIMITATIONS

The limitations of this Book are two-fold. First, as I indicated above, I have excluded the economic policy of the APC Government. Although this subject should have been the leading yardstick by which to judge the failure of the APC Government, yet I have excluded it, because (a) it is manifestly clear that Sierra Leone is on the verge of economic collapse, that it needs no emphasis; (b) more importantly, the economic mismanagement of the Sierra Leone Government by the APC, merits special attention, perhaps in a book called, "The economic consequences of the APC Government."

Second, it would perhaps have been useful if we proved our hypothesis by examination of the variable factors, *seriatim*. This has not been the case, because it is thought that a wiser course of action is, to present the prosecution's case in chronological order. In this way, we shall see quite clearly, the sequence of events, and the masterful manner in which the APC planned the onslaught on the peoples of Sierra Leone from the guerrilla base in Guinea, and the expert and meticulous way in which the plan was executed. In consequence, we have tried to list the variables in chronological order, and not in descending order of importance. We shall therefore, endeavour to substantiate the variables to the hilt.

The All Peoples Congress Party misled the electorates in 1967 that they were not seeking power for selfish reasons. In fact, they sought power because they felt that it was their turn to rule, not because the Sierra Leone Peoples Party, to which Siaka Stevens, their leader, originally belonged had been found wanting, but because they felt that it was time that they too enjoyed the fruits of independence, and the glamour of office. However, their record has shown abundantly clearly, that their denunciation of the Sierra Leone Peoples Party plan to introduce a one-party system of government was deceitful. As soon as they came to power, the All Peoples Congress Party introduced an executive presidency, abolished appeals to the

Judicial Committee of the Privy Council, so as to enable them to manipulate the judiciary, introduced a one-party system, all of which they had vehemently criticised when in opposition.

When they assumed the role of government, within 30 days, they unleashed a reign of terror. They continued the state of emergency which the Revolutionary Council of March, 1968 had declared, as if the civilian government and the military government, an interim one which handed over power to them as pre-arranged, were jointly administering the nation. Hundreds of Sierra Leone Peoples Party members, Paramount Chiefs, civil servants, members of parliament belonging to the Sierra Leone Peoples Party, were arrested without warrant and detained at Pademba Road Prison and Mafanta Prison, without preferring any charges against them, contrary to the Independence Constitution of 1961, and the rule of law. After 3 weeks, a writ of *Habeas Corpus* was issued against the Government. They hurriedly preferred charges of treason, treason felony, and misprision of treason against various detainees.

Since the APC came to power, Sierra Leone has been in a state of perpetual emergency, under the pretext that certain subversive elements are plotting, in collusion with external forces, to overthrow the Government. This is only an excuse for arresting the Opposition Members of Parliament and their supporters. In his first public broadcast to the nation, Siaka Stevens informed the people that the "kitty is empty". Twelve years afterwards, he spent over $200 million, hosting the Organisation of African Unity. This expenditure was the equivalent of the Annual Budget of Sierra Leone. Perhaps the kitty is now full.

When a political party forms the government and embarks on unconstitutional practices and perversion of the legal processes to harass, victimise and quash the opposition party, and these autocratic tendencies are not effectively challenged by the people, the government would resort to other authoritarian and illegal acts to stay in office FOREVER, as happened in the case of the All Peoples Congress Party of Sierra Leone, when they formed the government in April, 1968.

The first Opposition Party Government in Sierra Leone is a colossal failure. The introduction of the one-party system is the last straw that will break their backs. For these and other reasons, the people ought to have revolted to throw President Siaka Stevens and his confederates out of power. Various attempts are alleged to have been made resulting in the indiscriminate executions of innocent citizens.

Introduction Notes

1.   Clifford, Mary Louise; *The land and people of Sierra Leone*, J.P. Lippincott Company, New York.

2.   Collier, Gershon, *Sierra Leone, an experiment in democracy in an African Nation*, New York University Press, New York, 1970, pp. 14 & 15.

3.   Strachey, John, *The End of Empire*, Frederick A. Praeger, Publishers, New York, New York, 1959, p. 166.

4.   *West Africa*, West Africa Publishing Company Ltd., Holborn Viaduct, London EC1A 2FD, April 2, 1984 p. 703.

5.   Sartori, Giovanni, *Democratic Theory*, Wayne State University Press, Detroit 2, Michigan, 1962, p. 3.

6.   *Ibid*. p. 26.

7.   *Ibid*. p. 79.

8.   *Ibid*. p. 85.

9.   Laswell, H.D., The comparative study of elites,   Stanford, 1952, quoted by Giovanni Sartori, *Democratic Theory, ibid*. p. 96.

10.   Herodotus, History of the Persian Wars, trans. Rawlinson, Modern Library edition, Random House, New York, Bk 111 Chap. 80 1942, p. 252; Quoted by Roland Pennock in *Democratic Political Theory*, Princeton University Press, Princeton, New Jersey, 1979, p. 3.

11.   Thorson, Thomas Landon, *The Logic of Democracy*, Holt, Rinehart, and Winston, New York, 1962, p. 17.

12.   Quoted by Okon Edet Uya, *Monograph Series No. 2*, Published by Africana Studies and Research Center, Cornell University Press, New York.

13.   Quoted by Ali A. Mazrui, in *The African Condition*, Cambridge University Press, Cambridge, England, 1980, p. 6.

14.   Markovitz, Irving Leonard, *Power and Class in Africa - An introduction to change and conflict in African politics*, Prentice-Hall, Inc., Englewood Cliff, New Jersey 07632, p. 28.

15.   *Ibid*., p. 32.

16.   Williams, Chancellor, *The Destruction of Black Civilization, Great issues of a race from 2400 B.C. to 2000 A.D.*, Third World Press, Chicago, Illinois, 1976, p. 27.

17.   *Ibid.* p. 26.

18.   *Ibid.* p. 265.

19.   Quoted by Victor King, in *A Pamphlet entitled Unified Party System*, Freetown, Sierra Leone.

20.   *Ibid.* p. 15.

21.   Ed. by Gwendolyn M. Carter, *African One-Party States*, Cornell University Press, Ithaca, New York, 2nd Printing, 1964, p. 162.

22.   *Ibid.* p. 162.

23.   Sierra Leone Constitution, 1961, Printed by the Government Printer, Freetown, The Republic of Sierra Leone.

24.   Leviathan Chaps 14 & 24, Basil Blackwell, Oxford Oakeshott ed. 1946; Quoted by Roland Pennock in *Democratic Political Theory*, Princeton University Press, Princeton, New Jersey, 1979, p. 19.

25.   Lucas, J.R., The Principles of Politics, Clarendon Press, Oxford, 1966, p. 144; Quoted by Roland Pennock in *Democratic Political Theory, ibid.*, p. 133.

26.   Sartori, Giovanni, *Democratic Theory, ibid.*, p. 454.

27.   Quoted by Giovanni Sartori, *Democratic Theory, ibid.*, from Social Contract II, II.

28.   Laski, Harold Joseph, *Grammar of Politics*, George Allen & Unwin Ltd., London, 4th ed. 1937, p. 8.

29.   Quoted by Roland Pennock in *Democratic Political Theory, ibid.*, p. 13.

30.   Sartori, Giovanni, *Democratic Theory, ibid.*, 120.

31.   *Ibid.* p. 237.

32.   C.J. Allen Smith, The Growth and decadence of constitutional government, New York, 1930 chap. IV; Quoted by Giovanni Sartori in *Democratic Theory, ibid.*, p. 238.

33.   The Essential Lippman, ed. Clinton Rossiter & James Lare, Random House, New York, 1963 p. 229; Quoted by Roland Pennock, in *Democratic Political Theory, ibid.*, p. 153.

34.   *Ibid*. p. 153.

35.   Quoted by Thomas Landon Thorston, *The Logic of Democracy*, Holt, Rinehart and Winston, New York, 1962, p. 46.

36.   "Enforcing Equality: Two Statutory Attempts," in Gray Dorsey, ed. Equality and Freedom, 3:933-939, 939; Quoted by Roland Pennock, *Democratic Political Theory, ibid.*, p. 40.

37.   Laski, Harold Joseph, Grammar of *Politics*, George Allen and Unwin Ltd., London, 4th ed., 1937, p. 153.

38.   *Ibid*. p. 154.

39.   *Ibid*. p. 157.

40.   *The Rising Sun*, by the APC Secretariat, Siaka Stevens Street, Freetown, Sierra Leone, Produced by Impads, London, 1982, p. 307.

41.   *Ibid*. p. 309.

42.   *Ibid*. p. 373.

CHAPTER 1

THE DOWNFALL OF THE SIERRA LEONE PEOPLES PARTY

After Sir Milton Margai died in 1964, the Governor-General Sir Henry Lightfoot Boston, appointed Albert Margai as Prime Minister. Mr. Gershon Collier summarised the antecedent circumstances of the fall of Sir Albert as follows:

> Even though some of his closest friends and advisers were young Creole intellectuals... The Creoles, after less than 2 years of Albert Margai's leadership, embarked on a campaign of hate and vilification which surpassed anything that had occurred before, even in the particularly scurrilous record of Colony-Protectorate feeling. Known criminals instigated by a disbarred and dishonest lawyer joined in making extreme and sometimes imaginary accusations against him. The Creole dominated judiciary and the Civil Service were accused of open hostility to Albert Margai. He lost confidence in these institutions and the future of good government was seriously threatened. Politically, Albert Margai's government was accused of waste, corruption, and much else. The Creoles rallied around the APC and used it as the vehicle of vigorous dissent. They also as a group led the attack on Albert Margai's administration. Many Creoles in the Judiciary and the higher grades of the Civil Service were seriously accused of using their positions for subversive activities against Albert Margai's government and of both open and secret support of the opposition.[1]

Mr. Gershon Collier is one of the leading lawyers in Sierra Leone. He was Sierra Leone's Ambassador to the United States of America and Chief Justice of Sierra Leone.

These attacks against Sir Albert Margai led to the accusation that he was Menderising the Civil Service. Dr. John Cartwright, A Canadian lecturer, seconded to the University of Sierra Leone exposed the lie to these accusations in the footnote to his book that:

> By 1960, 245 of 583 senior service posts were filled by Sierra Leoneans, including such top posts as Secretary for Training and Recruitment, Solicitior-General, Permanent Secretary of Lands, Mines and Labour and Engineer-in-Chief of the Electricity Department. The Creoles still held a long lead over up-country people; only 53 of the Sierra Leoneans appear to have been of up-country origin. Data compiled from the Staff List, 1960.[2]

The Sierra Leone Peoples Party was accused of tribalism by the All Peoples Congress Party press. Undoubtedly, tribalism has been one of the main causes of political instability in Africa since independence. Dr. Martin Kilson holds the view that "Serious tribal political disturbances during the pre-independence period"[3] led to single party systems in Guinea, Ghana, Gabon, Dahomey, Congo Brazzaville. There were spontaneous, religious, tribal, or ethnic clashes in Guinea between 1946-1954. Similar disturbances erupted in Ghana especially between 1954-1958 supported and financed by chiefs, e.g., Nana Yirnorth, Asantehene-Kumasi, Okyenhene, Akim Abuakwa, became active party leaders. The leader of the National Liberation Movement was inflammatory in his address to the Ashanti people in 1954.

The Commission of Enquiry which investigated the matter, consisted of two Englishmen and Sir Tsibu Darku, a Paramount Chief. They reported that the General Secretary of the NLM and Apaloo were "guilty of conspiracy to carry at some future date in Ghana an act for an unlawful purpose revolutionary in character." Kwame Nkrumah passed the Avoidance of Discrimination Act of 1957, forbidding "the formation of political parties of a tribal, ethnic, religious, or regional character."[4] In Gabon, a north-south conflict led to the coalition of Union Democratique et Sociale Gabonaise (UDSG).

Religious differences between Muslims, Christians and animists in Dahomey, led to the merger of the ruling Rassemblement Democratique Dahomeen (RDD) under Hubert Maga and the Parti des Nationalistes in Dahomey (PND) under Sousou M. Apithy to form the Dahomeen d'Unite (PDU), a single party government in early 1961. In subsequent elections in April, 1961, the PDU banned the UDD.

Congo Brazzaville is another classic case in which tribal conflict in 1959 led to the death of 150 persons and 500 wounded. Dr. Martin Kilson wrote that the

> Union Democratique de Defense des Interests Africans (UDDIA) encouraged animosity among its Bakongo supporters toward the M'Bochi and Vili tribes, who supported the opposition Movement Socialiste African (MSA). It also instigated tribal violence against Bakongo and other supporters of the Matsounist Movement (a religious political cult) and on one occasion 35 persons were killed and 17 wounded.[5]

Following various political manoeuvres in which the UDDIA Government dissolved the MSA and coalitions followed, a single party government was formed in 1962.

Since colonial times there was no ethnic fragmentation nor was there any tribal wars in the country after independence. In point of fact the Sierra Leone Peoples Party was representative of a cross-section of all tribes. The SLPP Cabinet reflected this composition. The accusations of the SLPP Menderising the civil service was a fabrication by ill-disposed persons for personal ambitions.

As part of their campaign to discredit the SLPP, certain key members of the APC were assigned the duty of subverting top civil servants of the SLPP. They began preaching tribalism among Northerners. For example, one of them visited me on a Saturday before the General Elections and after lunch, he lectured me for an hour about the advisability of my joining the APC in secret. I reminded him of the Official Secrets Act under which I could be arrested and charged for violating the sacred trust of my office as Financial Secretary, with the disastrous consequences of losing my pension and gratuity if I was disloyal to the Government in power. He countered that the APC was formed to help Northerners and so as a Northerner, I should throw in my lot with it to help Northerners.

My wife was very angry with him for trying to subvert me. She assured him that we would continue to help Northerners who were in need, but that I could not possibly be a member of the APC. In his usual cynical laughter, he concluded in effect as follows:

> "OK brother. If you don't join us now while there is time, you will regret it later. You, Peter Tucker, Berthan Macaulay, John Kallon and Tejan Kabba are the pillars of Sir Albert. When we cut you down, Sir Albert will fall."

The following Monday, the headline of the editorial in the "We Yone" the APC newspaper, was, "Tucker and Daramy the highest paid civil servants - Le 13,000.00 each per annum." The editorial was devoted to vicious untruths, designed to create animosity against us.

My interviewer and I knew that there was no law that precluded civil servants from becoming members of the APC. He therefore, understood the context in which I reminded him of the Official Secrets Act. I could have joined the APC EVEN THOUGH I was Financial Secretary and voted for them at elections, so long as I did not participate actively in politics, and did not divulge official secrets to the Opposition.

The late Ibrahim Taqui contributed immensely to inciting the public against the SLPP. Another stalwart APC pamphleteer was T.S. Johnson a barrister-at-law. He wrote an article against me, that I had gone to Bo (where my mother lived), and was seen visiting various Lebanese shops. The imputation was clearly sinister.

When *We Yone* began publishing the contents of cabinet papers, Cyril Rogers-Wright then a cabinet minister, was suspected of passing on information to the APC. One day, he came to my office and reported that His Excellency Gershon Collier was by-passing him as Minister of External Affairs and his boss, and getting privileges direct from Sir Albert, the Prime Minister. He accused Collier of abuse of office and that I should advise Sir Albert that he should instruct Collier to observe protocol, and send his reports to him and not direct to the Prime Minister. If, he concluded, Sir Albert did not "discipline" Collier, he would ruin Sir Albert.

I asked him to accompany me to R.G.O. King, Minister of Finance, to discuss the matter. When we arrived, I reported what he had told me and concluded that, "I am requesting you to accompany me to the Prime Minister, as it is my duty to report matters of this nature to him forthwith. Mr. Rogers-Wright is a cabinet minister. If he threatens, in his own words, 'to ruin' the Prime Minister, I demand that it should be reported immediately to the Prime Minister." Mr. Rogers-Wright repeated what he had told me. We promised to take appropriate steps. After he left, we went and reported the interview to Sir Albert.

Leaks of secret cabinet documents to the press continued. Mr. Rogers-Wright was removed from cabinet. The intensity of the attacks against the SLPP became more scurrilous and provocative. As a result of the interview he had with me, I suspected that most of the articles were either written or inspired by him, because also he had been removed from cabinet.

The APC employed the most diabolical strategies to hold top civil servants associated with the SLPP Government to hatred, ridicule and contempt. There was open hostility towards us. They succeeded in sowing seeds of discord in the ranks of the SLPP, which deteriorated into intraparty squabbles. Sir Albert became the victim of the vilest lies and gossip against some of his most ardent supporters, whom he began to distrust. As the fortunes of the SLPP slumped, and the personal attacks on him intensified, he became less capable of differentiating gossip and self-serving interests from genuine advice.

Those who formed the back-bone of the SLPP like Kandeh Bureh, a Temne, remained loyal to the SLPP cause and suffered subsequently, because of their unflinching support of the SLPP and Sir Albert whom, most of us admired, and were prepared to be crucified on the SLPP alter, than to join Siaka Stevens, whom I personally knew, since I was 10 years old. When he was minister-in-charge of lands, mines and labour, I was a labour officer and worked closely with him. I had the opportunity of assessing him in a more mature manner. My impression was that he was very ambitious and would stop at nothing to achieve his aim.

President Siaka Stevens is a self-made man. He did not attend a university, nevertheless, he studied hard and the government awarded him a scholarship to Ruskin College in the environs of Oxford. There, he excelled himself and became a blue-eyed boy of the Colonial Office by the help of Edgar Parry, then Commissioner of Labour. He is handsome, and has a magnetic personality which radiates confidence and knowledge. He is quick-witted and has a repertoire of anecdotes which he exploits to maximum advantage, at times to the point of irritation.

When he visited the United States of America in 1980, Sir Albert and I reminisced closely over the past. One day, I drove him to Arlington Cemetery, as he had expressed a desire to pay his respects to "that great man", as he called the late John Kennedy. By the graveside of this illustrious son of America, victim of man's irrationality, greed and bigotry, we pored over the past. He had no doubts that under Siaka Stevens, Sierra Leone was well on the path to destruction. Siaka Stevens is, according to him, a man without principles. There is no depth too low for him to descend to achieve his ambition.

Sir Albert had no remorse for the past. He was obviously visibly shaken by the treachery of some of his closest friends. That a man could be indifferent to the consequences of his actions on his fellow man, was to Sir Albert, an inexplicable dilemma. This pain is the more unbearable, when inflicted by someone who is ones closest confidant. As we descended the steps from John Kennedy, Sir Albert was still confident that as our cause was just, history will vindicate us abundantly. He therefore, implored me to work hard to revive the SLPP in the Americas, because,

> Daramy, I mean when we go back home, the world will realize that Sierra Leone owes us a debt of gratitude. I bear no one malice, but that Siaka Stevens, that ungrateful fellow, will answer to God for all his misdeeds. As to whether there will be commissions of enquiry such as we suffered under the humiliation of the NRC, history will be the judge. (And we wept a third time since we arrived at Arlington).

FORTY YEARS RETIREMENT RULE

The Sierra Leone Peoples Party Government enacted legislation to enable civil servants in the prime of their career to retire after 40 years of age. This would enable them to seek jobs in the international market, particularly the United Nations Organization and its specialised agencies, in which Sierra Leone's quota was under-utilized. This legislation would also enable the Government to ask a civil servant to retire if it felt that the former had prematurely exhausted his capabilities, or that his work and conduct were incompatible with good government.

Again, there had been cases in which civil servants resorted to hazardous practices inimical to their health and which involved high medical bills, to retire from the Civil Service and to take on other employment elsewhere, e.g., Liberia, Ghana, Nigeria, international institutions. The Act facilitated early retirement with pension and gratuity rights, without a civil servant endangering his health to prove disability as a ground for retirement.

Nevertheless, this law was mischievously misconstrued as a weapon against the Creoles, although the Act was never enforced by Government against any one. Yet, like tendentious fiction, once it has had a start, it is difficult for the truth to overtake it. And so the image of the Sierra Leone Peoples Party was tarnished beyond recognition, while the consequences of the malicious propaganda against the Mendes are universal knowledge. Nonetheless, civil servants are now taking advantage of the 40 years retirement rule.

THE ONE-PARTY SYSTEM

Sometime in 1966, Sir Albert Margai announced his Party's intention to introduce a one-party system of government. This move was interpreted as the stepping stone to dictatorship by Sir Albert, and he was attacked vigorously in the press.

As his Financial Secretary, it was my duty to advise him on fiscal and financial policies. But since sound fiscal and financial policies flourish better in a healthy political system, like the Latin proverb, *mens sana in corpore sano*, at the height of opposition to the one-party proposal, I discussed it with

Sir Albert. In our discussion, I told him that it was being rumoured that he was the most ardent advocate of the one-party, because it was his ambition to be life president of Sierra Leone. He convinced me that infact, the matter was first raised in cabinet by a few ministers, and that it was not his brainchild. I warned him against misrepresentations that were being made that he was the protagonist of the one-party and that it was most unpopular and would cost him dearly. He told me that he was aware that some of his stalwarts were undermining him, for example, a member of cabinet was suspected of passing on cabinet papers to the Opposition. His sincere appreciation of my advice reinforced my conviction that he was under pressure to introduce a one-party constitution, but that he was not personally seriously keen on it.

Sir Albert Margai - prime minister of
Sierra Leone 1964-1967

When Dr. Raymon Sarif Easmon stepped up his attack of Sir Albert over the proposed one-party system, and it seemed as if it was going to deteriorate into a confrontation between Sir Albert and Dr. Raymon S. Easmon, I went and discussed it with him. We agreed that I should arrange a meeting between him and Sir Albert to discuss their differences over the one-party, and that Canon Harry Sawyer, Acting Vice-Chancellor of the University of Sierra Leone would be the chairman.

I went and spoke to Sir Albert, who readily agreed to meet Dr. Easmon. Canon Harry Sawyer expressed his willingness to chair the meeting, as he too was apprehensive of the outcome of a confrontation between these two leading personalities. Both of them were our mutual friends. Sooner or later we would have to choose between them. So the canon and I had our personal stakes in the gathering storm.

The meeting, which Peter Tucker (Secretary to the Prime Minister) and I attended, was cordial. There was a frank exchange of views. Although no rapprochement could be reached, a cooling-off period of one month was agreed, during which time Sir Albert agreed not to make broadcast speech or address public meetings on the one-party, while Dr. Easmon agreed not to publish any articles against Sir Albert relative to the one-party.

Dr. Easmon kept his side of the bargain, but the Sierra Leone Peoples Party press broke the truce after a month, and began replying to previous articles written by Dr. Easmon against the one-party. Canon Sawyer and I succeeded in pacifying Dr. Raymon Sarif Easmon to hold his reins and let time solve this delicate issue. Since the SLPP press were not represented at the meeting, we could only attribute their breach to innocent mistake.

In retrospect, perhaps we were able to arrange the meeting and agree on a suspension of hostilities, because we were dealing with two intellectuals who realized the overwhelming consequences of all-out press war between the leaders of Sierra Leone so soon after independence. As a lawyer, Sir Albert was accustomed to what Harold Laski in his address to us freshmen at the London School of Economics in 1948, called the "beauty of controversy." As a matter of fact, that was the title of his address. As I discovered later, Sir Albert Margai's enthusiasm for the one-party was a mere reflection of what his cabinet wanted and so perhaps, as *primus inter pares*, it was his duty to implement faithfully, the wishes of the majority, in the spirit of collective responsibility, which is a cardinal principle of British constitutional practice which we inherited. It is also arguable that his readiness to concede defeat and call off the one-party plan was the outcome of his personal disenchantment with the one-party as a system of government.

Nevertheless, even after he had realized the futility of pressing on with an ideological battle in which he would end up as the scapegoat, the party machine continued to grind on, rather sluggishly. Eventually, Sir Albert broadcast that his Party had abandoned plans for the introduction of a one-party system of government. But the harm had been done. He was suspected of playing for time, and that he would introduce the measure if his Party won the next election. Whatever the future held in store, it was great relief when the Party dropped the one-party idea.

DISAFFECTION IN THE ARMY

Several complaints were made to me by senior army officers from time to time against the Brigadier, David Lansana. As Financial Secretary, he held frequent meetings with me to iron-out problems relating to the Army Estimates, and so we became quite friendly. I was therefore, able to exploit our friendship by 'interfering' in military matters which he would have resented, but for our relationship, and as he said to me, his desire to expose some officers who were jealous of him and who felt that they could run the army better than he.

At a military cocktail party, an officer called me and my wife aside and advised us to go home, as they were planning to arrest the Brigadier that night. A cold shiver ran through my spine and my wife, with tears welling in her eyes said, "do ya...", meaning in Creole, "I implore you". I pulled her aside before she burst into tears. I advised him to see me together with Colonel John Bangura and some of his key officers concerned in their plan immediately at home, after the party. I assured him that their complaints would be investigated within 24 hours by the Prime Minister personally.

At midnight, Colonel John Bangura, Major Juxon-Smith, Captain Abdul Turay and Captain Sheku Tarawalli came to see me. I wrote down brief notes of their grievances and asked them to meet me at the Prime Minister's office at 10 a.m. Major Juxon-Smith who was their spokesman remarked that, "If there were 3 people in this country like you, this country would be on an even keel." I assured them that I derived my authority from the Prime Minister's concern about the Army which took precedence at all times. Colonel John Bangura assured his colleagues that he had no doubt whatsoever in my ability to arrange for them to see the Prime Minister as I had promised to do, as I had on a few occasions, settled disputes between him and the Brigadier.

After they left about 2 a.m., I reported my interview to the Secretary to the Prime Minister, Peter Tucker, who confirmed my action, which was approved by the Prime Minister that night. The meeting was held and relations between the Brigadier and his men began to improve, at least superficially.

A crucial criticism of Sir Albert was that by succeeding his brother as Prime Minister, it would appear as if the Sierra Leone Peoples Party had become the domestic property of the Margai family. This argument was touted by mischievous persons who were infact not members of the political party which tolerated this alleged Margai hegemony over the Party. Even if the accusations were true, it was the prerogative of the SLPP members to resolve this alleged irregularity.

The facts are that when an election was held for leadership of the Party by the Parliamentary Members of the SLPP caucus, Sir Albert won the election but gave way to Sir Milton for the sake of Party unity, and also because he was the elder one, who should take precedence according to native custom. But he was satisfied that he had established his status in the Party and that he was not in the Party on sufferance. From then onwards, he was for all intents and purposes, the leading contender in the line of succession. His being brother to Sir Milton was quite irrelevant to the issue. So when Sir Milton died, it was only but natural that he should succeed him. As a matter of fact Sir Albert was subsequently elected life chairman of the Party. Incidentally, Siaka Stevens' attempt to manipulate a similar election sparked off demonstrations and protests by Fourah Bay College students. In Sir Albert's case, his election was symbolic of his popularity in the country.

INCITEMENT OF THE ARMY

It was alleged in Government circles that the Opposition Party, APC, was inciting army officers to stage a coup d'etat. Colonel Bangura was suspected of master-minding an incipient coup, and so was arrested and detained at Pademba Road Prison. A court martial, chaired by Major Idrisa Kai-Samba, was appointed to investigate the allegations. Other army officers allegedly involved in the coup d'etat were Captain Sheku Tarawalli, Captain Seray Wurie, Captain Farrah Jawara, Lieutenant George Caulker, Lieutenant Kamara and Lieutenant Josiah. A number of non-commissioned officers were also detained.

In a broadcast to the nation on the 8th of February, 1967, reproduced in the *Daily Mail* the following day, the Prime Minister, Sir Albert Margai, warned that "We shall meet force with greater force." Extracts from the broadcast are as follows:

> My fellow Sierra Leoneans;
>
> May I start by apologizing for the delay in informing you of the discovery of a plot to stage a coup d'etat with the aim of overthrowing the constitutional government by armed force and seizing power by a number of Army Officers through the investigation (sic-instigation) of certain people in the community. There are two reasons for the delay....
>
> Secondly, at the time the plot was unearthed, the plotters having failed to strike a week earlier because of minor dissension amongst them were feverishly closing their ranks with the aim of striking on Wednesday or Thursday of last week....
>
> Many of you, fellow Sierra Leoneans, will recall that incessantly, both in the press and by public pronouncements, statements have been made that could be interpreted as blatant incitements to military personnel to overthrow the Government by force.

The Prime Minister cited articles in the press to substantiate his allegations.

> In the light of the writings and pronouncements of these gentlemen and others, it had long been obvious to me that the danger which we now face was sure to come and in fact has come upon us.
>
> The plot by Army Officers was aimed in the first instance at murdering the Force Officer, myself the Prime Minister and a certain number of Ministers and Civil Servants, take over the Government and appoint a Committee of Advisers, about seven in number.

The Prime Minister mentioned 4 persons who were to be members of the proposed Committee.

One Foreign African country has been mentioned as one of the sources from which help would be given to the plotters.

On learning of the plot, simultaneously with steps taken for internal protection and security of the State I contacted His Excellency Sekou Toure and requested him to be ready to keep the pledge which he had made to go to the aid of one another if requested in case attempts were made to overthrow the constitutional Government by intervention of armed forces.

The Prime Minister assured the nation that their lives and liberties are no longer seriously endangered chiefly due to prompt and vigilant action on the part of the Force Commander and his loyal officers and men, also by the Commissioner of Police and his force.

This broadcast was followed by a statement issued by the Government thus:

For sometime now, we have had cause to believe that certain sections of the community are planning to use violence when the House is dissolved for the General Elections in order to intimidate and terrorize peaceful citizens of this country.

Sir Albert warned such trouble makers that

if anyone threatens or attempts to use violence we shall meet force with greater force and we shall deal severely with any attempt.

He reminded the trouble makers that

The SLPP Government is the constitutional Government elected by the people and it is responsible to ensure the security and safety of every inhabitant of this country. As a Government we will not tolerate violence.

Having denounced violence as an instrument for securing the government of a country, the Prime Minister invited the Opposition Party APC, to do likewise. He concluded that the forthcoming General Elections provided the constitutional opportunities for every Sierra Leonean to seek election to Parliament and to form a government if selected in a majority party.

On the 13th February, 1967, several thousand SLPP supporters held a thanksgiving service at the Queen Elizabeth II Playing Field and reaffirmed their confidence in the Prime Minister, Sir Albert Margai and his government. Prayers were led by Rev. T. J. Stevens of the EUB Church and Alhaji Gibril Sesay, Organizing Secretary of the Sierra Leone Muslim Brotherhood. At the end of the Service, they expressed their confidence in the Prime Minister and his Government. A few days later, the Sierra Leone Muslim Pilgrims Welfare Association, led by their Secretary-General, El Hadj Abu B. Magba-Kamara, submitted a statement to the Prime Minister, pledging loyalty and support.

GENERAL ELECTIONS - MARCH, 1967

It was in this confused state of tension and uncertainty, that Sir Albert declared general elections. By that time, the popularity of the Sierra Leone Peoples Party was at its lowest ebb. Hooliganism was rampant. The suspicions that certain 'ill-disposed persons' had lists of cabinet ministers and 4 top civil servants, who were to be assassinated during the elections, persisted. It was suspected that the 4 civil servants were Peter Tucker, Sheikh Daramy, John Kallon, Tejan Kabba. There were also threats of plans to riot and to loot in several parts of the country during the elections.

Early in March, as reported in the *Daily Mail*, following "violent riots which broke out in Sefadu shortly after the close of nominations for the forthcoming election to the House of Representatives, last Monday,..."[6] a state of emergency was declared by the Sierra Leone Peoples Party Government in the Kono District. This was followed by the declaration of a state of emergency in the Western Area for three months. In the words of the Commissioner of Police, William Leigh;

> It would appear that my appeal has fallen into deaf ears. Since my broadcast, the Police have been on active duty throughout the 24 hours of each day dealing with unlawful processions, assaults of woundings, during political meetings, unlawful assemblies and many other breaches of the peace around the Western Area.
>
> Those who have been victims and suffered injuries are either in hospital or recovering from their wounds at home.[7]

The judiciary was not free from the upheavals gripping the country. Because he was dissatisfied with the way in which the judiciary was rapidly becoming politicized, the Prime Minister appointed His Excellency Gershon Collier, Sierra Leone's Ambassador to the United States and Permanent Representative to the United Nations, as Acting Chief Justice. In a letter to the *Daily Mail* published on the 9th February, 1967, Milton Gorvey wondered "why the hysteria about the appointment of Mr. G. B. O. Collier as Acting Chief Justice of Sierra Leone and the fear that seem to be passing from one man to another by a sort of contagion?"

Two barristers, T. S. Johnson and D. E. F. Luke took action against Gershon Collier and the Attorney General challenging the appointment of the former as Acting Chief Justice. Messrs. Livesey Luke, A. H. C. Barlatt, Dr. Marcus Jones and G. Gelaga-King, appeared for the plaintiffs.

Tension continued to mount as Election Day approached. In the circumstances, states of emergency were declared in all districts in the Provinces on the 15th, March 1967. Once again, the Commissioner of Police warned in a broadcast that the police would take drastic measures against law breakers.

> Also I have been informed, (he went on), and I have reasons to believe that there will be movements of persons from the Provinces to the Western Area and from one constituency to another in the Provinces on Polling Day to vote under various guises.

> Within the past few weeks, large numbers of persons have been transported to various places in the Provinces to create trouble on Polling Day. Already clashes between political parties, some very serious, have occurred in a number of towns. I have also been informed that a number of school boys under the age of 21 will attempt to vote.[8]

The Commissioner concluded that any school boy found voting in this way would be arrested.

MARCH 17TH 1967 – GENERAL ELECTIONS OF ORDINARY MEMBERS OF PARLIAMENT

The general elections of Ordinary Members of Parliament were held on the 17th of March, 1967. On Election Day, pandemonium broke out in Kroo Town Road, Freetown. The cause of the trouble was the opposition to Foulahs voting, because they were regarded as foreigners from Guinea. The *Daily Mail* reported that a Foulah was beaten up at another polling station in Freetown.

On the 29th of March, 1967, the *Daily Mail* published the results of the elections as Sierra Leone Peoples Party 31, the All Peoples Congress Party 28, Independents 2.

According to the *Daily Mail* of 21st March,

> About 50 persons including school children and women were rushed to the Connaught Hospital, Freetown, yesterday afternoon for treatment following a gun and knife incident along Kroo Town Road, Freetown). About 20 of them were ... put on the danger list. The Foulah Chief and over 100 Foulahs were arrested and taken to the Central Police Station,

while their shops were looted in their absence. The *Daily Mail* reported that infact, before the incident, a large crowd of political supporters danced along Kroo Town Road, provoking Foulahs by threatening remarks. Foulahs were known to be supporters of the Sierra Leone Peoples Party. About 60 of the 100 Foulahs arrested were taken to the hospital for medical treatment.

20th MARCH, 1967 - GENERAL ELECTIONS OF PARAMOUNT CHIEF MEMBERS OF PARLIAMENT

The general elections of Paramount Chiefs were held on the 20th of March. By midday, the results of ordinary members showed that both parties were dead-heat at 32/32. In the light of these results and the hooliganism, vandalism and wide-spread disturbances all over the country, the Governor-General, Sir Henry Lightfoot Boston, invited Sir Albert Margai and Siaka Stevens to State House. He told them that in view of the state of the Parties, in his opinion, the elections' results showed that the elections had been conducted on tribalistic lines, the two largest tribes, Mendes and Temnes and their respective supporters being equally divided. In the circumstances, it would be advisable for them to form a coalition government. He advised them to go and consider the necessity for such coalition and to see him about 10 a.m. on the 22nd of March.

That night, certain influential persons paid, what the Governor-General's secretary, O. P. A. Macaulay described at the first treason trial in Sierra Leone as, a "social visit". In his book, Gershon Collier wrote that "When on March 21, 1967, the Governor-General yielded to pressures from the Colony Creole elements and appointed Siaka Stevens Prime Minister, events dramatically reached a climax."[9]

DECLARATION OF MARTIAL LAW - 21ST MARCH, 1967

On the morning of the 21st March, 1967, the Governor-General invited Brigadier David Lansana to the State House and told him that he had decided to appoint Siaka Stevens as Prime Minister. The Commissioner of Police, William Leigh, was present. Brigadier David Lansana informed the Governor-General that the country was on the brink of civil war and that he should postpone the appointment to enable him to deploy his soldiers to cope with the civil disturbances which he said, had already started. He left.

Mr. Siaka Stevens then arrived with his entourage, including, Dr. Mohammed Forna, Ibrahim Taqui, Cyril Rogers-Wright, S.A.J. Pratt, for the swearing-in ceremony. Lieutenant Norman told Brigadier Lansana of developments. He also informed him that a large and unruly crowd had surrounded the State House. The Brigadier instructed him to seal-off the State House and that he should not allow any one to enter or leave it.

At the treason trial, the Brigadier explained, in answer to the Acting Chief Justice, Okoro-Cole, that he took those steps in order to protect the Head of State, in view of the hostile mob that had gathered outside State House. In reply to the Acting Chief Justice, he said that he would under similar circumstances in future, take similar steps to protect the Governor-General. The Acting Chief Justice told him that his "conduct stinks". His lawyer intervened to protect his client, but was told by the Acting Chief Justice, "and you add stench to it." Mr. Berthan Macaulay, the 12th accused in the treason trial of which I was the 11th accused, protested against the learned Acting Chief Justice's remarks and added that, but for the fact that other people were involved, he would have asked him to recuse himself from the trial, as he felt that those remarks coming from a trial judge, were prejudicial to the accused persons.

After the swearing-in ceremony, the Governor-General gave Tommy Decker, the then Permanent Secretary, Ministry of Information and Broadcasting, a press release announcing the appointment of Siaka Stevens as Prime Minister. He took it to Brigadier Lansana at Flag Staff House.

That evening, Brigadier Lansana declared Martial Law. In his declaration of Martial Law at 5:55 pm. on the 21st of March, 1967, Brigadier David Lansana told the nation;

> We are now operating under Martial Law. (This action was taken to) protect the constitution and to maintain law and order (following) wide-spread rumour put out by the APC that the Governor-General has appointed Mr. Siaka Stevens as Prime Minister. I want to assure the public that if this rumour is true, it is unconstitutional because the results of the elections have not yet all come in. And at this very moment I am speaking, the election of Paramount Chiefs is going on. No party has yet got sufficient number to form an overall majority of the Members of Parliament. Only this morning, March 21, at about 10:30 the Governor-General assured me that he will not proceed with the appointment of Prime Minister until he has had consultation on Wednesday (today) March 22.
>
> This rumour being spread by the Opposition is an attempt to ignore the Constitution and seize power by force. This as I assure (sic) the Governor-General this morning will lead to chaos and civil war. As custodian of State Security, I have decided to protect the Constitution and to maintain law and order.
>
> Therefore from now on, we are operating under Martial Law. From now on the army is in control and will use all its power to see that the Constitution is not violated (Parenthesis mine).

He advised the people to remain calm, because "The last thing we want in this country is bloodshed. Please let us all avoid it by remaining calm and awaiting for (sic) the results of the elections".

Top players in Sierra Leone. See Matchet, page 2400

WHY THE ARMY STEPPED IN

The issue of the *Daily Mail* of 23rd March, 1967, carried a full statement by the Force Commander, Brigadier David Lansana, explaining why the Army stepped in. The Constitution, he said, and the laws made there under, provided for 12 Paramount Chief Members and 68 Ordinary Members. The Governor- General appoints as Prime Minister some one who commands a majority of these members, i.e., "someone who has the following of at least 40 Members of the House of Representatives."

He recounted the procedure followed during the last general elections. After the elections of Ordinary Members had been known on the 18th of March, 1967, the state of the Parties was 32 seats for the Sierra Leone Peoples Party, 32 All Peoples Congress Party, and 2 Independent Members. These results showed a clear tribal division of the country between Mendes and Temnes and their associates. The country was therefore, not divided according to political ideologies, and neither Party had a majority over the other.

The Brigadier had a meeting with the Governor-General and was assured by him that "he did not intend to do anything unconstitutional and that he would wait until the elections" results of Paramount Chief Members were known to him before appointing a Prime Minister. He went on,

> I again informed him that I would not be able to contain any trouble which might arise if he acted unconstitutionally. Two hours after my interview with him, he decided to make an appointment when neither Party had a majority and elections (of Paramount Chief Members -mine) were still in progress.

Brigadier David Lansana then reiterated his assurances that

> I want to make it clear that the Army-and I say this after consultation with my senior officers -does not, I repeat does not, intend to impose a Military Government on the people of Sierra Leone. This country has a record for Constitutional Government.

> Nevertheless, as soldiers, when the Constitution is violated and violation is likely to lead - and in this case was actually leading - to a breakdown of law and order, I and my officers felt that, in accordance with established practice, we should come to the aid of the civil power to restore Constitutional Government

and law and order. Our attitude and action are fully supported and backed by the Commissioner of Police.

I am now despatching, by cable, a copy of this my statement to the Queen of Sierra Leone in England. Fellow citizens, we are all aware of the serious dangers of tribalism now current in our country. This unfortunate trend which we had feared all along came into full evidence during and after our recent elections. We are all familiar with the fact that the tribal split in our country has been clearly reflected in the election results. This situation became dangerous when it appeared obvious, as the results of the first elections came in, that in response to the propaganda that the SLPP was a Party of the South and the APC a Party of the North supported by the Western Area, both Parties had equal strength in the country.

Even while the votes were still being cast, tribal feelings rose to such a height that serious incidents of violence occurred and we today find ourselves on the brink of inter-tribal warfare. On the first polling day hundreds of voters were dragged out of the queues and beaten. Since that date Fullahs and other nationals have been attacked and looted.

The Fullahs, too, in a desperate mood to protect their lives and property, took counter measures and a serious disaster was only avoided by the timely intervention of the Army in support of the Police

This situation was brought to the notice of the Governor-General by a number of responsible people including myself. And I requested the Governor-General to suspend any action regarding the appointment of a Prime Minister until all the results were known. The Governor-General promised me as Chief Custodian of State Security that he would follow my advice.

Not only was he aware of the highly explosive situation but he himself expressed concern about the fact that the elections were apparently fought on a tribal basis. He said as much to both Sir Albert Margai and the Honourable Siaka P. Stevens at a meeting with them on the 20th of March, 1967, and advised them to consider the formation of a coalition Government.

He further asked them to see him again on the matter at 1000 hours on Wednesday, 22nd of March, 1967.

One of the things I had planned to do in the interim period was to make a reassessment of the security position should a confrontation develop and the ability of the Police and the Army to cope with such an emergency and prevent it from escalating into a widespread conflict, with results with which we are all familiar from the experiences of other countries.

I have reproduced the foregoing and similar documents verbatim, because of their historical importance. To paraphrase them would vitiate from their value and might do injustice to the dramatis personae. Reported speeches are often prone to the slant which the narrator puts on them, depending on his predilections. This is even more so in politics.

The circumstances leading to the interventions of the army in the administration of Sierra Leone are of historical importance. I have therefore, decided, where appropriate, to reproduce the full text of declarations, proclamations, so that the reader would be able to assess the validity of my interpretations and the conclusions which I draw from them.

BRIGADIER DAVID LANSANA IN CUSTODY - 23RD, MARCH, 1967

On the 23rd of March, 1967, Brigadier David Lansana was arrested by his senior officers and detained at Pademba Road Prison. They then formed the National Reformation Council. On their behalf, Major Charles Blake broadcast the following statement on the day of his detention:

> Fellow citizens, this is Major Charles Blake speaking. You will recall Brigadier Lansana's statement to you last night in which he outlined the irregularities surrounding the Governor-General's unconstitutional action in the appointment of Mr. Siaka P. Stevens.
>
> He also said that he as custodian of state security had decided to protect the Constitution and to maintain law and order and for this reason, he had assumed control. Fellow citizens I want to make this quite clear that we, the senior officers did not intend to impose a military government on the people of this our beloved country.
>
> We had, therefore, agreed with the Force Commander that since the election results had demonstrated a clear tribalistic attitude of the country motivated and aggravated by the propaganda campaigning of the two parties, the safest and surest solution for the benefit of our beloved country was to bring both parties to the conference table to discuss the establishment of a national government representative of every section of the country.

We, the senior officers had since noticed that the attitude of the Brigadier was not to bring about the creation of a national government but to impose Sir Albert Margai as the Prime Minister of this country.

We the senior officers dissociate ourselves from the Brigadier's line of action and in the interest of this country have no alternative but to divest the Brigadier of control of this country. The Army and the Police are now in complete control.

I appeal to all civil servants and to all citizens of our beloved country to remain calm and to remain at their posts. I take the pledge to assure all my fellow citizens that the Army does not propose to take cognisance of the past, to mount exhaustive inquiries into the liberty and possessions of the individual but to turn a new page in the history of our beloved country.

As an interim measure there shall be a National Reformation Council comprising of the following: Lt. Col. A. P. Genda, Chairman; Mr. William Leigh, Commissioner of Police has been invited to be the Deputy Chairman; Lt. Col. A. T. Juxon-Smith, Major A. C. Blake, Major B. I. Kai-Samba, Major S. B. Jumu, Major A. R. Turay and Mr. Alpha Kamara, Assistant Commissioner of Police has also been invited to become a member.

There shall also be a National Advisory Council to the National Reformation Council which will comprise of eminent civilians in the country. The nominations of these civilians will be deliberated at the first sitting of the N.R.C.

As from this moment, the Constitution is suspended; all political parties are dissolved and all political activities prohibited.

The Governor-General is under house arrest, the Force Commander and the leaders of the two political parties, Sir Albert Margai and Mr. Siaka P. Stevens are in protective custody....[10]

THE NATIONAL REFORMATION COUNCIL PROCLAMATION

As soon as the NRC was formed they issued the following Proclamation:

Whereas it is a fundamental duty of the Sierra Leone Police Force to maintain and secure public safety and public order.

And whereas the actions and utterances of the political parties and their leaders have resulted in tribal factions and brought about a situation which has led to an almost total break down of law and order, bloodshed and imminent tribal war.

And whereas it is expedient in the situation aforesaid that due provision should be made for the maintenance of law and order in Sierra Leone, and the proper administration by law of the State of Sierra Leone.

Now therefore, we the members of the Sierra Leone Military Forces and the Sierra Leone Police Force in cooperation with the people of Sierra Leone in order to ensure the maintenance of law and order, ensure domestic tranquility, the future enjoyment of the blessings of liberty to citizens of Sierra Leone and all persons living therein and their posterity, do hereby proclaim as follows....[11]

Then followed the usual trappings of a new government. Judges of the Appeal and Supreme Courts took the Judicial Oath of Allegiance to the National Reformation Council at the Officers' Mess Wilberforce on the 26th March in the presence of the Council, presided over by William Leigh, Commissioner of Police, and Deputy Chairman of the Council.

Chapter 1 Notes

1.   Collier, Gershon: *Sierra Leone: An experiment in Democracy in an African Nation*, New York University Press, New York, 1970, p. 63.

2.   Cartwright, John R: *Politics in Sierra Leone*, 1947-1967, University of Toronto Press, Toronto, 1970 p. 121.

3.   Kilson Martin L. Authoritarian and single party tendencies in African politics, *World Politics* January, 1963, p. 272.

4.   *Ibid.*, 275.

5.   *Ibid.*, 276.

6.   *Daily Mail*, March 2nd 1967 Sierra Leone.

7.   *Daily Mail*, March 4th 1967 Sierra Leone.

8.   *Daily Mail*, March 16th 1967 Sierra Leone.

9.   Collier, Gershon, *Ibid.*

10.   *Daily Mail* March 27th 1967, Sierra Leone.

11.   *Ibid.*

CHAPTER 2

THE DOVE-EDWIN COMMISSION OF INQUIRY

In order to avert, what Brigadier David Lansana honestly believed was internecine war, he declared Martial Law which authorised him to assume extraordinary powers over the civil authority. According to him, his officers were fully in agreement with the steps he was taking. Colonel Charles Blake explained in his broadcast, after they had arrested Brigadier David Lansana, and detained him at Pademba Road Prison, that they were motivated by the fact that they suspected that the Brigadier was planning to impose Sir Albert Margai on the nation.

When they formed the first military government in Sierra Leone, the officers immediately appointed a Commission of Inquiry which we shall now discuss. Other crucial constitutional issues relating to the Brigadier's action and the appointment of Siaka Stevens as Prime Minister by Sir Henry Lightfoot Boston, the then Governor-General, will also be discussed.

The terms of reference of "The Dove-Edwin Commission of Inquiry into the conduct of the 1967 General Elections in Sierra Leone", were, to investigate, in particular,

    (i)   the compilation and operation of the Register of Voters;
    (ii)   the custody of Ballot Papers;
    (iii) the conduct of Political Parties;
    (iv) the results of the, aforesaid General Elections.[1]

We shall consider the points that are germane to our immediate problems, namely, the propriety of Brigadier David Lansana's action and the constitutionality of the Governor-General's action in appointing Siaka Stevens as Prime Minister.

POSITION OF PARAMOUNT CHIEFS

With reference to the Governor-General's action, Justice Dove-Edwin's Commission recommended as follows:

> 104.   In not waiting for the results of the Paramount Chiefs' Elections before acting under his powers the Governor-General, Speaker Sir Henry, was manifestly right.

> 105.   One seems to forget that quite apart from his qualifications Sir Henry was, until his appointment as Governor-General, Speaker of the House and used to all the rights and conventions of the House.   We are satisfied that Paramount Chiefs represent their Districts and by and large support the Government.

> 106.   It has been said that the Governor-General in exercising his powers under Section 58 (2) of the Constitution cannot in Law exclude the Paramount Chiefs when making his assessment of who appears likely to command the support of the majority of the Members of the House, and that the Paramount Chiefs are "persons" as provided for in Section 22 of the Constitution which provides for the protection of freedom of assembly and association.

> 107.   This opinion is probably responsible for the statement that the Governor-General acted unconstitutionally, one of Brigadier Lansana's reasons for his action since the results of the Paramount Chiefs' Elections had not been announced.

> 108.   We think that the Governor-General was right. The result of the Paramount Chiefs' Elections would not have helped him at all in coming to his decision.   The most those Elections would reveal is that twelve Paramount Chiefs had been elected, each for his own District and nothing to do with the Parties.   We have dealt with the meaning of "declared for the S.L.P.P." It simply does not mean a thing.   In the Assembly all Independents who wish to can cross over to the Party of their choice and it is then that the change of loyalties can be of any value.

109.   In 1964 when Sir Albert was appointed the then Attorney-General, who remained Attorney-General till the take-over by Brigadier Lansana and for some time after, gave a written opinion about the Governor-General's discretion acting under Sections 58 (2) and 64 (I) (b).

110.   He said that it could not be questioned except in a Court of Law and the Privy Council is the final Court to determine matters of interpretation of our Constitution. Whether he advised Brigadier Lansana or not is not clear.

111.   If we understood Sir Albert Margai properly when he was cross-examining some witnesses, his point is that there is nothing in the Constitution to prevent any Paramount Chief declaring for the Party of his choice. We hope we have dealt with this. We repeat, no Paramount Chief could change his place as a representative of his District to say he is a Paramount Chief S.L.P.P. Member or A.P.C. He cannot be any more than an Independent with leanings towards the Government in power. If at all he wants to change over he should do this in the House.

The Commission vindicated the Governor-General as follows:

120.   We must stress that as the Constitution reads the Governor-General is not bound by figures although they go a long way to help.

121.   Sir Albert was appointed and no one counted how many persons in the House would support him and yet the Governor-General was right in his appointment. The then Attorney-General, Mr. Berthan Macaulay, said so.

122.   When Brigadier Lansana took over the true position of the Parties and the *true* results of the Elections were: (Emphasis supplied)

S.L.P.P. - 22 contested seats and 6, unopposed

A.P.C. - 32 contested seats and none opposed

Independents - 6

123.   On the above figures the Governor-General could appoint a Prime Minister. He acted constitutionally and to say it was unconstitutional is to miss the point.

124.   The section under which the Governor-General acted has been quoted time and again and must be known by all who care by now.

125.   The Governor-General's duty is to appoint a member of the House who appears to him *likely* to command the support of the majority of the Members of the House, acting in accordance with his own deliberate judgment. (Emphasis supplied)

126.   It was, on the wording of the Constitution, not open to Brigadier Lansana to interfere. Why did Sir Albert not go to the House and defeat Mr. Siaka Stevens? Why did the Brigadier not tell him to do so? Perhaps because it was known that the Governor-General was right.

The statement of the National Reformation Council on the foregoing is as follows:

POSITION OF PARAMOUNT CHIEFS

27.   The National Reformation Council does not agree with the conclusions reached by the Commission as regards the position of Paramount Chiefs in the House of Representatives. It is the view of the National Reformation Council that, since the House of Representatives consists of Ordinary as well as Paramount Chief Members, no House of Representatives can be legally constituted before elections of both categories of members have been duly concluded in accordance with section 30 of the Constitution.

28.   The Paramount Chief Members are therefore an integral and essential part of the House of Representatives.

29.   Also, although as a matter of practice and expediency, Paramount Chief Members may be expected to throw their lot in with the party in power, it is legally possible, having regard to the entrenched provisions of the Constitution with regard to freedom of association, for such members to exercise their right to support any political party of their choice.

30.   Accordingly, the Commission's statement in paragraph 101-"Whilst we concede that in the House the Chief might find himself occasionally voting with the Sierra Leone Peoples Party, he cannot join any party in his own and his District's interest" is not acceptable.

31.   The Commission's statement in paragraph 105 to the effect that-"We are satisfied that Paramount Chiefs represent their Districts and by and large support the Government" is not entirely an accurate statement.

32.   Similarly, the statement in paragraph 108 of the Report that the results of the Paramount Chief Members election would not have helped the Governor-General at all in coming to this decision, is incorrect, because he would not have been competent to appoint a Prime Minister if in fact no election was held for Paramount Chief Members.

33.   While it is conceded that the Governor-General can use his deliberate judgment in the appointment of a Prime Minister, it would have been more in accord with the spirit of the Constitution if the constituent members of the House of Representatives (Ordinary Members and Paramount Chief Members) had been elected before such appointment was made. (parenthesis supplied)

34.   There is in fact nothing in the Constitution to prevent the Governor-General appointing a Paramount Chief Member as Prime Minister if a Paramount Chief Member appears to the Governor-General a person likely to command majority support of the members of the House. Therefore, in appointing the Prime Minister before the election of the Paramount Chief Member, the Governor-General inadvertently deprived the Paramount Chief Members of their right to have one of their members elected as Prime Minister.

35.   Regrettably, the Governor-General in appointing the Prime Minister on the 21st day of March, 1967, never took notice of a single Paramount Chief Member (*see* paragraph 136(2) of the Report). In this respect the National Reformation Council cannot accept this part of the Report. (Emphasis and parenthesis supplied).

THE APPOINTMENT OF PRIME MINISTER

36.   When the Commission started its sittings, sufficient evidence was received by the National Reformation Council that several eminent citizens of the then Western Area including high-ranking Judicial Officers, the clergy and commercial people had thronged the State House and pressurized the Governor-General to appoint Mr. Siaka Stevens as Prime Minister before the completion of the election of Paramount Chief Members to the House of Representatives.

37.   The National Reformation Council was both shocked and surprised to learn during the course of the Inquiry, that Mr. Justice Dove-Edwin, the Chairman of the Commission, had been one of the people who had been present at the State House at the material time.

38. This fact was brought out in the evidence of Lieutenant Norman before the Commission that Mr. Justice Dove-Edwin himself was present at the State House on the 21st of March, 1967.

39. It is the view of the National Reformation Council that the Chairman of the Commission, having been confronted with this evidence, should have tendered his resignation. However, the National Reformation Council did not take the alternative of revoking the appointment of the Chairman, because at that time the Council felt that this involvement of Mr. Justice Dove-Edwin was immaterial, since the issue of the constitutionality or otherwise of the appointment of a Prime Minister was outside the terms of reference of the Commission. The National Reformation Council was therefore surprise (sic) to find several paragraphs in the Report devoted entirely to this issue, including the communications between the Governor-General and the then Prime Minister (Sir Albert Margai) and Mr. Siaka P. Stevens.

40. There is no evidence either in the manuscript or in the Report of the Commission that the people who pressurized the Governor-General were called upon to give evidence to refute the allegation of Lieutenant Norman. In the absence of anything to the contrary, the National Reformation Council is of the view that the Governor-General did not exercise his deliberate judgment, free from outside pressure, in appointing Mr. Siaka P. Stevens as Prime Minister on the 21st day of March, 1967.

41. The National Reformation Council, from its inception, has always held the view that the Governor-General can only exercise his discretion when the occasion arises. It is the considered view of the Council that the occasion for the Governor-General to exercise his discretion had not yet arisen on the 21st of March, 1967, when he purported to exercise this discretion.

42. This untimely action of the Governor-General gave rise to an increasing tension throughout the country. The situation was aggravated when the Senior Officers of the Royal Sierra Leone Military Forces realized that Brigadier Lansana wanted to impose Sir Albert Margai as Prime Minister on the people of Sierra Leone. This would have led to utter chaos and bloodshed in the country.

43. The National Reformation Council's intervention on the 23rd day of March, was a rescue operation and was not intended permanently to impose a Military Government on the people.

44.   The issues raised in paragraphs 118 to 132 are outside the terms of reference of the Commission.

We have had cause to quote, extensively, the Dove-Edwin Commission Report because it is the main cause of all the misconceptions that have led to the erroneous conclusions that the APC won the 1967 General Elections and particularly, that the Governor-General acted constitutionally in appointing Siaka Stevens as Prime Minister on the 21st of March, 1967 while the elections of Paramount Chief Members of Parliament were in progress.

Having stated the Dove-Edwin Report and the National Reformation Council's White Paper thereon, we shall now outline the All Peoples Congress Party's actions on the fundamental issues raised by the Report.

THE ALL PEOPLES CONGRESS PARTY CONSTITUTION ON THE ROLE OF PARAMOUNT CHIEFS IN THE LEGISLATIVE PROCESS.

According to Section 44 of the APC One-Party Constitution No. 12 of 1978, to be eligible for election to Parliament, a Paramount Chief shall be required to be a member of the Recognised Party, the All Peoples Congress Party. This Section is a direct refutation of the Dove-Edwin Commission's Recommendation 108 that "the meaning of 'declared for the S.L.P.P.'....simply does not mean a thing." If it did not mean a thing by convention of the 1961 Constitution, it does mean everything under the 1978 One-Party Constitution which makes it mandatory for him to be a member of the One-Party, namely, the All Peoples Congress Party. He is not now required to declare but compelled to belong to the APC. Furthermore, Section 44 clearly over-rules the Commission's paragraph 111 which recommends that

> We repeat, no Paramount Chief could change his place as a representative of his District to say he is a Paramount Chief S.L.P.P. member or A.P.C.

The role of Paramount Chiefs in the appointment of a Prime Minister under the 1961 Constitution is so important and crucial that to ignore them has led to misinterpretation of the Constitution and therefore, to the erroneous conclusion that the APC won the General Elections in 1967, which they did not win. The National Reformation Council Statement on the Report quite correctly made nonsense of the Dove-Edwin Commission Report.

Finally, and this is the pith of the matter, that Sir Henry was manifestly wrong in appointing a Prime Minister while the elections of Paramount Chief Members were in progress, has been endorsed by Siaka Stevens. Realising the enormity of his crime in instigating prominent citizens of Sierra Leone to pressurise the Governor-General to appoint him as Prime Minister prematurely, as soon as he became Prime Minister, in 1968, he tried to expiate his guilty conscience by enacting in Section 50(1) (c) of the All Peoples Congress Party 1971 Constitution of Sierra Leone Act No. 6 that

> No person shall be appointed Prime Minister during a dissolution and before all the results of the General Election held under Section 48 have been declared....

We shall deal with this point more fully in the next chapter.

Two important principles of English common law are raised by the National Reformation Council Statement on the Dove-Edwin Commission Report, namely, (a) a man cannot be a judge in his own cause, (b) justice must not only be done, but must be manifestly and palpably be seen to have been done.

At paragraph 37 of the National Reformation Council Statement on the Dove-Edwin Report as reproduced above,

> The National Reformation Council was both shocked and surprised to learn during the course of the Inquiry, that Mr. Justice Dove-Edwin, the Chairman of the Commission, had been one of the people who had been present at the State House at the material time.

Mr. Justice Dove-Edwin did not resign from the Commission, when he was 'confronted' with this evidence by Lieutenant Norman, at the material time, nor did the National Reformation Council revoke his appointment

> because at that time the Council felt that this involvement of Mr. Justice Dove-Edwin was immaterial, since the issue of the constitutionality or otherwise of the appointment of a Prime Minister was outside the terms of reference of the Commission. The National Reformation Council was

therefore surprise (sic) to find several paragraphs in the Report devoted entirely to this issue... (Paragraph 39 of the Report above).

His commission should have been terminated forthwith by the National Reformation Council. We shall explain this point later.

The learned Mr. Justice Dove-Edwin ought to have realised that he was seriously compromising himself by accepting chairmanship of the Commission set up to investigate a matter in which he was intimately associated. He was in State House at the material time when

> several eminent citizens of the then Western Area including high-ranking Judicial Officers, the clergy and commercial people had thronged the State House, and pressurised the Governor-General to appoint Mr. Siaka P. Stevens as Prime Minister before the completion of the election of Paramount Chief Members to the House of Representatives (paragraph 36 of the Report above).

If he participated in pressurising the Governor-General as it was alleged above, then he violated the first canon above, by subsequently becoming a judge in his own cause. He should therefore, not have accepted chairmanship of the Commission, nor even become a member, as to do so, would be a clear case of conflict of interest. On the other hand, if, although he was at the Governor-General's residence that night, yet did not participate in the alleged pressurising of the Governor-General, nevertheless, because of the scandal surrounding such allegations, the course of justice would not be manifestly and palpably be seen to have been served, by his chairmanship of a Commission investigating the events relating to the Governor-General at the material time that he was there. Either way, Mr. Justice Dove-Edwin disqualified himself from membership, nay more, chairmanship, of the Commission.

Little wonder that the value of the Report is vitiated by these facts. The National Reformation Council, in short, did not accept the crucial part of the Report, which is, the legality of the Governor-General's action in appointing Siaka Stevens as Prime Minister, which precipitated all the trouble in March, 1967. Furthermore, the constitutionality or otherwise of the appointment of a Prime Minister was outside the terms of reference of the Commission. (NRC Statement)

And so the NRC were surprised "to find several paragraphs in the Report devoted entirely to this issue." (Paragraph 29 of the Report).

Why did Mr. Justice Dove-Edwin devote so much time on a matter clearly outside his terms of reference?

In the case of Jones v. The National Coal Board; Appeal Case, 1953, London, Lord Justice Denning gave judgment, inter alia, that

> We much regret that it has fallen to our lot to consider such a complaint against one of Her Majesty's judges; but consider it we must....

> No one can doubt that the judge, in intervening as he did, was actuated by the best motives.

> Nevertheless, we are quite clear that the interventions, taken together, were far more than they should have been. In the system of trial which we have evolved in this country, the judge sits to hear and determine the issues raised by the parties, not to conduct an examination or investigation on behalf of society at large, as happens, we believe in some foreign countries....

> Lord Greene M.R. who explained that justice is best done by a judge who holds the balance between the contending parties without himself taking part in their disputations....

> In the very pursuit of justice our keenness may outrun our sureness, and we may trip and fall. This is what has happened here. A judge of acute perception, acknowledged learning, and actuated by the best of motives, has nevertheless intervened so much in the conduct of the case that one of the parties-nay, each of them-has come away complaining that he was not able properly to put his case, and these complaints are, we think, justified.

Another outstanding case on the points we are discussing is Sudan Government v. Omer and another, High Court of Justice in the Sudan on the 1st July 1972. Justice Abdel Imam held that:

> natural justice requires judicial and quasi-judicial activities to be carried out in good faith, and the Court will quash a decision which has clearly already been arrived at maliciously

...'bias is to denote a departure from the standard of even-handed justice which the law requires from those who occupy judicial office or those who are commonly regarded as holding a quasi-judicial office, such as an arbitrator.'

Where objection is taken on the score of bias, the question is not whether the justices were really biased, or in fact decided partially, but whether there was real likelihood of bias. Actual bias on the part of the authority need not be proved, nor need it be proved that the actual decision is biased....

Moreover it is an admitted principle that justice should not only be done but should be manifestly and undoubtedly be seen to be done....

Even if a magistrate having an interest sat along with others but took no part in the proceedings, they must be quashed.

The pith of the judicial principles enunciated above are that

(a)   ....justice is best done by a judge who holds the balance between the contending parties without himself taking part in their disputations....

(b)   ....the question is not whether the justices were really biased, or in fact decided partially, but whether there was real likelihood of bias...Actual bias...need not be proved,....

(c)   Even if a magistrate having an interest sat along with others but took no part in the proceedings, they must be quashed.

The Honourable Mr. Justice Dove-Edwin more than anyone else, knew after the swearing-in of Siaka Stevens as Prime Minister that he was directly or indirectly associated with alleged person or persons who pressurised the Governor-General into appointing Siaka Stevens as Prime Minister contrary to the line he had mapped out the previous day, when he instructed Sir Albert Margai and Siaka Stevens to consider forming a coalition government. It is immediately conceded that, *presence* at the scene of a crime does not predicate complicity, but it is a serious presumption of *knowledge*, which again, is not sufficient to send a man to the gallows, although, curiously, it would have been, to convict of misprision of treason, as the pundits were straining strenuously to prove at our treason trial.

Was his presence at the alleged pressurisation of the Governor-General sufficient to constitute the likelihood of bias? Will a jury of 12 men agree that it does constitute the likelihood of bias?

The National Reformation Council "was both shocked and surprised to learn during the course of the Inquiry, that Mr. Justice Dove-Edwin, the chairman of the Commission had been one of the people who had been present at the State House at the material time." It was their view that, the chairman of the Commission "having been confronted with this piece of evidence should have tendered his resignation." He never did. This fact vitiated whatever value the Commission's Report might have had. It is precisely for these reasons that the learned judges said above that, "justice should manifestly and undoubtedly be seen to be done....", that is, that it should be free from the "likelihood of bias".

That was not the end of the matter. The Honourable Gentleman went on to expatiate on matters outside his terms of reference. Why? When Lieutenant Norman confronted Justice Dove-Edwin with evidence of his presence at State House, it was the duty of the NRC to have investigated Lieutenant Norman's evidence. If proved, then Justice Dove-Edwin's Commission should have been terminated forthwith. He should not have been allowed to continue in the Commission. The NRC allowed him to continue in the Commission

> because at that time the Council felt that this involvement of Mr. Justice Dove-Edwin was immaterial, since the issue of the constitutionality or otherwise of the appointment of a Prime Minister was outside the terms of reference of the Commission.

The NRC's reasons for allowing him to stay on the Commission are not convincing. They gambled and the consequence for the history of Sierra Leone has been catastrophic. The Dove-Edwin Report confirmed Siaka Stevens in his diabolical schemes which he later pursued by unleashing a holocaust on the Sierra Leone Peoples Party as soon as he became Prime

Minister, for alleged interference with his appointment to mis-rule Sierra Leone from 1967.

I submit with respect to the learned Honourable Mr. Justice Dove-Edwin that, by entering into extraneous matters, matters outside his terms of reference, "there was real likelihood of bias." Quite apart from that, he had no business on that Commission.

Concluding the above case:

> His Lordship emphasized...that the law should not be allowed to be used for collateral or extraneous purposes, nor should it be allowed to be an instrument of political or any kind of oppression. In a civilized community, its sole purpose was the preservation of peace and order. (Jones v. The National Coal Board)

The legal principles which we inherited from the British were not all tainted with the curse of imperialism. They were laid down primarily for the protection of English settlers and their vested interests. If we continue to apply them, let us do so faithfully. The judiciary should be our last hope. If a man cannot go to court with reasonable certainty that his case is going to be heard impartially, then let us stop paying hypocritical lip-service to sacred injunctions like the "impartiality of the judiciary." It should not have double meaning for Mende and Temne, or Kuranko and Sherbro for that matter. The judiciary is an essential, infact the most important part of a democracy. The impartiality of the judicial system should at all times be beyond suspicion, in short, it should be inviolate. The office of judge is sacrosanct and should not be made into a political foot-ball. Judges can do a lot by preventing this from happening. As soon as people lose confidence in the judicial system, the rule of law would be in danger. It was his impartiality and aloofness from the intrigues of Freetown that made Sir Henry such a jewel in the Supreme Court of Sierra Leone, and an eminent substitute for the colonial Governor-General. That he should have been pressurised into appointing Siaka Stevens in a manner inconsistent with his original plan, is lamentably sad.

President Siaka Stevens atoned for this interference. That was why as soon as he took over the reins of government, he immediately amended the relevant section by providing that the Governor-General shall not appoint a Prime Minister UNTIL all the results have been declared after general elections have been held. This might perhaps avoid the recurrence of several innocent people, including the author languishing in gaol for 3½ years while his wife and other wives strove painfully to eke out bare subsistence.

With this back-ground to the events of the 21st of March, 1967, we shall now consider the constitutionality of the Governor-General's action in appointing Siaka Stevens as Prime Minister.

Chapter 2 Notes

1.   National Reformation Council: Report of the Dove-Edwin Commission of Inquiry into the conduct of the 1967 General Elections in Sierra Leone and the Government Statement thereon; Printed and published by the Government Printer, Sierra Leone, 1967, p. 1.

CHAPTER 3

THE CONSTITUTIONALITY OF THE GOVERNOR-GENERAL'S ACTION

There has been and will continue to be concerned debate over the constitutionality of the Governor-General's action in the appointment of Siaka Stevens as Prime Minister in the prevailing circumstances in Sierra Leone, on the 21st of March, 1967. We shall now consider the constitutional provisions that relate to this matter.

Sections 29 and 30 of the Constitution of Sierra Leone 1961, relating to the "Establishment of parliament", and the composition of the House of Representatives are as follows:

Section 29 - Establishment of Parliament

> There shall be a Parliament of Sierra Leone which shall consist of Her Majesty and a House of Representatives

> Section 30 (1) The House of Representatives shall consist of a Speaker and the following members (who shall be known as 'Members of Parliament,') that is to say

> (a)   One member for each District who shall, subject to the provisions of this Constitution, be elected in such manner as may be prescribed by or under any law from among the persons who, under any law, are for the time being Paramount Chiefs; and

> (b)   such number of other members as Parliament may prescribe who, subject as aforesaid, shall be elected in such manner as may be prescribed by or under any law:

Provided that

(i)   the number of members to be elected in pursuance of paragraph (a) and the number of members to be elected in pursuance of paragraph (b) of this sub-section shall not together be less than sixty;....

With regard to the appointment of Prime Minister, Section 58 (2) of the Constitution reads as follows:

Whenever the Governor-General has occasion to appoint a Prime Minister he shall appoint a member of the House of Representatives who appears to him likely to command the support of the majority of the members of the House. (Emphasis mine)

On the 23rd of March, 1967, the Army and the Police staged a coup d'etat. The Dove-Edwin Commission of inquiry into the conduct of the general elections reported that

In not waiting for the results of the Paramount Chief Elections before acting under his powers (in appointing Siaka Stevens as Prime Minister), the Governor-General Sir Henry was manifestly right.[1] (Parenthesis mine)

The National Reformation Council which appointed this Commission did not accept this recommendation, because it was revealed to the Commissioners that the Governor-General was pressurised into appointing Siaka Stevens as Prime Minister. Mr. Gershon Collier former Ambassador of Sierra Leone to the United States of America and the United Nations, and former Chief Justice of Sierra Leone, wrote in his book on Sierra Leone, that

When on March 21, 1967, the Governor-General yielded to pressures from the Colony Creole elements and appointed Siaka Stevens Prime Minister, events dramatically reached a climax.[2]

Sir Henry, a Bastow Scholar, former Judge of the Supreme Court of Sierra Leone and former Speaker of Parliament was, undoubtedly also, one of the most outstanding jurists in the British Commonwealth. Nevertheless, whether he was manifestly right or not on this occasion is open to debate. It is precisely for such problems, that the Judicial Committee of the Privy

Council was established because, in their decisions, the most learned judges may err. Therefore, the All Peoples Congress Party Government hastily abolished appeals to the Privy Council while the treason trial was in progress, as they realised that if the accused were convicted and they appealed to the Privy Council, it would uphold their appeals.

Within the parameters of the Constitution as outlined above, we shall examine the constitutionality of Siaka Stevens' appointment.

First, whenever the Governor-General has occasion to appointment "for Prime Minister...." a such occasion never arose on the 21st, of March, as the National Reformation Council stated, when the Governor-General appointed Siaka Stevens as Prime Minister, because the criteria in Section 30 had not been fulfilled. That is to say, that the Governor-General shall appointment a Prime Minister only when the House of Representatives is constituted. The House of Representatives means, a House consisting of a Speaker, Paramount Chief Members and Ordinary Members. The Ordinary Members Elections were held on the 17th while the elections of Paramount Chief Members were held on the 20th of March. At the time of the Governor-General's conference with Sir Albert Margai and Siaka Stevens, the results of the Ordinary Members were known to him. The Sierra Leone Peoples Party won 32 seats and the All Peoples Congress Party, 32 seats. When he was apprised of the widespread disturbances in the country by the Force Commander, Brigadier David Lansana, he advised Sir Albert Margai and Siaka Stevens to consider the formation of a coalition government. At that time, the Paramount Chiefs' Elections were being held, that was why the learned Governor-General, without any interference whatsoever, or influence by any person or persons, advised the two leaders of the parties to consider the need for rapprochement.

Sir Henry Light-foot Boston was recommended to Her Majesty the Queen to become Governor-General by Sir Milton Margai, when Sir Maurice Dorman's tenure of office ended, because of his sterling qualities as a scholar, his impartiality as a Judge of the Supreme Court, and his unique exclusion from the hustle and bustle and idle gossip for which the capital is noted. Infact, he was known as a recluse. He was therefore eminently suited to replace Sir Maurice. Without any interference, as disclosed by the

National Reformation Council Statement on the Dove-Edwin Commission of Inquiry, discussed more fully in the last chapter, and by Gershon Collier above, he would most certainly have stuck to his advice to Sir Albert Margai and Siaka Stevens, waited until the results of the Paramount Chiefs' Elections were known to him, and therefore, the House of Representatives constituted, and then appointed a Prime Minister under Section 58(2), in accordance with his advice to both leaders. It is only after all the results of the (a) and (b) Members have been furnished to His Excellency the Governor-General, and the fact published in the Royal Gazette, can there be said to be a House of Representatives, and those who won elections referred to as Members of such House. Until such time, there can be no House of Representatives within the constitutional definition above.

When the House of Representatives is assembled and the new Members sworn in, then the House of Representatives becomes legally constituted, and the Members become de jure Members of the House of Representatives. After the House has been legally constituted according to the provisions of the Constitution, the Governor-General's choice of Prime Minister could then be tested. If the majority of the Members support him, in the constituted House, they would be endorsing the "member of the House of Representatives who appears to him (the Governor-General) to command the support of the majority of the Members of the House." (Parenthesis mine).

But when, according to the National Reformation Council and Gershon Collier, he "yielded to pressures" and appointed Siaka Stevens as Prime Minister, *in medias res*, he was not appointing "a member of the House of Representatives who appears to him likely to command the support of the majority of the Members of the House," in accordance with Section 58 (2), but someone who appeared to the "pressure cookers" to command the majority of a non-existent house.

It is quite out of character for Sir Henry to have taken a decision and reversed himself midstream. If he had not been pressurised, he would most certainly have held the conference with the two leaders as he had proposed to them, and resolved the impending catastrophe. A significant and disturbing aspect of this sordid and unfortunate interference in the unfettered prerogative of the Governor-General was the fact that the Paramount Chiefs were excluded from the selection. Again the National Reformation Council drew attention to this fact. Section 58 (2) speaks of a "member of the House of Representatives who appears to him". This includes Paramount Chiefs. According to the National Reformation Council, there is no provision in the Constitution which excludes Paramount Chiefs from holding the post of Prime Minister. And why should they not be considered for appointment to this high office?

In defining the House of Representatives, the Act quite rightly gave precedence to Paramount Chiefs, because of their historical importance as the natural rulers of Sierra Leone. They are the "(a)" Members. Colonial powers humiliated Paramount Chiefs, and so their subjects tended to disrespect them, particularly, when they were privileged to attend high institutions of learning.

President Siaka Stevens agrees with the contention that by appointing him as Prime Minister while the elections of Paramount Chiefs were being held, Sir Henry Light-foot Boston was manifestly wrong. To remove all doubts, Section 50 (1) (c) of the All Peoples Congress 1971, Constitution of Sierra Leone Act No. 6 states that

> No person shall be appointed Prime Minister during a dissolution and before all the results of the general election held under section 48 have been declared, except that, if the Prime Minister dies during the said period, the President shall appoint any person who was a member of Parliament immediately before the dissolution as Prime Minister.

It has been argued also outside Sierra Leone that the All Peoples Congress Party won the General Elections, 1967. Because of this confusion of the facts as they existed at the time and as revealed at the treason trial, I wrote the following letter to *West Africa* and reproduced by them on the 2nd February, 1981.

> I would like to refer to the correspondent's statement on the 1967 General Elections in Sierra Leone that "the voters showed plainly that the SLPP as led by Sir Albert Margai no longer commanded the trust and support which it had had for 15 years. So much so that the Governor General, Sir Henry Lightfoot Boston, invited Mr. Siaka Stevens to become Prime

Minister. This prompted the Army Commander, Brigadier Lansana to declare martial law and veto the Governor General's decision."

This is a gross distortion of the facts. The results of the Ordinary Members General Elections of 1967 showed that the voters were divided by 32-32 plus the late Messrs. Kai Samba and Luseni Brewah, SLPP members: thus giving the SLPP two more over the APC. That was why the APC mounted frantic efforts to poach these two gentlemen who became the centre of feverish political manoeuvring by both parties-the Sierra Leone Peoples Party attempted to retain them, and the All Peoples Congress tried to poach them. The results of the 12 Paramount Chiefs elections were never known. It is therefore quite clear that the balance of advantage would appear to have been in the lap of the SLPP and not the APC. Only God knows what the final outcome would have been had there been no coup d'etat.

Secondly, Brigadier David Lansana did not declare martial law because Mr. Siaka Stevens was appointed Prime Minister and so vetoed the Governor General as alleged by the correspondent. He declared martial law to protect the Governor-General and Mr. Siaka Stevens, to stave a bloodbath, and prevent civil war.

During the treason-trial presided over by the Acting Chief Justice, Okoro Cole, it was brought out in evidence that on the 20th of March, 1967, the Governor General invited Sir Albert Margai and Mr. Siaka Stevens to State House and told them that in view of the tribalistic division which the elections results showed (32 SLPP and 32 APC as shown in the Exhibit tendered by Mr. Joseph Findlay, the prosecution witness), they should consider the formation of a coalition government. They were to report to the Governor-General on the 21st by which time the results of the elections of Paramount Chief Members would have been known to the Governor General, Parliament properly constituted, after which he could legally "appoint a member of the House of Representatives who appears to him likely to command the support of the members of the House." (Section 58(2) of 1961 Constitution).

A prosecution witness said that after Sir Albert Margai and Mr. Stevens left some persons including prominent personalities, paid the Governor-General a "social visit" that evening of the 20th March. At 10 am on the 21st March, the Governor-General appointed Mr. Siaka Stevens Prime Minister. The legality of the Governor-General's action at that point in time, comes into question. By his appointment of Mr. Siaka Stevens while the elections of Paramount Chief Members were in progress, he precluded the Paramount Chief

Members "from his own deliberate judgement" (Section 64) in the selection of someone who appeared to him to command a majority in Parliament. Someone "who appears to him likely to command the support of the members of the House," includes Paramount Chiefs, since the House of Representatives consists of the Speaker, Paramount Chief Members and Ordinary Members, and there is no section in the 1961 Constitution which precludes a Paramount Chief from becoming Prime Minister.

According to Brigadier Lansana, as soon as Mr. Siaka Stevens was appointed Prime Minister, jubilant APC supporters and indignant SLPP supporters converged on State House, as reported to him by the Governor-General's ADC. In his judgement as Chief Security Officer, the Governor-General's life was in danger. He instructed the Governor-General's ADC, a lieutenant, to seal the gates of State House-not to allow anyone to enter or leave State House.

Brigadier Lansana declared Martial Law that night. In his evidence, Brigadier David Lansana said, according to my notes which I took while in the dock:

'If a similar situation were to arise today, I will not alter that decision as I realised it was necessary to save lives and property and I am now prepared to stand by it.'

He then asked Mr. Justice Banja Tejansie, the Speaker of Parliament to convene a meeting of Parliament to resolve the constitutional impasse. In his broadcast summoning candidates who had won the elections, Mr. Justice Banja Tejansie, assured them of Brigadier Lansana's bona fides.

The legality or otherwise of the Governor-General's action in appointing a Prime Minister while the results of the elections of Paramount Chief members - Class A Members - were unknown to him and thus pre-empting their candidature for Prime Ministership; the propriety of Brigadier Lansana's intervention in averting imminent internecine war with Mendes and Temnes slaughtering one another; and of course, the propriety of paying the Governor-General a "social visit" while on a battlefield charged with explosives, will be debated for years to come... Maryland, USA Sheikh Batu Daramy.

On the question of the constitutionality of the Governor-General's action in appointing Siaka Stevens as Prime Minister, John Cartwright who had written two books on Sierra Leone, holds the view that

In this situation, the only impartial course the Governor-General could follow would be to choose the Prime Minister with no reference to the Paramount Chief's whatsoever, and given the relative support for the two party leaders among the ordinary members, there can be no doubt that he made the constitutionally correct choice.[3]

His argument in support of the exclusion of the Paramount Chiefs is that they could be dismissed from office by an executive action of the Prime Minister.

To allow Sir Albert to remain in office until the Paramount Chiefs elections results were known the Governor-General, according to Cartwright, "would be ensuring that an additional twelve members of Parliament would declare their support for Albert." This is a typical inference from the discredited Justice Dove-Edwin Report.

First, the argument that if Sir Albert were still in office after the elections of Paramount Chiefs they would vote for him applies also to Siaka Stevens. Therefore, by his appointment as Prime Minister before the conclusion of the Paramount Chiefs' elections, the Governor-General, according to John Cartwright's argument, was "ensuring that an additional twelve members of Parliament would declare their support for" Siaka Stevens. If Siaka Stevens, why not Sir Albert Margai?

This is precisely our contention. Mr. Siaka Stevens realised that if Sir Albert remained in office after the elections were over the latter would get an overwhelming majority. That was why he precipitated a crisis by getting influential people to pressurise the Governor-General to appoint him immediately, because time was running out. This action turned out to be illegal.

Second, Sir Albert had no power to dismiss Paramount Chiefs. The constitutional practice during Sir Albert's time was, that a Paramount Chief was removed after a judicial inquiry. The report of the judicial commission was sent to the Prime Minister who made his recommendations to the Governor-General. If a Governor-General approved the Prime Minister's recommendations then the Paramount Chief was removed. But the Governor-General could reject the Prime Minister's recommendation. It is conceded that invariably, the Governor-General accepted the Prime

Minister's recommendation. If he rejects it, he could be creating a constitutional crisis, either immediately, or in due course. This law applied to whoever became Prime Minister. It was not exclusively reserved for Sir Albert, as Cartwright would appear to infer.

Third, that the Governor-General should appointment a Prime Minister "with no reference to the Paramount Chiefs whatsoever", on the grounds of the reasons adduced above, is a naive colonialist mentality which strove hard to humiliate Paramount Chiefs, as if they counted for naught.

Paramount Chiefs are the embodiment of everything that is left of African traditional custom of the people. They are the repository of the peoples' conscience and the custodians of their properties. The functions of a Paramount Chief and his courtiers include investigation and settlement of disputes relating to ownership of farm lands, matrimonial causes, all of which vary from chiefdom to chiefdom. Most educated Africans, would have been divorced from the customs of their people by the time they graduated from universities. Thereafter, they invariably spend most of their time in the cities and remain ignorant of their heritage. The burden of caring for their people in the villages falls on the chiefs and their courtiers. The late Franz Fanon of Martinique stressed the need, in *The Wretched of the Earth*, for associating the peasants with the nationalist movements. Too often, they are neglected. They, therefore, have no one to turn to but the Paramount Chief.

Paramount Chiefs mean more to the Africans because they are elected to office and therefore, signify the peoples will and trust, than members of the British House of Lords, who are not elected and therefore, are not responsible to the electorate. To the Labour Party, the British House of Lords, is an anachronism. Yet they are still there and John Cartwright, a Canadian, pays homage to them from time to time. The Queen's visit is an occasion to renew their allegiance. To dismiss the Paramount Chiefs of Africa in such cavalier manner is a betrayal of ones ignorance of what chieftaincy means to the average African.

Dr. Cartwright's categorical remarks that "the only impartial course the Governor-General could follow would be...." is highly presumptuous.

That there were other courses open to the Governor-General was borne out by the fact that he suggested the formation of a coalition government. The facts as we know them from the findings of the National Reformation Council are that the Governor-General was not impartial. He was pressurised by prominent citizens of Freetown. The Governor-General's Secretary gave evidence in the witness box at the treason trial that certain prominent personalities paid the Governor-General a "social visit", at the material time when 'things' were happening. These facts and Lieutenant Norman's evidence at the Dove-Edwin Commission, discussed in the last Chapter, destroy Cartwright's "only impartial course" argument. Lord Fenner Bockway was also misguided by the Dove-Edwin Report when he wrote that "In the election of March, 1967, when Siaka Stevens won by three, the Commander of the army, Brigadier David Lansana intervened to retain Margai in power."[4]

Finally, from the morass of charges and counter-charges by the SLPP and the APC, emerge the fact that both parties, were equally determined to win the general elections. That is what political parties are for, so long as they employ legitimate means within the parameters of the electoral laws of the country, they are entitled to entice, cajole and persuade fence-sitting candidates to join their party; so long as they employ legitimate democratic means. That the APC transgressed these elementary tenets of parliamentary democratic practices, was quite evident in 1966 and 1967. Subsequent elections also confirm this charge.

The Dove-Edwin Commission alleged that Brigadier David Lansana "intervened". The National Reformation Council stated that the Dove-Edwin Commission had "sufficient evidence... that several eminent citizens... pressurized the Governor-General to appoint Mr. Siaka Stevens as Prime Minister...."While we have concrete evidence that certain influential persons pressurized the Governor-General, we also have corroborated evidence that when Brigadier David Lansana intervened, he consulted the Speaker of Parliament, thereafter, and the latter convened a meeting of Parliament. In the light of these evidence the APC was highly culpable. As a matter of fact, as soon as the army officers led by Colonel Blake, interfered and formed a government, the APC went to Guinea to raise a guerrilla army to invade Sierra Leone, which they did, by proxy of the other ranks. Therefore, the APC and not the SLPP committed treason against the state of Sierra Leone.

The propaganda that the APC won the general elections in 1967 should now "be laid to rest." Since the APC assumed the reins of power in 1968, they have proved beyond any doubt that they are incapable of winning fair elections. We shall further substantiate this charge. In the meantime, we shall consider another misguided notion that Brigadier David Lansana planned to impose Sir Albert on the people of Sierra Leone.

Chapter 3 Notes

1.   National Reformation Council: *"Report of the Dove-Edwin Commission of Inquiry in the Conduct of the 1967 General Elections in Sierra Leone and the Government Statement Thereon;"* printed and published by the Government Printer, Sierra Leone, p. 1.

2.   Collier, Gershon; *Sierra Leone: An Experiment in Democracy in an African Nation*; published by New York University Press, New York; 1970.

3.   Cartwright, John: *Politics in Sierra Leone 1947-1967*, University of Toronto Press, 1970, p. 252.

4.   Brockway, Lord Fenner, *The Colonial Revolution*, St. Martin's Press, Inc,, 175 Fifth Avenue, New York, New York 10010, 1973, p. 331.

CHAPTER 4

THE PROPRIETY OF BRIGADIER DAVID LANSANA'S INTERVENTION

Brigadier David Lansana intervened on March 21st, 1967 by the declaration of martial law, when in his judgment, the security situation was deteriorating rapidly and, unless the army went to the aid of the police force, Sierra Leone would be plunged in civil war. This action has sparked off tremendous controversy among Sierra Leoneans and Africans generally. This intervention has been interpreted as an atrocious challenge of the authority of the Governor-General and a flagrant exaggeration of his role as Chief of Security.

As Governor-General of Sierra Leone and Commander-in-Chief of the Armed Forces, it is arguable that the Force Commander cannot question his action. Even if he reversed his own decision to form a coalition government of the Sierra Leone Peoples Party and the All Peoples Congress Party, it was his prerogative to do so. Any one who felt aggrieved, could challenge his action in a court of law. That is what courts are for.

Prima facie, this argument is attractive as an academic exercise while Rome burns. Given the political situation in Sierra Leone at the time, when, for example, the leaders of the SLPP had lost confidence in the so-called impartiality of the judiciary, any suggestion of seeking remedy through the courts would have been ludicrous. For example, about 99% of SLPP parliamentarians lost their seats following election petitions. You will recall that Sir Albert Margai recalled Gershon Collier from America and appointed him as Acting Chief Justice, and later as Chief Justice, when his acting appointment was challenged in court. Even when the National Reformation Council came to power and Colonel Charles Blake assured the people that "the Army does not propose to take cognisance of the past to mount exhaustive enquiries into the liberty and possessions of the individual, but to turn a new page in the history of our beloved country..." yet the commissions of inquiry which were appointed rocked the SLPP from whatever adventitious roots were left of its foundation. Some cabinet ministers were arrested, humiliated and detained at Pademba Road Prison, while the properties of leading SLPP members were confiscated by the National Reformation Council. Even Paramount Chiefs were not spared these brutal treatment. These occurrences were manifestations of the built-in hostility against the SLPP that even the National Reformation Council which was hailed as a rescue operation turned out to be an inquisition on the SLPP.

Given these antecedent circumstances, one can visualise the state of affairs in March 1967. With this background, we shall now consider the propriety or otherwise of Brigadier David Lansana's action in declaring martial law on the 21st of March, 1967.

First, Brigadier David Lansana did not question the intentions of the Governor-General to appoint Siaka Stevens as Prime Minister. When the Governor-General told him that he was going to appoint Siaka Stevens, the Brigadier advised him to postpone the appointment in view of the explosive situation, to enable him to redeploy his soldiers in readiness for the escalation of the civil unrest which had begun all over the country. In Chapter 1 we saw confirmation of the chaotic state of affairs in Sierra Leone at the time which necessitated declarations of states of emergency all over the country. In fact, subsequent events proved him right, because as soon as Siaka Stevens and his entourage arrived at State House for the appointment, a mammoth crowd surrounded the House. Some were celebrating the forthcoming appointment of Siaka Stevens as Prime Minister, while an equal number were protesting what was about to happen. Under those circumstances, the Brigadier was compelled to seal off all entrances and exits to and from State House.

Second, he declared martial law in order to cope with the imminent civil war, e.g., gun fights began in Kono District, at Kroo Town Road in Freetown, when some hooligans started looting the stores of Fullah traders, and the latter armed themselves with cutlasses and shotguns to protect their families and properties.

Third, the facts prove abundantly clear, that Brigadier Lansana never contrived to obstruct the All Peoples Congress Party. Following his declaration of martial law, he consulted Acting Chief Justice Banja Tejansie who was then Speaker of the House of Representatives. The Speaker broadcast an invitation to all members of Parliament to a meeting to resolve the political impasse. The Acting Chief Justice's broadcast vindicates the Brigadier in unequivocal English.

Brigadier David Lansana's action is hardly consonant with the actions of a soldier who wants to meddle in political matters in the interest of his friend, or for personal gain. What is unique and highly laudable about his action was the fact that, if he had conspired with Sir Albert, after his declaration of martial law, he could have formed a Government and later handed it over to Sir Albert. Whenever there has been military intervention, the soldiers go the whole hog. For example, after his officers took over from him, they staged a coup d'etat and formed a government, viz., the National Reformation Council. There are abundant examples all over the world that, when soldiers intervene, they form governments, e.g., Nigeria, Ghana, Cameroon, Mali, Guinea, Liberia.

Fourth, it has been argued that the Governor-General's action should have been endorsed and obeyed by the Army, and that any aggrieved persons could test his action in a court of law. We have examined this point, suffice it therefore, to say, that this argument is a naive and infantile one, verging on hypocrisy. It is tantamount to saying that the Army should have allowed the country to be plunged into a full-scale civil war. After the leading contenders had exterminated one another, then the police should arrest the survivors and charged them with murder, arson, maiming, et cetera. That is, let Freetown and other cities in the hinterland burn, while the purists plan to assemble Parliament, and to celebrate the appointment of the first APC cabinet, if any one of them survived the carnage.

It was precisely because of the flammable situation created by the APC, that they subsequently ignored the agreement to form a coalition government. They were apprehensive that the SLPP would emerge triumphantly again, and overshadow them. Furthermore, several cache of ammunition which they are alleged to have brought into the country from Guinea, and the proliferation of automatic weapons with the guerrillas over which they had no control, caused them some concern. It was alleged that some of them had hidden large quantities of ammunition in the Provinces, presumably also, in readiness for any internecine battle which the power struggle among them might precipitate. The leaders of the APC were in a quandary. In their frantic fear, they carried revolvers for a long time, because they realized that they were sitting on powder kegs of their creation.

Fifth, if his officers had not intervened, a meeting of elected members of Parliament, including Paramount Chief Members, would have assembled under the chairmanship of the Acting Chief Justice, and Speaker of the House and *in* Parliament as agreed by Brigadier David Lansana and the Acting Chief Justice Banja Tejansie. The members would have resolved the impending disaster. About fifty percent of the crowd who were outside State House were demonstrating because a Prime Minister was about to be appointed in glaring disregard of the claims of Paramount Chiefs, as if they did not matter. That is to say, while the results of Paramount Chief Members had not yet been known, a Prime Minister was being appointed, as if they were not eligible for appointment. Whatever arrogant and supercilious attitudes the African elite might have about the so-called 'illiterate' (in European education) Paramount Chiefs, the peoples revere their Paramount Chiefs as the fountain of justice, the embodiment of their customs, usages and mores. They are the cohesive force which binds the people. Together with their courtiers, Paramount Chiefs as Kings, ruled African Empires, centuries before the advent of outsiders. In West Africa, they ruled the Empires of Ghana, Mali and Songhai. There were empires in other parts of Africa, from the north to the south.

Educated Africans who ape their former colonial masters, followed in the footsteps of Europeans in derogating and humiliating Paramount Chiefs. Some of them have the effrontery to suggest that Paramount Chiefs should not be members of Parliament, but should be relegated to the backyards of their *barries* (courts).

Sixth, the argument that anyone aggrieved by the appointment of Siaka Stevens as Prime Minister should have tested the appointment in a court of law, also assumes that the courts were isolated and insulated from the upheavals in the country, and therefore, could be relied upon to dispense justice. Again, this point has been touched upon in the preamble to these arguments. Finally, supervening events did not allay the apprehensions of the SLPP that they were the victims of unfounded propaganda.

All the SLPP members of Parliament lost their seats following the elections petitions. Since the majority of the casualties were Mendes and their allies, they suspected that the judges of the Supreme Court were in league with the APC caucus. It was an unfortunate conclusion. The Dove-Edwin Commission Report did not allay their suspicions. Nor did the Foster Commission Report of Inquiry, both of which were set up by the National Reformation Council, even though the latter had broadcast that they would not "mount exhaustive enquiries." In his report, Justice Foster highlighted the names of some of the persons he investigated with asterisks against their names, and with a footnote, that they were the blue-eyed boys of Sir Albert Margai, the former Prime Minister, a Mende, as if it was a crime to be the blue-eyed boy of the Prime Minister. On the whole, the Commissions set up by the National Reformation Council turned out to be onslaughts against the Mendes, and persons associated with them. That was the feeling in Mende land.

When at the first treason trial the Acting Chief Justice Okoro-Cole overruled Berthan Macaulay (Q.C.) the 12th accused, the latter was so infuriated this time, that he hinted that the point at issue, and in fact the whole case, would be tested in the Privy Council. The learned Chief Justice replied, "you can go to heaven or to hell," et cetera. To the Mendes, such outburst by a Judge of the Supreme Court, is incompatible with his high office. They could not understand, nay more appreciate, that the judicial immunity which the learned Chief Justice enjoyed, and infact judges of the Supreme Court enjoy, was perhaps limited only by the skies above. Whether judicial immunity covers cases where the judges remarks are clearly malicious and prejudicial to an accused person at a trial for his life, needs clarification by the lawyers. The inference which the jury might draw from the learned Acting Chief Justice's reprimand of Brigadier David Lansana when he was in the dock that, "Your conduct stinks", and when his lawyer objected to the alleged prejudicial language of the Acting Chief Justice, he told him, "And you add stench to it," is anybody's guess.

By a combination of fortuitous circumstances which President Siaka Stevens would have attributed to God's moves in mysterious ways, his wonders to perform, the composition of the Appeal Court of the first treason trial consisted of Justice Tambia, a Ceylonese on temporary assignment to the Government of Sierra Leone as Chairman, Justice Bridges, Chief Justice of the Gambia, an Englishman, and Justice Beccles-Davies of the Judicial Department of Sierra Leone. He is a Creole, who is renowned for his impartiality, punctuated with arrogance, and a bearing that insinuates that he is the only blue-blooded Creole alive. That he could have given judgement against the APC Government in the prevailing atmosphere in Sierra Leone, makes Beccles-Davies one of the most courageous judges any where in the world. It should also go a long way to re-assure the Mendes that there are still Sierra Leonean judges, like Justice Agnes Macaulay who will tell Siaka Stevens and his APC cabinet the truth, regardless of the consequences. We may not understand the fine points of the law and the way in which the wheels of justice turn, but in our ignorance, we can smell the rat when it stinks,

In summary, if Brigadier David Lansana had not sealed off State House after the swearing in ceremony of Siaka Stevens, there would have been civil war in Sierra Leone, and such whole sale slaughter, that would make the 1898 Hut Tax War look like a jamboree. By his declaration of martial law, Brigadier Lansana therefore staved off civil war, as the country realised that the Army were in control of law and order, and would take drastic steps to punish any malefactors, regardless of ethnic origin or political affiliations. The National Reformation Council allowed both political parties a cooling-off period. And so we were spared, for 12 months, the APC executions which they had planned and which they carried out later.

In post-colonial Africa, when politicians cannot govern, soldiers stage a coup d'etat and take over the government. Sierra Leone is no exception, as we already know. We shall now consider Sierra Leone's experience of military governments.

CHAPTER 5

MILITARY INTERVENTIONS

(a)   THE FIRST MILITARY GOVERNMENT - 23RD MARCH, 1967

On the morning of the 23rd of March, 1967, Majors Charles Blake, S.B. Jumu, and Idrisa Kai-Samba, assembled the soldiers at Wilberforce Barracks and addressed them about the situation in the country. About midday, when Brigadier David Lansana did not see his officers for the usual consultations and plans for the day, he drove to the Barracks. On arrival, he was arrested and taken to Pademba Road Prison where Colonel John Bangura was still in detention.

On the same day, Majors Blake, S.B. Jumu, Idrisa Kai-Samba, and Commissioner of Police, William Leigh, formed the National Reformation Council. The total members were about eight. They appointed Colonel Genda as Chairman, and sent cablegrams to him and Colonel Juxon-Smith to return home immediately. When they arrived at Las Palmas, Colonel Genda received a cablegram to return to London, Colonel Juxon-Smith was received home as Chairman of the National Reformation Council.

It was rumoured that the switch in leadership of the NRC was engineered in Freetown by persons who were afraid that another Mende Brigadier in the saddle would not be in the best interest of Northerners and their allies. Colonel Juxon-Smith who was believed to be partly Creole (father) and Sherbro (mother) with Oku connections, would be a suitable compromise.

The National Reformation Council released Brigadier David Lansana from detention and sent him to New York as Sierra Leone's Counsellor to the United Nations Organisation, while Colonel John Bangura was sent to Washington as Charge d'Affaires in the Embassy of Sierra Leone. Colonel Genda was also made Ambassador.

RECORD OF THE NATIONAL REFORMATION COUNCIL

The "*Statement on the Budget for 1967/68 - Broadcast by Colonel A.T. Juxon-Smith. Chairman. National Reformation Council on 30th June, 1967*", the equivalent of a civilian government's Budget Speech by the Minister of Finance to Parliament, contains the main task of the NRC.[1]

STANDBY ARRANGEMENT

Following the investigations and recommendations of the Mission (the International Monetary Fund), a Stand-by Arrangement was signed with the International Monetary Fund for a Period of one year, with effect from the 1st of November, 1966....

Specifically, Government undertook to carry out the following measures:- Measures agreed upon with the IMF:-

(a) the freezing of all vacancies, with the exception of essential services; (b) reductions in the budgetary appropriation for travel and supplies; (c) the introduction of certain tax measures; (d) the avoidance of any future prefinance agreements and short-term loans which are inconsistent with our ability to repay these loans; (e) the revision of company tax law, the improvement of tax administration, and the renegotiation of certain concession agreements... (parenthesis mine)

These were the STABILIZATION MEASURES agreed with the IMF. Liquidity crisis in the Sierra Leone Produce Marketing Board was saved by loans arranged by the National Reformation Council.

Economic Advisory Committee

They set up an Economic Advisory Committee consisting of Dr. G. Conrad, Economic Adviser to the NRC, as Chairman; S.B. Daramy, Financial Secretary, as Secretary to the Committee; S.B. Nicol-Cole, Governor of the Bank of Sierra Leone, and V.A.W. Nylander, Secretary, Development Planning Division of the NRC Secretariat.

National Development Bank

The National Development Bank which was in preparation and for which the bulk of the capital had been obtained by the SLPP Government was formally launched by the NRC, "to mobilize local capital resources for economic development..."

Phasing out the Sierra Leone Railway

The NRC took steps to implement a controversial IMF recommendation to phase out the Sierra Leone Railway, because it had outlived its economic usefulness and was becoming a mill-stone around the economy.

(b)   THE SECOND MILITARY GOVERNMENT - MARCH, 1968

When the National Reformation Council was formed, Sir Albert Margai and Siaka Stevens left Sierra Leone. It was learnt that both went to London.

In September, 1967, Colonel Idrissa Kai-Samba who deputized the Chairman of the NRC as Member in Charge of Finance, S.B. Nicol Cole, Dr. Gunther Conrad and I, attended the World Bank and Fund Meetings in Rio de Janeiro. After the meeting, the Colonel and I went to Washington to negotiate loans with the World Bank.

His Excellency Ade Hyde was then Ambassador to the United States of America and resident in Washington. We did not see Colonel John Bangura his Charge d'Affaires at the Embassy. On enquiring, His Excellency Ade Hyde informed us that his wife informed him, that he had a boil on his head and had gone to see his doctor in New York.

On her invitation, Colonel Kai-Samba and I went to pay Mrs. John Bangura a social visit in the evening. As soon as we had exchanged courtesies, she immediately informed us that Colonel John Bangura was ill and had gone to New York for medical treatment. The story was not properly concocted, because it sounded so hollow, that I was firmly convinced that he had gone to Guinea to train guerrillas for the All Peoples Congress Party to invade Sierra Leone, as was being rumoured in official circles in Sierra Leone.

Colonel John Bangura and Dr. Mohamed Forna, who were officers in Siaki's Guerrilla Army, trained spies whom they sent to infiltrate the Sierra Leone Army. Colonel John Bangura is alleged to have gone to Freetown *in cognito* and conducted the clandestine operations from Murray Town. They 'convinced' the non-commissioned officers to stage a coup or else the guerillas would attack and wipe them out. This rumour tied up neatly with allegations that when the NRC was formed certain civilians began to make plans, in concert with some soldiers, to overthrow the NRC. Almost to the day, after the NRC had been in office, warrant officers led a countercoup against the National Reformation Council and brought their rule to an end, twelve months after they had been in office.

1st Day

At 10:00 p.m. we heard gun-shots from all directions of our residence. Shortly afterwards, while the shots were being fired, Warrant Officer Emadu Rogers, my cousin-in- law, rang and told us that the warrant officers and other ranks had staged a countercoup, arrested all their officers, and senior police officers, and detained them at Pademba Road Prison; that the situation was fluid and tense, and that they would be coming to see me for consultation.

By that time, there were sporadic outbursts of gun-fire from Wilberforce Barracks and Murray Town Barracks. From our residence at Signal Hill, we could see large military lorries full of soldiers going towards the city. The shooting went on till the small hours of the morning. At 2:00 a.m., Warrant Officer Emadu Rogers rang me and said that as soon as it was practicable, they would be coming to see me.

2nd Day

At 8:00 a.m., the following day, two military land-rovers drove to my house and Warrant Officers Conteh, Emadu Rogers, Kengenyeh and about ten soldiers alighted. The latter had automatic guns which they call, oozie.

After the usual formalities, Warrant Officer Conteh who was the most senior officer, led the discussions. He informed me (a) that they had arrested the National Reformation Council Members and other senior military and police officers and detained them at Pademba Road Prison, because, the NRC members were corrupt, (b) that they had formed the Anti-Corruption Revolutionary Council, (c) that the soldiers had demanded more pay immediately, and unless their demands were met, the situation would go out of hand, (d) that they wanted to restore the country to a civilian government by the appointment of a Governor-General.

I advised them as follows: (a) that I could not at that stage, comment on items (a) and (b); (b) that I would have to consult my colleagues before I could reply to the demand for more pay; (c) that after consultation with my colleagues, particularly, the Attorney-General, I would be able to advise them about the appointment of a Governor General. In the meantime, I advised tentatively, that according to the Constitution, in the absence of a Governor-General, the Chief Justice has to perform this function in the capacity of Acting Governor-General, until a substantive Governor-General has been appointed.

That in the present circumstances, having appointed an Acting Governor-General, it would be his duty to convene a meeting of members of parliament to appoint a Prime Minister.

We agreed to meet at Murray Town Barracks at 8:00 p.m. that night. After they left, I summoned Lamin Sidique, Acting Secretary General to the former NRC, who was also head of the Civil Service; Albert Metzger, Acting Attorney General; John Kallon, Establishment Secretary; T.A.L. Decker, Permanent Secretary of the Ministry of Information and Broadcasting, to my residence for consultation. On arrival, I informed them what had transpired between the soldiers and me.

After discussing the matter, we agreed: (a) that I should offer them 10 percent pay increase; (b) that Albert Metzger would explain the constitutional solution to the appointment of an Acting Governor-General, after having endorsed my interpretation of the Constitution to the soldiers.

Meeting Between the Anti-Corruption Revolutionary Council and the Civil Servants Listed Above.

A meeting was held in the warrant officers' mess. We were surrounded by a large crowd of soldiers, most of whom carried automatic guns. After tedious negotiation with the soldiers, we agreed: (a) that I should authorize the Accountant General to pay the soldiers and police an increase of 10 percent with effect from 1st March, 1968; (b) that Chief Justice Banja Tejansie be appointed Acting Governor-General, and that his immediate duty was to convene a meeting of parliamentarians to appoint a Prime Minister; (c) that I should inform the Chief Justice of the agreement at (b) and convey his approval to them, that Albert Metzger should prepare the necessary legal instrument to effectuate the Council's agreement; (d) the Council accepted my suggestion to substitute the Revolutionary Council for the Anti-Corruption Revolutionary Council. I pleaded with the soldiers that the adjective "Anti-Corruption" was an allegation which would give the erroneous impression in international circles that the NRC members had been tried and found corrupt. Until it could be proved in a court of law, they were presumed innocent.

I then asked them what their intentions were with regard to the officers who were detained at Pademba Road Prison. There were various suggestions ranging from indefinite imprisonment to facing firing squads. I advised that the best solution would be for them to retire the officers of the NRC and appoint them as ambassadors to various countries. This would save them the embarrassment of keeping them in prison, as their sympathisers in the army and the police could stage a countercoup against them. There appeared to be general agreement to my suggestion among the leaders of the soldiers. After conferring among themselves, Warrant Officer Conteh directed that the future of the officers in Prison would be considered later. He personally appeared to be sympathetic to my suggestion, but as the hostility against the officers seemed to be pretty high, he could not over-rule the general feeling on the matter.

3rd Day

At 8:00 a.m., I went to see Chief Justice Banja Tejansie and informed him about the discussions we had had with the soldiers and their requests. He willingly agreed to be Acting Governor-General.

I went to see Warrant Officer Conteh about arrangements to get some food for the army and the police. They got armed escorts for me in a land-rover, and I went to Freetown and arranged for 20 bags of rice, 2 drums of palm oil, 2 cows, which I divided equally between the army and the police.

4th Day

After the legal formalities, Chief Justice Banja Tejansie became Acting Governor-General. I instructed the Accountant-General to take necessary action to increase the pay of the soldiers and the police non-commissioned officers by 10 percent, with effect from 1st March, 1968.

A couple of days later, Colonel Genda arrived in Freetown. Colonel John Bangura also arrived at Jui Airport Hastings in a car, ostensibly having travelled from Conakry by road. We welcomed him like a head of state.

On the evening of his arrival, Abu Koroma (substantive Attorney-General who had been away from Sierra Leone), Lamin Sidique, John Kallon and I, held a meeting with Colonel John Bangura and the Revolutionary Council at Murray Town Barracks. As the middle man between the soldiers and the civil servants, I was the spokesman for our group. I narrated what had happened up to the time of his arrival. After he had thanked us for the part we played in bringing tranquility in the country, he advised us to continue to perform our duties in our respective posts as civil servants.

For the next two weeks, Colonels Bangura and Genda visited me regularly and had lunch with me. I reciprocated their visits. After lunch one day, Colonel Bangura assured me that any attempt to victimize me would be over his dead body. He then went outside, took an automatic weapon from one of his soldiers, and fired about 10 rounds in rapid succession.

While we were in the process of preparations for the return to civilian rule, the Governor-General summoned Lamin Sidique, Abu Koroma and me in his office. He showed us a cablegram which he had received from Siaka Stevens in Guinea to the effect that

> Sierra Leone does not belong to the Koromas, the Sidiques, and the Daramys. They should be warned not to take any action which would not be supported by the boys.

We interpreted the boys as the guerrillas who had infiltrated the Sierra Leone Army.

We were indignant that Stevens should send us such a cablegram, after the hard work we had done to return the country to civilian rule without bloodshed. We therefore, wrote a joint letter to the Governor-General protesting the unwarranted attack on us by Stevens, notwithstanding the fact that we knew that he was directing operations from Guinea for his return to Sierra Leone to form a Government.

I recalled the difficulties I encountered in explaining the Constitution to the soldiers on the appointment of a Governor-General when they came to see me on the 2nd Day of the coup. While their leader, Warrant Officer Conteh seemed to endorse my suggestion to appoint the Speaker of Parliament and Acting Chief Justice as Acting Governor-General, one of the soldiers insisted that Paramount Chief Adikali Modu of Port Loko should be appointed Acting Governor-General and not Sir Banja Tejansie. When Siaka Stevens sent his cablegram from Conakry, I suddenly realized that the soldiers who insisted on the appointment of Paramount Chief Adikali Modu as Acting Governor-General were operating in accordance with Siaka Stevens' instructions. Mr. Siaka Stevens preferred Paramount Chief Adikali Modu, because it would be easier and quicker for him to remove the Paramount Chief once he became Prime Minister than Sir Banja Tejansie, for obvious reasons. Furthermore, there was no love lost between Siaka Stevens and Sir Banja Tejansie. These nuances are ever so crucial in politics that ignorance of their existence could cause serious problems for civil servants charged with the responsibility of interpreting regulations according to set rules. The irony of this case is that when he became Prime Minister, Siaka Stevens detained Paramount Chief Adikali Modu at Pademba Road Prison. While there, he and I were not on proper speaking terms and I suspected that he was not too keen to speak to me even though we had been on cordial terms before then. It might have been due to my objection to his appointment as Acting Governor-General. Unfortunately, he could not appreciate the legal implications nor the insuperable difficulties he would be assuming.

From the traditional point of view, it was distressing when Siaka Stevens started detaining Paramount Chiefs. It is against traditional custom for a paramount chief to bathe with his subjects. An extension of this custom is that a *gborka* is not allowed to see the naked body of a *sohini*[2] below the waistline. Paramount Chiefs who were detained at Pademba Road Prison were not accorded any privacy or preferential treatment in keeping with their dignity as natural rulers. Commoners, non-society members bathed together with paramount chiefs, in full view of one another.

History we are told, repeats itself but in a different setting. It is a pathetic irony that when revolutions take place in Africa, the natural rulers become the victims of the new regime. Colonial governments humiliated African kings to the level of paramount chiefs. When they resisted, they were banished from their kingdoms to some outlandish island, to perish in the wilderness. When the All Peoples Congress Party took over the government of Sierra Leone, some paramount chiefs were beaten up, arrested and detained like common criminals, even though in most cases, they were political prisoners.

Chapter 5 Notes

1. & 2. A *gborka*, according to the Temnes, is someone who has not been initiated in the secret society for men or women. A member of this society is called *sohini* in Mende. In both cases, membership of this society is a prerequisite for appointment or election to public office, such as paramount chief. The women have their counterpart, called *sandei* in Mendeland. In Mendeland, they also have the *Wonde* society.

All these institutions and more are sacred to the people. Any government which assumes power in Sierra Leone would be well advised to recognize their preeminence. In pre-colonial times they were the foundations of the society. For example, the elections of kings were planned in the *poro* bush, where all differences were ironed out, and the contending parties and candidates reconciled to the wishes of the elders who spear-head subsequent general elections.

CHAPTER 6

THE RETURN TO CIVILIAN RULE - NOW OR NEVER

By 1966, Siaka Stevens realized that time was running out. If he did not become Prime Minister after the General Elections, it might be too late. So the motto of the All Peoples Congress Party became "NOW OR NEVER." The APC had to win the elections at all cost, or else they would have to spend another five years opposing.

When the first batch of detainees were released from detention cum gaol in 1971, I had a careful appraisal of the political upheaval, vandalism, and lawlessness in our country, with my close confidant. I was astounded when he said, in words to the effect:- S.B., we should all thank Allah that David declared martial law, there was a coup, Pa Siaka went to train guerrillas in Guinea, that there was a countercoup, and the All Peoples Congress Party came to power. The APC had to take over from the SLPP after the last elections, or else you, me, Bra Albert, Peter Tucker, the whole lot of us, would have been slaughtered in cold blood. To crown it all, the APC would have taken over the country in any case. So what? You languished in gaol for 3½ years, Hawa, your children and your mother starved for a while; but in his good time, Allah rescued you from the jaws of Satan. Let us thank Allah, and shut up. As you are aware, the APC slogan during the General Elections was, NOW OR NEVER. They meant it figuratively and in reality. As an Ex-Serviceman, I ought to be abreast of the currents and cross-currents. Let the All Peoples Congress Party govern

Sierra Leone. Posterity would be able to compare, contrast, and pass judgment. When I recalled what had happened before the General Elections and my release from detention cum gaol, I thanked Allah for our deliverance.

Having assumed the office of Acting Governor-General, Sir Banja Tejansie convened a meeting of members of Parliament to elect a Prime Minister.

On the directions of Colonel John Bangura, Lamin Sidique, Gunther Conrad and I prepared a speech which Colonel John Bangura delivered at State House in the presence of the Acting Governor-General, and members of Parliament. He ended by saying that he hoped that the members of Parliament would elect a Prime Minister, so that he could return to the Barracks where he belonged. Mr. Siaka Stevens was 'elected' Prime Minister, and Colonel John Bangura concentrated on military duties. With the exception of one soldier who was killed in the latter, the coup and countercoup were without the usual fatalities that accompany coup d'etat.

In an interview with the journal *West Africa* in London, in April, 1984, Sir Banja Tejansie who was the Governor-General who approved the appointment of Siaka Stevens as Prime Minister, revealed the following salient facts about that historical event:

Q. So you were. (removed) from office? (Parenthesis mine).

A. Oh yes, absolutely! First of all Stevens refused to go to the country as required by constitution because he feared that he would lose. Boys like S.I. Koroma they had no time for that. In fact it was clear from the moment they assumed power that they had disrespect for the constitution...they lied.

For example, before I appointed Stevens as prime minister, he signed an undertaking in my office at State House declaring that he would at all times retain a certain number of SLPP members (because it was a national government) until the next general elections were held. I said 'sign the paper before I make you prime minister', he signed and appointed a number of SLPP members in his government but then he soon began sacking them one after the other claiming to have won elections petitions against them. He got Luke to do all the dirty work for him. I also had people like A.B.S. Janneh and Mohammed Taqi coming to me shouting, 'please sir we want all the Cabinet posts because we won the elections and we simply didn't want more opposition? The same pressure was also put on Stevens who yielded. He was very weak in that respect.

Q.   Sir Banja you have never, at least publicly, made any comment about Stevens' one party state... does your silence mean a compromise or an approval of the one party?

A.   I have never been in favour of a one party government for Sierra Leone. Of course, as you know, it was (Albert) Margai who started this one party business and appointed me as chairman to consider the possibility of a one party state. I collected all the information I needed and I went personally to meet him. I told him bluntly that any talk of a one party was most unpopular and ill-advised...so he dropped it. (Emphasis mine).

Earlier in the interview, Sir Banja Tejansie stated that when Siaka Stevens was on a state visit to Zambia,

trouble began. So I telephoned him in Lusaka to say 'look, come home there was trouble'.

He immediately returned home; but as soon as he got back he questioned me why was it that people had stoned and attacked his house and not mine. I tried to explain to him how people had advised me that there was shooting and I was not to come out otherwise I would be killed, But Stevens kept on asking me the same question why his house was fired upon and not State House, my official residence. He accused me of being behind a coup to oust him. But that was nonsense because I wouldn't have telephoned him in the first place to come home,

I had received intelligence reports about people who wanted to kill me and of course he, Siaka Stevens, was behind it. Stevens regarded me as standing in his way of ambition.

That was a microscopic sketch of Siaka Stevens' machinations and ungratefulness to those who helped to enthrone him.

As soon as Siaka Stevens had been sworn in as Prime Minister, and ensconced at State House, rumours started circulating that plans were being made to arrest some people. One evening, George Panda, former Commissioner of Labour and Secretary to the Prime Minister and personal friend to Siaka Stevens, summoned me to his residence, and in his usual lift-hearted manner, he said, "S.B., you have heard the latest eh-ha ha ha?"

"No?" I replied. "Well," he went on, "it is being rumoured that the SLST (Sierra Leone Selection Trust Company - a diamond mining company), had given me Le 30,000 ($30,000) to give you to bribe the soldiers to overthrow Siaki's Government." "Is that so?" I asked. "Yes Mr." He laughed for a minute, pacing up and down, like a lion in its lair. "Then why didn't you give me?" I asked. "You go and ask them," he mocked.

About a couple of months after he and I had been arrested and detained at Pademba Road Prison, the rumour persisted. The SLST issued a warning in *West Africa*, a journal published in London, that they had heard the rumour. They denied having given anybody money to overthrow the Government, and challenged anyone who could prove the allegation to report the matter to the police immediately. If anyone was caught making such malicious slander against them, they threatened to take appropriate legal action.

While this gossip was gaining currency, another equally alarming rumour spread like wild fire, that the APC Government was planning to victimize some civil servants. The Secretary to the Prime Minister, G.L.V. Williams, asked the Prime Minister to address permanent secretaries.

On our behalf, he pledged our loyalty to the Government, et cetera. As the next senior civil servant to him, I seconded the motion and made a suitable speech. In his reply, the Prime Minister, Mr. Siaka Stevens, lied that his Government was not contemplating, nor would they victimize any civil servants. Although I was not particularly enarmoured by the APC Government, yet, since they had now achieved their goal by means of guns, I had no immediate premonition of impending danger, either to my person or interference with my job. So I resolved to prove that civil servants should be loyal to the political party in power, whatever their predelections might be.

My resolution was not put to the test.

(A)   THE REIGN OF TERROR BEGINS WITH MASS ARRESTS

In compliance with my wife's wishes, I left for Goderich beach accompanied by Morkeh Yamson a long time friend at about 5:00 p.m. on the 28th of May, 1968 to buy fish. We returned home at approximately 7:30 p.m. About 200 yards from my bungalow at Signal Hill, Wilberforce, I saw a long line of huge military lorries full of soldiers with automatic weapons sticking out of the lorries.

The sun had set and it was already dark. A couple of taxis that had overtaken me while I waited for the lorries to proceed were reversing fast. One of the drivers told us that the road was full of military lorries carrying armed soldiers and police, and that the officers would not allow any vehicles to proceed to Freetown by Signal Hill.

After thirty minutes, I became quite impatient, and began to drive on to my house. Sub-Inspector Vincent pointed his torchlight on the number plate of my car. Having assured himself that it was SB250, their quarry, he walked up to me. "Good evening, Sir," he greeted. "Good evening." I replied. "Are you going in Sir?" "Yes," I replied. He allowed me to proceed. Driving slowly to negotiate the narrow 90 degrees precipitous entrance to my residence, I overheard a soldier in a land-rover reporting. "He has just arrived, over," That was an ominous message, I thought. I passed seven military lorries before I entered my home, They were fully armed with automatic weapons whose deadly noses pointed menacingly towards the starry heavens.

As soon as I alighted, Deputy Commissioner of Police, Tinga Sesay walked up to me, saluted and greeted, "Good evening, Sir," I murmured something. "It is a painful duty to arrest one's elder brother," he said. I inquired, "Have you come to arrest me then?" "Yes Sir." He replied. "On whose authority?" I again inquired. "I have been instructed by the Prime Minister and the Force Commander (Brigadier John Bangura) to come and arrest you." (Parenthesis mine) I could see him vaguely in my minds eyes standing almost at the same spot that Tinga Sesay was standing, firing the salvo from the automatic weapon, and after which he assured me that if any one attempted to arrest me, "It would be over my dead body." "Where is your warrant?" I pressed. "I have no warrant." "O.K., let me speak to my wife, before we leave."

I sent for some cigars which a friend had recently brought for me from Havana, and after giving my wife the contents of my pockets, I advised her not to forget to remove the fish from the boot (trunk) of the car, and let her driver park my car.

She shouted and slumped on the ground, and began to cry. My mother and my children who had gathered around us began to cry. My father-in-law (an Arab from Morocco) who had come to visit us from Pujehun for medical treatment looked out of his window and said, "Allah go with you." I lit a cigar, hugged Hawa goodbye, waved to my children and my mother, shook hands with Morkeh Yamson, and I was helped into the land-rover which led the storm troopers.

We drove down Signal Hill. When we reached Congo Cross, we turned left into Wilkinson Road. As I had suspected, the lorries halted outside George Sulayman Panda's house. He was former Secretary to the Prime Ministers, Sir Milton and Sir Albert. After thirty minutes, I heard Mrs. Rachel Panda swearing that God Almighty will punish those people who have arrested her husband for no justifiable reason.

"Hello S.B., so you are here too?" and Bra Panda laughed in his usual infectious manner. "Actually, they picked me up as soon as I returned home with all that fish." "Ah ha, good show, Hawa and the children will eat yours on your behalf," he mocked me.

We drove away while Rachel continued her prophecy. "George, God will protect you. May the Lord punish those wicked people."

The lorries stopped outside Migore Kallon's house. Mr. Migore Kallon was former Minister of External Affairs, he was not at home. Later, he informed me at Pademba Road Prison, that while at a friend's home, he learnt that the arrests that were contemplated, and which had become common knowledge, had begun, and that his brother and I had been arrested. On his friend's advice, he decided not to go home that night for fear of being man-handled by the police in the process of arresting him. So he went to the Central Police Station the following morning and surrendered himself.

Having left his place, they went and arrested Thomas Decker, Permanent Secretary of the Ministry of Information and Broadcasting. They then went and arrested John Kallon, Establishment Secretary, A.B. Paila, former Mende Tribal Headman. When the convoy headed for Kroo Town Road, Panda and I speculated, "who next." We were clueless until we heard

Mrs. Zainabu Kamara's booming invectives, outside her home by Kroo Town Road Bridge.

When she was arrested, she had a long argument with the Internal Security Unit, while at the same time she went on insulting and swearing. We were carted to the former Elder Dempster Lines Building, Water Street, where elaborate security arrangements had been made for our reception. The station was full of soldiers with automatic weapons. As we passed them they pointed the guns menacingly and grinned sheepishly at us, as if they were awaiting orders to dislodge their burden.

Well over 100 armed soldiers were involved in the operations. In retrospect, one wonders, why such unnecessarily elaborate show of force was displayed? It was part of the Government's plan to terrorize the people because at most, two land-rovers would have been sufficient to take seven of us to the police station.

Shortly after our arrival, they brought in Abu Koroma, the Attorney General. When he joined us as a prisoner, I had a sadistic sense of relief that by arresting the Attorney General, they were burning the bridge behind them. It is the kind of feeling which a soldier gets when his comrade is shot dead by his side in a trench-sorrow for the death of his friend, and relief that at least he was still alive. Then followed Kandeh Bureh, former Temne Tribal Headman and former Cabinet Minister of the SLPP Government who also acted as Prime Minister quite a few times.

Since it had been rumoured for sometime that the All Peoples Congress Party were planning to victimize and harass members of the Sierra Leone Peoples Party, we were not surprised when the mass arrests began. That it should have begun with such primitive fanfare and flourish, could be due mainly to the Government's desire to whet the appetite of the sadists in the Party, and those who planned with the APC caucus to annihilate us, for diverse reasons.

While we were ruminating on these strange phenomena, alien to the civilized traditions of our fore-fathers, time had come to a stop. Every hour seemed like a day, as the night inexorably wore on slowly but surely. At 5:00 am., the Commissioner of Police, Malcolm Parker, arrived at the station. He glanced at askance at us, and wafted away into a room. We sat up anxiously, awaiting whatever was in store for us. Shortly afterwards, he came to us and said, "Ladies and Gentlemen, I have been instructed to take you to Pademba Road Prison." That was the last time that we were addressed as Ladies and Gentlemen, or Mrs., or Mr.

We were again herded into the lorries and driven to what turned out to be our inferno for the next three years and more.

RECEPTION AT PADEMBA ROAD PRISON

When the convoy arrived at the Prison, the Deputy Director and his officers were at hand to welcome us to Her Majesty's Prison. In accordance with the Prisons Ordinance and Rules made thereunder, we were divested of the articles we had in our pockets.

I asked Deputy Commissioner of Police, Tinga Sesay, to arrange for me to get my medication, which I had to take every night before going to sleep. Two hours later, Tinga Sesay brought a bottle for me from my wife. These courtesies to a prisoner whose guilt had been decided long before our arrests, perhaps in the training camps in Guinea, are worth every commendation.

After our records had been completed, we were led to our cells. For seven days and seven nights, we were kept in solitary confinement and treated worse than convicted prisoners who were allowed to roam about in the prison. While we were at the reception desk, our arrival was flashed by the warders to all the blocks.

There are four blocks at Pademba Road Prison - Clarkson, Wilberforce, Granville and Hudson. Each had two floors - ground and first. The National Reformation Council and the commissioned officers of the Army, and Police Officers, were at the first floor in Clarkson Block, They too had heard of our arrival, and as we were being shepherded into our cells, I could hear their excitement. Some of them jumped and hung onto the ventilation bars, to get a glimpse at us.

As soon as our cells were locked, Tiger Bone, one of the most dangerous criminals going, arranged a reception party for us. They assembled outside our ventilation bars and began to insult us. For the next seven days and seven nights, they woke us early in the morning with their melodies of insults.

Subsequent events convinced us that our reception must have been planned "from above", and the Director of Prisons instructed accordingly. Otherwise, such disorderly conduct would not have been tolerated by the Prison Officers, who were adept at enforcing discipline against dangerous prisoners. The attitude and behavior of the officers lent support to this suspicion. Most of them were extremely hostile and rude to us as if they themselves had personal animosity against us, and now had to settle old scores.

We were supplied Hungarian blankets to cover our bodies while we lay on the bare cement floor for seven days and seven nights. The routine was that the cell was opened in the morning and each prisoner was allowed five minutes to run to the iron gate, wash his face and mouth without soap or tooth brush and paste, and return to his cell immediately.

Breakfast consisted of a loaf of bread with margarine spread thinly inside it, and a mug of tea. For lunch, we had rice and sauce that were not properly cooked. Our dinner consisted of two or three tiny Irish potatoes, a tablespoonful of stew, containing one or two tiny pieces of meat.

There were two zinc buckets in each cell with water. One was drinking water, while the other was for toilet. Both had no lids, and so the flies flew freely from bucket to bucket. After four days, I saw circles of white zinc oxide on the inside of the bucket with drinking water. I was apprehensive that it had been planned to kill us by zinc poisoning. When the warders brought our food, they put the basin on the floor, opened the door and kicked the basin into the cell. At times some of the food spilled on the floor, and so one got only a fraction of the meagre food which was not sufficient in the first place. We were locked up in our cells for 24 hours, and came out only to wash our faces and mouths in the morning. This solitary confinement lasted for seven days and seven nights. On the seventh day our wives were allowed to visit us. Not having washed for seven days and seven nights and our hair full of cheap Hungarian blanket wool, we must have looked to our wives like Rip Van Winkle's children, from the Catskill Mountain.

When Hawa saw me, she burst into tears and began to cry. The Prison Officer warned her not to make noise in the prison. According to her, I looked like an animal and she could smell the stench from my body as soon as she saw me, "Hawa," I said to her, "this is the prelude to despotism. During the Second World War, we read about Mussolini and Hitler and the methods which their soldiers employed to extract 'confessions' from prisoners. This is the way in which they softened their prisoners before interrogation. By such inhuman treatment, they break one's morale and endurance. After that, one is tortured further, to admit whatever they suggest to the prisoner." When I stopped, she said, "The Lord God Almighty will be the judge."

After seven days' and seven nights' solitary confinement, we were transferred to Wilberforce Block, given mattresses each and taken to the bathroom, for showers for the first time since our captivity. We greeted one another like long lost brothers and discovered that more people had been arrested after the 28th May swoop. When I saw Berthan Macaulay, former Attorney General, who I did not know had been arrested and slept with me in the same block for seven days and seven nights, I had a second sadistic satisfaction, that I was not alone. That they could arrest two attorneys general with us, was to my mind the most stupid thing they did. It meant that they were in for a long drawn out battle to accomplish their satanic plans, if ever. "Whatever happens," Berthan Macaulay said from time to time, "there is the Privy Council in London."

Up to that time, we did not have the slightest notion as to the reason for our arrest, other than that the APC caucus and people associated with it, had gone back on their promises and decided to victimize SLPP members and associates and to harass the populace generally, into complete submission. Mr. George Panda and I discussed the alleged Le 30,000 from day to day and consoled each other with the prospect of exposing the APC fabrications.

After we had washed off the week's dirt, and flees, Dr. Olu Thomas came to see us. We described the inhuman conditions under which we were living. Because of my poor health, he recommended that I should be supplied with a bed and mosquito net. Incidentally, I was the only one he recommended on his first visit to be supplied with a bed and a mosquito net. According to the officers, although they had beds in store, yet they were supplied only to special prisoners.

One month after his recommendation, I was supplied a bed and three months later, I was supplied a mosquito net which Henneh Shamel had rejected. Mr. Henneh Shamel was arrested and brought to prison for allegedly having organized gangsters who robbed the Sierra Leone Selection Trust Company diamond cargo at Jui Airport, Hastings, at gun point. The diamonds stolen were variously estimated at Le 5m-Le 10m ($5m-$10m).

Mr. Henneh Shamel received the most V.I.P. treatment when he arrived in prison. He was given a bed, mattresses and mosquito net the same day. He is alleged to have rejected the first mosquito net which was hurriedly sewn for him, that evening, because it was not properly made. Another one was made for him the same night. The rejected net was passed on to me. That a man alleged to have robbed diamonds partly owned by the Sierra Leone Selection Trust Company and the Sierra Leone Government at gun point, worth about Le 5m-Le 10m, should be given such V.I.P. treatment by the prison officers, while we, former cabinet ministers, Paramount Chiefs, parliamentarians, top senior civil servants, dignitaries, should be treated worse than murderers, was - beyond our ken. Mr. Henneh Shamel was never brought to trial, but was expelled from Sierra Leone under suspicious circumstances.

MAFANTA

We shall take a journey to Mafanta Prison in Magburaka, and back to Freetown to continue our story. While we were being rounded up in the Western Area, SLPP members and sympathizers, including Paramount Chiefs, were being arrested in the Provinces and detained in the local prisons, e.g., Mafanta, Kenema, Bo.

At Bo, the army and the police raided the home of the Honorable Samuel Toma Navo, a prominent barrister-at-law, in the small hours of the morning. He had been alerted that he would be arrested that night. He and his guest, Julius Cole, the editor of the SLPP newspaper, *Freedom*, retired early that evening, in readiness for the ordeal that lay ahead, but naturally, could not sleep.

When the army and the police arrived, Navo quickly welcomed them, changed into his working dress and jumped into the truck. "Lord have mercy, Sergeant," one of the soldiers shouted when he forced open the door of the room where Julius Cole was browsing over his next article. He snatched it from him and continued, "So so lie. E high pass himself. Na you people day spoil this country with your lies. B.A., M.A., Bo School all so so lies and trouble. You make me nor see me pikin dem. Ah nor even sleep with me wife for two weeks now. Bo School nonsense. Kpata kpata." "Shut up," the Sergeant-in-charge warned him. "Don't you know the Brigadier (meaning Brigadier John Bangura) went to the Bo School?"

Mr. Julius Cole was thrown into the lorry and he landed with such a bang that his host was apprehensive that he might have broken a limb or two. "Sit down on the floor you bush man." A soldier commanded. They could not object to the orders, although the floor was soaking wet.

Within a flash, the news of their arrest had spread in Bo. The wonde boys (warrior society) began grouping for an assault on the police station to rescue their lawyer and the champion of whatever freedom of speech was left in the nation. On instructions from Freetown, they were rushed to Mafanta Prison in Magburaka. But for this timely action, there would certainly have been an insurrection in Bo, as subsequent events proved.

At Mafanta, the prisoners saw other prominent SLPP members and Paramount Chiefs, including Dr. Drissa Yilla, Honorable Salia Jusu Sheriff. The food was so bad that some of the inmates died of diarrhoea. The food was badly cooked, and what is more, sand was thrown into the rice. For days on end, the prisoners were not allowed to take their bath in the same way in which we were treated in Pademba Road Prison, The prison officer in charge was notoriously wicked to prisoners. Prisoners were assaulted for no apparent reasons, while some of them were locked up in their cells for days on end.

That Siaka Stevens could descend so low, astounded even his admirers. Why this inordinate show of force and brutality? After his release from detention, one of the detainees went to visit Prime Minister Siaka

Stevens. He enquired why he was detained. The Prime Minister replied that they had planned to detain sharks. If in the process, minnows (tiny fishes) got caught in the nets, it was unfortunate for them. But in times of war, all rules are suspended. This is a typical APC ideology which is still in vogue under the APC emergency regulations.

These flagrant, irresponsible and frivolous abuse of executive authority were signals of the kind of government that had assumed the reins of power in Sierra Leone. Regrettably, a vocal sector of the elite who openly identified themselves with the fortunes of the SLPP switched their allegiance to the APC as the party that had emerged to save Sierra Leone from Mende hegemony. Whatever were their true motives, they openly endorsed the reign of terror that had begun and the rape of the Constitution as the treason trials revealed, so long as they were unaffected by the atrocities.

(B)   TREASON TRIALS GALORE

Mr. Siaka Stevens was sworn in as Prime Minister, the first opposition party Prime Minister in Sierra Leone in April 1968. In May, the All Peoples Congress Party unleashed a reign of terror by arresting hundreds of Sierra Leone Peoples Party Members, Paramount Chiefs, parliamentarians, top civil servants, and sympathizers. They began a series of treason charges unprecedented in the history of any country. Within a year, they preferred three treason charges against Kandeh Bureh and six others, Brigadier Andrew Juxon-Smith and seven others, Brigadier David Lansana and seventeen others.

In ten years of their reign, the APC had instituted six treason trials, and hanged several persons including Paramount Chiefs; Brigadier John Bangura who trained the APC guerrillas in Guinea; Brigadier David Lansana who was alleged by the Dove-Edwin Commission of Inquiry to have forestalled Siaka Steven's appointment as Prime Minister; Dr. Mohammed Forna, the APC physician of the Guerrilla Army and Minister of Finance of the APC Government; Ibrahim Taqui, the APC Minister of Information and Broadcasting; and architect of the 'overthrow' of the SLPP; Colonel Farrar Jawara; Major Korlu Gbonda and others.

Treason is the most serious offence and carries the death penalty. As if the blood that had been spilt during the 1967 General Elections was not sufficient, Siaka Stevens and his Executive Committee of the APC now embarked on a systematic policy to exterminate the opposition party in Sierra Leone and their sympathizers. In view of the length of these cases it is not proposed to discuss them in detail. We shall therefore, summarize the salient points.

Months before the 1967 General Elections, the All Peoples Congress Party intensified its policy of systematic propaganda of false-hood, half-truths, unfounded slander of political opponents, and down-right deception of the electorate. The caucus indoctrinated its followers to hate and ridicule any one who did not belong to the All Peoples Congress Party.

By 1976, the imprisonment of political opponents and sympathizers gained added momentum. According to Amnesty International, by 1976, there were 500 political prisoners, the majority of whom had not been tried. Sierra Leone became the laughing stock, like Uganda, in international circles. President Siaka Stevens' visits abroad were greeted with protests by Sierra Leoneans. For instance, on his visit to the United States of America, Sierra Leoneans in Washington D.C., demonstrated against him. As reported in the Washington Post, of May 29, 1976,

> The president said he was aware of the 25 or so pickets who paraded on lower Connecticut Avenue yesterday to protest his visit. 'This is a democratic country and they may express themselves freely,' he said. He added that they were a very small percentage of the students from Sierra Leone in this country.

> One of the pickets carried a sign that read, 'Go home Killer Stevens,' apparently referring to the execution of nine anti-government former cabinet members almost a year ago.[1]

When they formed the Government in April, 1968, following the counter-coup of private soldiers against their officers which the All Peoples Congress Party Executive Committee planned and directed from their guerrilla headquarters in the Republic of Guinea, they embarked on a vicious and unprecedented vendetta of incalculable dimensions.

From 1968 when the APC came to power to 1974, they instituted six treason trials, viz.,

(i)   R. V. Kandeh Bureh and 6 others

(ii)   R. V. Brigadier Andrew Juxon-Smith and 7 others

(iii)   R. V. Kombe Kajue and Paramount Chief Madam Ella Koblo Gulama

(iv)   R. V. Brigadier David Lansana and 17 others

(v)   R. V. Brigadier John Bangura and 3 others

(vi)   R. V. Dr. Mohamed Forna and 14 others

These treason trials became the scene of full scale legal battles in which Berthan Macaulay as usual excelled himself with superlative expertise.

(i)   R. V. KANDEH BUREH AND 6 OTHERS

Kandeh Bureh and six others were arraigned before Magistrate Donald Macaulay and indicted with treason.

The Acting Attorney General applied to the Acting Chief Justice Okoro Cole for authority to transfer the case to a judge of the Supreme Court. The Acting Chief Justice granted the application and so ordered.

Mr. Berthan Macaulay one of the accused in this trial, appealed.

The Appeal Court consisted of Sir Samuel Bankole Jones, Judges G.P. Dove-Edwin, and S.C.W. Betts.

Preamble

The question for the Appeal Court to decide was whether an indictment for treason could be preferred by written direction or consent of a Supreme Court Judge under Section 136(i) of the Criminal Procedure Act No. 32 of 1965 which reads as follows:

> 136(i) No indictment shall be signed or filed in respect of any criminal offence unless there has been a committal for trial consequent upon a previous preliminary investigation in accordance with the Provisions of Part III...except in the case of indictments which by law maybe preferred by the direction or with the consent in writing of a judge.

FACTS

Kandeh Bureh and six others, including Berthan Macaulay former Attorney General, were charged with treason under the Treason and State Offences Act No. 10 of 1963 before Magistrate Donald Macaulay.

The accused appeared before the Presiding Magistrate on the 25th of September, 1968. After the charges were read, the case was adjourned to 3rd October, 1968. Before hearing commenced, Brigadier Juxon-Smith issued subpoenas for over 50 witnesses.

When hearing began, Berthan Macaulay objected to Donald Macaulay presiding and applied to the Supreme Court for the case to be transferred to another Magistrate. The Motion was to have been heard by a judge on 7th November, 1968.

On the 6th November, 1968, the Acting Attorney General applied *ex parte* to Justice Okoro Cole, Acting Chief Justice for indictment for the case to be heard instead before a judge of the Supreme Court, on the ground that a speedy, fair and impartial trial may be had. Speedy indeed. Justice Okoro-Cole granted consent and an order issued.

Mr. Berthan Macaulay appealed against this order as it was a contravention of his fundamental rights as entrenched by sections 12 and 19 of the 1961 Independence Constitution, in that Treason cannot be preferred by written direction or consent of a judge. The requirements of Section 136 (i) of the Criminal Procedure Act, 1965, reproduced above, is mandatory.

In his characteristic legal style, the appellant buttressed his legal submissions by decided cases in the House of Lords and the British Commonwealth, to prove that, as was held by the House of Lords in another case,

> Procedural sections are usually mandatory and there is nothing which point to the contrary in this case.

The Acting Attorney General conceded, that with the exception of the Perjury Act of Sierra Leone, there is no law in Sierra Leone which enables a judge of the Supreme Court to order preferment of indictment for treason without a previous preliminary investigation in accordance with the provisions of Part III of the Criminal Procedure Act of 1965.

HELD

In granting such order, Justice Sir Samuel Bankole Jones held, that the learned Acting Chief Justice Okoro-Cole was wrong. The appeal was allowed and the Order of Justice Okoro-Cole set aside.

Justice H.M. Tambia concurred with Justice Samuel Bankole Jones, and added:

> Where an accused is prosecuted for a serious crime the intention of the legislature is to have preliminary investigation proceedings before he is arraigned before any trial court.

In this way,

> He will know the nature and contents of the charges which will be framed against him. He will have the right to cross-examine the prosecution witnesses and demolish their evidence...where there is a trial without preliminary investigation accused loses all these advantages... The Treason and State Offences Act No. 10 of 1963 contains no provision authorizing a judge to consent in writing or direct a prosecution for the offence of Treason, one of the heinous offences in Sierra Leone...

> The learned Acting Solicitor General frankly conceded that there is no provision in law to warrant the illegal procedure adopted in this case...

> The learned Acting Chief Justice was of the view that there was no provision to quash an illegal indictment. The learned Acting Chief Justice has offered the trial to proceed on an illegal indictment...

> For those reasons I hold that the indictment presented against the accused is illegal and accordingly quash it.

> The appeal is allowed.

The flush of victory had gone into the heads of the APC executive. They had misled the electorate into believing that the SLPP was a Mendeman's party that was bent on monopolizing power for the benefit of Mendes. Now that they were in power they had to prove their charges quickly, even if it involved hasty trumped up charges, speedily manipulated through the courts, even in violation of the Criminal Procedure Act. The foregoing is the first case in point.

Although this first treason trial floundered, it reveals the vindictive propensity of the APC. That as soon as they came to power they began to reveal their diabolical ideology, the systematic elimination of the SLPP and therefore, the suppression of all opposition to the APC. Having failed in this first attempt, they went on to the next treason trial.

(ii)   R.V. Brigadier Andrew Juxon-Smith - Royal Sierra Leone Military Forces
Major Charles Blake - Royal Sierra Leone Military Forces
Major Idrissa Kai-Samba -Royal Sierra Leone Military Forces
Major M.M. Koroma - Royal Sierra Leone Military Forces
Captain Foya - Royal Sierra Leone Military Forces
Berthan Macaulay Q.C., - former Attorney General

With the exception of Berthan Macaulay, the rest were members of the National Reformation Council which governed Sierra Leone for one year, when the soldiers took over in March, 1967. Brigadier Andrew Juxon-Smith was then the Chairman and William Leigh, the Deputy Chairman.

They were all charged with two counts of treason, alleging that they overthrew the government and usurped the executive powers of the state.

When the Preliminary Investigation began, Brigadier Andrew Juxon-Smith subpoenaed 35 persons to give evidence on his behalf, including the following:

1.   His Excellency the Acting Governor-General, Mr. Justice Banja Tejansie

2.   Mr. Siaka P. Stevens - Prime Minister

3.   Madam Honoria Bailor-Caulker, Paramount Chief, Kagboro Chiefdom and a contestant in the Moyamba District, Paramount Chief Member bye-election

4.   Sir Bankole Jones, President of the Sierra Leone Court of Appeal

5.   Dr. Davidson Nicol, former Principal of Fourah Bay College and Vice-Chancellor of the University of Sierra Leone

6.   L.A.M. Brewa, Sierra Leone's present Minister of External Affairs

7.   The Attorney General

8.   G.L.V. Williams, Secretary to the Prime Minister

9.   Colonel John Bangura, Force Commander

10.   Malcolm Parker, Commissioner of Police

11.   S.B. Daramy, Financial Secretary

12.   Albert Metzger, who acted as Attorney General and is
      now in the Crown Law Office

13.   Lt. Colonel West of the R.S.L.M.F. (expatriate)

14.   C.B. Rogers-Wright, one of the prosecution counsels in
      the first stage of the treason trials.

This list was culled from one local newspaper.

By this list, the Brigadier obviously dropped a cat among the pigeons. There was frantic flurry in Court among the prosecution, and the hearing was adjourned to October 25, 1968. This charge died a natural death. It reappeared in R. V. Brigadier David Lansana and seventeen others, when Brigadier Andrew Juxon-Smith was dropped out this time to reappear in another treason trial, in which the author was his principal witness.

In this ruthless manner of bringing forth countless number of charges of treason designed to annihilate prominent members of the SLPP and others, harass innocent citizens, the Government set about to prostitute the law of the land. Treason, as we have said, is the most heinous crime on the statute book, and should not be prostituted to satiate the sadistic motives of politicians. To have resorted to it as a political weapon to pulverise the opposition political party, only proved once again that the political ideology of the All Peoples Congress Party was to eliminate all opposition to its rule and so pave the way for declaration of a one-party state.

For good measure, we shall consider one more treason trial before we settle to 'the' treason trial, the cause celebre of Siaka Stevens' reign.

(iii)   R. V. KOMBE KAJUE AND PARAMOUNT CHIEF, MADAM
        ELLA KOBLO GULAMA

On the 7th of July 1969, Robert Kombe Kajue an SLPP opposition member of parliament for Moyamba South Constituency was arrested shortly after Parliament adjourned as he was driving away from Parliament. He was taken to the CID Headquarters where he was charged with Treason Felony and Misprision of Treason.

He was charged jointly with Paramount Chief Madam Ella Koblo Gulama who was at the time detained at Pademba Road Prisons and who had already been charged in another Treason Trial along with 17 others.

The Government controlled Newspaper *Unity*, reported that Kombe Kajue and Paramount Chief Ella Koblo Gulama might have been arrested following investigations which the CID were conducting as a result of the disclosures of Winston Mima Popai in his evidence in the Treason Trial of Brigadier David Lansana and 17 others that

> In March 1967 while in the compound of Madam Gulama at Moyamba, he saw ex-Premier Sir Albert Margai take out piles of two leone notes from a briefcase, and handed Le 40,000 to Robert Kombe Kajue telling him that he should proceed to Liberia to purchase arms.

> Last Thursday, in answer to a question raised by the opposition leader, the Prime Minister, Dr. Siaka Stevens told Parliament that fresh charges against Madam Gulama were imminent.

In August 1969, a pamphlet called *Freedom*, associated with the Sierra Leone Peoples Party, wrote in its editorial column that

> During the last session of Parliament, Siaka Stevens said with an air of delightfulness and unconcern that one Sierra Leonean is languishing in a Liberian cell...Jonathan Bindi, the man in the Liberian cell, is a Kono man.

> Mr. Siaka Stevens said that Jonathan Bindi was caught with the handsome amount of Le 40,000 ($40,000). He further asserted that Bindi was involved in the arms deal.

That was another of Siaka Stevens' perennial lies against the SLPP and persons associated with them, which most of the prosecution witnesses like Winston Mima Popai were taught to memorize. Again, as this case floundered, the Government now concentrated on their biggest treason trial. In that trial, Brigadier David Lansana and 17 others, Winston Mima Popai and Kortu-wa-teh-bu were among the star witnesses, When they were being cross-examined by Berthan Macaulay, Popai explained that *popai* is a

Mende word which means, a swamp which inevitably swallows its victims. He refused to answer Berthan Macaulay's suggestion that, in like manner, he had come to court to swamp the accused persons with his lies from which they would never extricate themselves. Mr. Kortu-wa-teh-bu also explained that his name means, if you substitute stones for the eggs of a hen, it would never hatch them, Again, Berthan Macaulay suggested that his story was as incredible as that a hen can hatch stones. He murmured cynical denial.

Like his predecessor and some of the witnesses which the prosecution mustered, their stories put together, were insufficient even to swing a cat, nay more to convict any one of treason.

(iv)   R. V. BRIGADIER DAVID LANSANA AND 17 OTHERS

Three weeks after our arrest without warrants, Mrs. Berthan Macaulay applied for a Writ of Habeas Corpus directed to the Director of Prison to show cause why he was holding Berthan Macaulay in Pademba Road Prison illegally. The Writ sparked off immediate retaliation from the Government. Section 17 of Cap. 39, An Ordinance to Consolidate and Amend the Law relating to Criminal Procedure No. 2 of 1908 to No. 38 of 1959, relating to Habeas Corpus, arraignment and indictment, stipulates that

> All arrested persons to be brought before the Court without delay. Subject to the provisions of Section 72 all arrested persons shall be brought as soon as possible before the Court having jurisdiction in the case, or the Court within the local limits of whose jurisdiction any such person was arrested.

Section 72 relates to the

Power of the Police to admit to bail.

It stipulates that

> (1)   Notwithstanding anything in the last preceding section contained, any police officer or constable in charge of a police station may take bail by recognisance conditioned for the appearance of an accused person before the Magistrate's Court, on a day and at a place to be mentioned in such recognisance, there and then to be dealt with according to law, in the following cases-

The "last preceding section," i.e, Section 71, relates to "Admission to Bail."

A couple of days after the Writ of Habeas Corpus had been served, over twenty of us were taken to the Central Investigation Department at 8 p.m. Statements were written down, following interrogations by police officers. While I was being interrogated, a police constable was standing with an automatic weapon pointed at me. The Sub-Inspector had a list of questions which he asked me, and as I replied, he wrote down answers which purported to have been made by me. When we completed the questions, he left the room and went to another room to get further instructions from Cyril Rogers-Wright, a disbarred lawyer referred to elsewhere above, who scrutinized the statement.

As soon as he left the room, the police guard started provoking me by pointing the gun at me, as if he was going to shoot at any moment. "These people have stolen all our money," he began, "built houses and bought Mercedes Benz cars. It is a waste of time to put them on trial. They should all be taken out and lined up, and we spray them with bullets, rather than Pa Rogers-Wright wasting our time writing questions for them to answer." It was then that I knew that the questions and answers were being vetted by Cyril Rogers-Wright.

By the time the officer returned with another list of questions, I was frightened stiff not knowing when the irate police constable would pull the trigger. I hurriedly answered his questions, signed the statement, and was taken to the main room where we arrived. When we returned to the prison, I was unable to sleep until the small hours of the morning.

We the undermentioned were arraigned before Senior Police Magistrate Donald Macaulay on charges of treason, treason felony, and misprision of treason, namely, (1) Brigadier David Lansana, Former Ambassador to the United Nations Organization; (2) Colonel Augustine Blake, Former Member of the National Reformation Council; (3) William Leigh; Former Deputy Chairman of the National Reformation Council, and Commissioner of Police; (4) Kandeh Bureh; Former Cabinet Minister in the SLPP Government; (5) Colonel Bockarie Kai Samba; Former Member of the National Reformation Council; (6) George Sulayman Panda; Former Secretary to the Prime Minister; (7) Thomas Decker, Permanent Secretary, Ministry of Information and Broadcasting; (8) Captain Samuel Norman,

A.D.C. to the Governor-General; (9) Momoh Foh, Director of the Elections Commission; (10) John Kallon, Establishment Secretary; (11) Sheikh Batu Daramy, Financial Secretary; (12) Berthan Macaulay Q.C., Former Attorney General; (13) Abu Koroma, Attorney General; (14) Samuel Margai, Brother of Sir Albert Margai; (15) A.B. Paila, Former Mende Tribal Headman; (16) Maigore Kallon, Former Cabinet Minister in the SLPP Government, and Minister of External Affairs; (17) Paramount Chief Madam Ella Koblo Gulama, Paramount Chief and Former Cabinet Minister in the SLPP Government.

A large crowd of hooligans had been mustered by the APC to heckle us. As soon as the prison lorries arrived at the Court House, there was thunderous applause from SLPP members to boost our morale, as we were hurriedly herded into the Court House. The APC hooligans responded with boos and insults. They sang:

"Tiffy tiffy, Jan koni ko," meaning, "thieves, dance."

The court was overcrowded. The Senior Police Magistrate, Donald Macaulay read the charges against us.

The "Fundamental Rights and Freedoms" of Sierra Leoneans were at that time protected by the Constitution of 1961 as follows:

Section 13(1) Protection from arbitrary arrest or detention.

No person shall be deprived of his personal liberty save as may be authorized by law...

(2) Any person who is arrested, or detained, shall be informed as soon as reasonably practicable, in language which he understands, of the reasons for his arrest or detention.

Section 16 Protection from inhuman treatment.

(1) No person shall be subjected to torture or to inhuman or degrading punishment or other treatment.

Section 19 Provision to secure protection of law.

Every person who is charged with a criminal offence shall be *presumed to be innocent until he is proved or has pleaded guilty.* (Italics mine).

Notwithstanding the above protections, an individual's fundamental liberty may be curtailed under Section 13(5) " during a period of public emergency." Section 25(4) interprets "period of public emergency," as any period during which

(a)   Sierra Leone is at war; or

(b)   there is in force a resolution of the House of Representatives declaring that a state of public emergency exists.

DEPRIVATION OF PERSONAL LIBERTY

During the army interventions, they suspended the Constitution and governed by decrees. As soon as Siaka Stevens was sworn as Prime Minister in April, 1968, and formed his Cabinet, his first duty should have been, the restoration of the Constitution and the immediate abolition of the emergency decrees of the military government. If a state of public emergency existed, and he wanted to take appropriate action, he should have done so in accordance with the Constitutional provisions as outlined above, or other legislation empowering him to do so, such as, the Public Order Act.

No such action was taken by the APC Government and so the ludicrous situation existed, wherein a civilian government was governing Sierra Leone, side by side with the army. This was not an oversight, because Siaka Stevens is too astute not to have seen the ambiguity and ludicrous nature, not to speak of the unconstitutionality, of such a coalition, He chose to shut his eyes deliberately to the Constitution, so as to carry out his diabolical plans under the cloak of military emergency.

Mr. Siaka Stevens became Prime Minister in April, 1968. We were arrested on the 28th May, 1968, and yet our detention order was not issued until 17th July, 1968, namely,

PUBLIC NOTICE

Supplement to Sierra Leone Gazette Extraordinary Vol. XCIX, No. 47 dated 17th July, 1968

Public Notice No. 29 of 1968 Published 17th July, 1968

THE ADMINISTRATION OF SIERRA LEONE

(NATIONAL INTERIM COUNCIL) PROCLAMATION, 1968 (P.N. No. 21 of 1968)

THE NATIONAL INTERIM COUNCIL (DETENTION) (AMENDMENT) Short title. ORDER, 1968

1.   This Order shall be deemed to have come into force on the 19th day of April, 1968. Commencement

2.   The Schedule to the National Interim Council (Detention) Order, 1968 is hereby amended by the addition thereto of the following names:

E.A. George	Okere Adams
J.S. Moiwo	Kai Dumbuya
E.A. Coker	Zainabu Kamara
J.N.E.G. Smith	Bindi
A.S.D. Kallon	T.A.L. Decker
E.A. Bangura	B.A. Kargbo
J.C. Tucker	J.H. Saffa
S.T. Kamara	H.B. Kanneh
F.A. Jalloh	M.S. Kanneh
W.B. Davies	N. George
T.T. Jusu	S.K. Salu-Bao
T.A. Konteh	O.A. Smith
C.V. Roques	J.B. Macarthy
S.A. Taylor	M.B. Jawara
A.W. During	T.A. Walker
D.W. Quee	F.L. Seisay
J.O.C. Thomas	J.F. Koroma
D.E. Fitha	J.S. Gottor
E.M. Harding	M.J.A. Tucker
T.B. Mannah	H.D. Bangura
H.W.O. Shyllon	W.Y. Kanu
J.A. Grant	H. Swarray
E.G.O. Cauker	A.M.D. Bangura
A.B. Seisay	Sampson Caulker
D.D.K. Vandy	Eric Musa
K.D. Bangura	Gbassay Kamara
M.A. Seisay	O.J.C. Williams
Maigore Kallon	J.E. Johnny
F.S. Josiah	Berthan Macaulay
S.M. Conteh	Joseph Boumie
J.S. Momoh	M.F.O. Spencer
M.M. Kosia	J.R. Koroma
John Kallon	I.R. Golley-Morgan
G.S. Panda	Emadu Rogers
Samura Sesay	Patrick Conteh

A.B. Paila	P.C. Bai Makaray Ansilk
A.B. Paila	P.C. Alikali Modu III
Prince George	Momoh Foh
Sam Margai	Abu Koroma
P.C. Ella Koblo Gulama	Bai Makari II Alex Koroma
Mrs. Regina James	Daramy
Kande Bureh	M.S. Tarawally
S.B. Daramy	S.H. Norman
Kandeh Luseni II	Saffa Kengenyeh
	Bockarie Sambama
	John E. Kuyembeh

Made and Issued this 20th day of April, 1968

COL. JOHN A. BANGURA
Chairman, National Interim Council

Printed and Published by the
Government Printing Department, Sierra Leone
GAZETTE EXTRAORDINARY NO. 47 of 17th July, 1968

The above detention order states that we were arrested and detained on the Orders of the National Interim Council, and signed by Colonel John A. Bangura, Chairman on the 20th of April, 1968. That is to say, that although a civilian government was restored by the appointment and swearing in of Siaka Stevens as Prime Minister in April, 1968, the country was being governed by a civilian government and a military government jointly, since April 1968 to July 1968.

When Siaka Stevens was sworn in as Prime Minister the APC assumed control immediately, and began their massive arrests of SLPP members and sympathizers. When the legality of his arrest and detention were challenged by Berthan Macaulay, he produced such startling documentary evidence that Justice Roland Harding said: "Mr. Crown Council, do you see what I see? I shall see that justice is done, even if it costs me my job," or words to that effect. Undoubtedly, the learned Judge was astounded by the fraudulent documents the government had prepared to cover up their illegal actions.

Second: Information for arrest as soon as possible.

We were never "informed as soon as reasonably practicable...of the reasons for...(our) arrest or detention," as required by the Constitution. (parenthesis mine). The first time that we knew the reason for our arrest and detention was when the Senior Police Magistrate read the indictment to us in court, weeks after our arrests and detentions.

Third: Torture, inhuman and degrading punishment.

Since the 28th May 1968 when we were arrested up to the 19th of October, 1971, when some of us including me, were released, we were subjected to the most cruel and inhuman treatment. After breaking us in by seven days' and seven nights' solitary confinement, we were transferred to Wilberforce Block.

There was relaxation in the solitary confinement. When we did not go to court, we were allowed two hours for breakfast, two hours for lunch, and two hours for dinner. Otherwise, we were locked up in our hot and humid cells all the time for over six months during which period we were allowed to go to the field for exercise for two hours each day. The time for exercise was extended gradually as time went on.

We were at the first floor. Below us, there were over 200 prisoners. That was, an average of five prisoners in one cell, intended originally by the colonial government for one prisoner. They had their own vessels for water, and for toilet; both of which had lids. At 5 a.m., three large drums were placed one at each end of the Block, and one in the center. All prisoners emptied their overnight toilets in the drums which were carried away by 8 a.m., after we had had sufficient time to inhale the effluvia, as we were located up in our cells above them. To be confined for the best part of the day in a hot, humid, mosquito infested cell with no windows, except small ventilation bars at the top, in a bedlam of noises till midnight, and woken up at 5 a.m. by the stench of faeces and urine, amidst indescribable pandemonium, are far beyond the prohibitions contemplated in Section 16(i) of the Independence Constitution, namely torture, inhuman and degrading punishment.

The government cannot pretend ignorance of these torture, inhuman and degrading punishment to which we were subjected, because they authorized our arrests and must have been aware of the reasons of our arrests and detentions, which were preceded minutes before the infamous 'subversive elements' broadcast by the Prime Minister, Dr. Siaka Stevens. The indictments which followed, lend color to this knowledge. Furthermore, when ever we complained against the inhuman treatment meted out to us, the Director of Prisons explained that they received their instructions from above. Therefore, from the day of our arrests and detentions, the Government was aware that we were political prisoners who should be treated as such under International Law, and not be subjected to cruel and unusual punishment. Yet, they chose to behave in the most callous, primitive, and uncivilized manner, consonant only with the creed of their Party NOW OR NEVER, and at all cost, in blatant defiance of human rights.

The solitary confinement imposed on us for seven days and seven nights, and the partial solitary confinements that followed thereafter, were not only a violation of International Law, but an infraction of the Sierra Leone Prisons Act and Rules made thereunder. Since the Government elected to ignore these edicts, little wonder that the Deputy Director of Prison, could violate these Rules with reckless abandon. For instance, he imprisoned me falsely in my cell contrary to the Prison Act, i. e., without trial, because my wife kissed me. He then proceeded to put me on trial; thereby putting the cart before the horse. So I was subjected to double jeopardy-imprisonment in gaol.

During our incarceration, I saw two dead bodies carried away to the mortuary. They had fungus all over their bodies. These men were ill and without proper medical treatment, they died slowly when their frail frames could bear the stings and bites of mosquitoes, ground bugs, overcrowding, and the general insanitary conditions no more, that prevailed in the prison.

It is a cardinal principle of Anglo-Saxon legal system, that an accused man is presumed innocent, until his guilt is proved beyond all reasonable doubt. This principle was embodied in the Sierra Leone Independence Constitution. For all practical purposes, from the time I was arrested - incidentally, I was the first person to be arrested during the notorious "subversive elements" broadcast - our guilt was presumed beyond all reasonable doubt. By and large, the people had been attuned to that conclusion. Therefore, our captors, (soldiers), prison officers, police guards when we were interrogated at the Central Investigation Department, were hostile to us. The APC propaganda machinery was in full gear, and the Government was determined to hang not less than seven of us, as Cyril Rogers-Wright told Berthan Macaulay in the Supreme Court; "You wait, when your neck will be swinging in the gallows, you will speak your Queen's English." This was an aside, when Berthan Macaulay teased him that he had problem in understanding the Queen's English. Cyril Rogers-Wright was speaking for the hard-core of APC members and associates. According to the Director of Prisons, prisoners are not addressed as "Mr.", as if they lose all their self-respect as soon as they are arrested and are treated as convicted criminals, regardless of the Constitutional provision that they are presumed innocent.

That Cyril Rogers-Wright should have been selected by the Prime Minister, Siaka Stevens, to prosecute us was an important indication of the policy which he was going to pursue in governing Sierra Leone, as the following facts demonstrate.

Mr. Siaka Stevens published a document in 1961 in London entitled "Sierra Leone's forthcoming Independence - Points to Ponder," on behalf of the APC Working Committee, *inter alia*, castigating Cyril Rogers-Wright,

> the lawyer, who had been sacked from his profession for such serious offences, had now been promoted by the Prime Minister and the Governor to be a pillar of the Government.

> Worse still, the inclusion in the Coalition of an individual who was twice suspended from practice as a lawyer for dishonest practices, and was on the third occasion debarred altogether, has made a good many people wonder whether this is the standard of honesty and integrity which is to be set for independence. It might not have been so bad if the offence for which the ex-lawyer was debarred were some remote one, but it concerned illiterate electors in the Northern Province who during the 1957 disturbances, hired the man to put their case against the chiefs and after receiving payments from them, went and took monies from the Chiefs also. This appointment has also baffled the poor illiterate people who were alarmed when they heard that the lawyer, who had now been promoted

130

by the Prime Minister and the Governor have the right to appoint anyone whom they choose to be a Minister, Since the Governor is in Sierra Leone as a representative of the British Government the APC cannot but believe that the British Government approves of the appointment. We therefore now bring this matter to the direct notice of members of Parliament, the British Press and public in order that they may know the kind of Independence to which Sierra Leone is moving.

The above quotation was culled from *Freedom*, Vol. 1, No. 38 of July 5, 1969, published by Alimamy H. Conteh. This paper went on to comment that

Indeed, here is an instance of history repeating itself with ironic pungency at the expense of the present Prime Minister, Mr. Stevens, and his APC Government. If our inference is correct that the reference is to Rogers-Wright, then this is a very poor reflection indeed on the integrity of the principles of Mr. Stevens and his party.

Today, under the government of these same people and party, Mr. Wright was made to retrieve his WIG, and beyond that, assumes total charge of Sierra Leone's historic TREASON trials, which involve the lives of many top-ranking citizens, (Capitals supplied).

Freedom went on to quote the following from the above document written by Mr. Siaka Stevens on behalf of the APC Working Committee, while he was in London.

The British Government has brought us up all along on the principle of government and opposition in the Governmental machinery, but just at this time when it is handing over power, it is handing the country over to a government which has practically no Opposition. Thus we are to move into an entirely new arrangement which the country has not been trained for and which is a puzzle to most people.

This was the Cyril Rogers-Wright whom Siaka Stevens now selected to prosecute us. It is quite evident that Cyril Rogers-Wright was therefore, selected by Siaka Stevens to lead the prosecution of the treason trials because, Siaka Stevens knew of his "dishonest practices," as he described them, and was determined that the treason trials shall be prosecuted in a dishonest manner, to ensure our conviction.

It is against this background of official presumptions that we were to be treated as if we were guilty, until our innocence was established beyond all reasonable doubt, that the reader should read the next treason trial.

Furthermore, Siaka Stevens was complaining to the British Government and public in 1961, that the British Government was "handing the country over to a Government which has practically no Opposition," and yet in 1978 when he crowned himself monarch of Sierra Leone, he imposed a one-party state on that nation in the teeth of the most violent opposition. President Siaka Stevens' political *volte face* is so blatant and transparent that we need no microscope to penetrate them. He will go down in history as the most unscrupulous Machiavellian Prince that ever 'trod on neat's leather.'

After the preliminary investigations, Senior Police Magistrate, Donald Macaulay, committed our case to the Supreme Court, presided over by Acting Chief Justice Okoro Cole.

At the end of the usual preliminary legal battle, the Acting Chief Justice C.O.E. Cole ruled that

> the expression 'prepares or endeavours' contained in Section 3 (1)(a) and (b) and in Section 4 of the Treason and State Offences Act 1963 (Act No. 10 of 1963) creates one and indivisible offence...

> In the circumstances, I order that the expression 'prepared or endeavoured' be substituted in Count 1; 3; 5; 7; 9; and 11 for the expressions 'prepared' and 'endeavoured' where so used in this Count.

The amended indictment reads as follows:

> Amended by Order of Mr. Justice C.O.E. Cole; Acting Chief Justice on the 7th day of February, 1969 and on the 1st day of July, 1969.

> Count 1 Statement of Offence: Treason contrary to Section 3(1)(a) of the Treason and State Offences Act, 1963.

Particulars of Offence:

That between 1/1/67-3/23/67 in the Western Area

1.   David Lansana...
2.   William Leigh...
3.   Augustine Blake...
4.   Bockarie Idrissa Kai Samba...
5.   Samuel Einga Norman...
6.   Kandeh Bureh...
7.   George Sulaiman Panda...
8.   Thomas Decker...
9.   Ella Koblo Gulama...
10. John Kallon...
11. S.B. Daramy...
12. Berthan Macaulay...
13. Abu Aiah Koroma...
14. Momoh G. Foh...
15. Sam Margai...
16. A.B. Paila...

'prepared or endeavoured' to overthrow the Government of Sierra Leone by unlawful means.

2.   Conspired together and with other persons unknown to overthrow the Government of Sierra Leone in that they agreed

(a)   To imprison the Governor-General, Sir Henry Lightfoot Boston and Mr. Siaka P. Stevens who had been appointed and sworn as Prime Minister and Ibrahim Taqui who had been sworn as Minister

(b)   To seize control of the State House in Freetown...the seat of the Executive Head

(c)   To seize and take control of the transmitting station at New England and Goderich and the SLTV at New England

(d)   To suppress the publication and announcement over the SLBS of a press release by the Governor-General concerning the appointment of a new Prime Minister in the person of Mr. Siaka Stevens

(e)   To declare Martial Law in Sierra Leone and take over the Government of Sierra Leone

(f)   To impose and enforce the Curfew Law in Sierra Leone

(g)   To assemble members of Parliament

(h)   To delay and suppress the publication of the results of the 1967 General Elections

(i)   To falsify the results of the 1967 General Elections

3.   That between 16/3/67 and 21/3/67 at Hill Station

William Leigh, Kandeh Bureh, George Sulaiman Panda, Thomas Decker, John Kallon, S.B. Daramy and Berthan Macaulay incited David Lansana to overthrow the Government of Sierra Leone by unlawful means.

4.   That between 16/3/67 and 21/3/67 David Lansana, Augustine Blake and Bockarie Idrissa Kai-Samba incited the said Samuel Hinga Norman, Lieutenant Gbassa, Sapha Steven Jande Kengenyeh, Captain Foyah and other members of the Royal Sierra Leone Military Forces to overthrow the Government of Sierra Leone by unlawful means.

5.   That on 21/3/67 at the State House in Freetown, David Lansana and Samuel Hinga Norman arrested and falsely imprisoned the Governor-General, Sir Henry Lightfoot Boston, Mr. Siaka Stevens who had been appointed and sworn as Prime Minister and Ibrahim Taqui who had been sworn as Minister. That on 21/3/67 David Lansana declared Marital Law in Sierra Leone.

7.   That on the 21/3/67 David Lansana, Augustine Charles Blake, Bockarie Idrissa Kai-Samba and Samuel Hinga Norman by force of arms took control of the State House Freetown.

8.   That on or about 21/3/67, David Lansana, Augustine Charles Blake, Bockarie Idrissa Kai-Samba and others by force of arms, took over control and complete charge of the then SLBS transmitting Stations at New England.

9.   That David Lansana, Leslie William Leigh...Charles Blake, Bockarie Idrissa Kai-Samba, Kandeh Bureh, George Sulaiman Panda, Thomas Decker, John Kallon, S.B. Daramy, Berthan Macaulay and Sam Margai on 21/3/67 at Hill Station conspired together and with other persons unknown to suppress and did suppress the publication and announcement of a Press Release by the Governor-General concerning the appointment on that day of a new Prime Minister in the person of Mr. Siaka P. Stevens.

10.   That on or about 21/3/67 Leslie William Leigh, incited the members of the Sierra Leone Police Force to join the Military Force to overthrow the Government of Sierra Leone.

11.   That on or about 21/3/67 and between that day and 23/3/67, the said David Lansana, Leslie William Leigh, Augustine Blake and Bockarie Idrissa Kai-Samba imposed and enforced the Curfew in Sierra Leone.

12.   That on or about 21/3/67 at Hill Station David Lansana, Berthan Macaulay, Augustine Charles Blake, Bockarie Idrissa Kai-Samba, Thomas Decker and Sam Margai met and after the said meeting Berthan Macaulay was heard to say "David Lansana has made his mind to take over."

13.   That on or about 21/3/67 at Flagstaff House, Hill Station, Kandeh Bureh, David Lansana, Leslie William Leigh, Berthan Macaulay, Augustine Charles Blake, Bockarie Idrissa Kai-Samba, John Kallon, S.B. Daramy, George Sulaiman Panda and Sam Margai were heard to say "David Take Over, Take Over."

The jurors found us guilty and the Acting Chief Justice sentenced ten of us to be hanged and two to seven years' imprisonment, with hard labor. We appealed and our appeal was heard by Justice Tambia (Judge of the Sierra Leone Appeal Court - Chairman), Justice Bridges (Chief Justice of the Gambia), and Justice Beccles Davies, a Judge of the Supreme Court of Sierra Leone. Our lawyers submitted legal arguments in our defence at the end of which, we were all acquitted. The Government re-arrested us and we were again imprisoned, as published hereunder:

Public Notice No. 32 of 1971

Published 8th May, 1971

THE PUBLIC EMERGENCY REGULATIONS, 1971
(P.N. No. 18 of 1971)

THE PUBLIC EMERGENCY (DETENTION)
(NO. 11) ORDER, 1971 Short Title

WHEREAS, the Minister of Defence is satisfied, with respect to the persons named in the Schedule hereto, that it is necessary to make an Order directing that the said persons be detained in order to prevent such persons acting in any manner prejudicial to public safety:

NOW, THEREFORE, in exercise of the powers conferred upon him by Regulation 7 of the Public Emergency Regulations, 1971, the following Order is hereby made:-

Commencement

1.   This Order shall come into force on the 8th day of May, 1971

Certain persons
to be detained

2.   The persons named in the Schedule hereto shall be detained in such place or places, and for such period as the Minister shall determine.

SCHEDULE

David Lansana   Berthan Macaulay
Thomas Decker   George Panda
John Kallon   Augustine Charles Blake
Kande Bureh   S.B. Daramy
L.W. Leigh   M.G. Foh
A.T. Juxon-Smith   Bockarie Idrissa Kai-Samba
Samuel Hinga Norman

Made this 6th day of May, 1971.

SIAKA STEVENS
President and Minister of Defence

After three and a half years in gaol, seven of us were released, including me. The rest were released later. Since this book seeks to survey general perspectives of the ideology and performance of the First Opposition Party Government in a newly emergent nation, space would not permit a detailed study of the prosecution's case, examination and cross-examination of the army of witnesses they mustered, presentation of our evidence in chief and the government's efforts to discredit us. Suffice it to say, that we won our appeal. The prosecution charged that we "prepared or endeavoured" to do a host of illegal acts, as we saw in the indictments above. The Appeal Court held, *inter alia*, that the indictments were bad for duplicity. That is to say, that the prosecution should have divided the overt acts of preparation and endeavour. As they stood, one could not say what the jurors convicted us of. Was it 'preparation', or 'endeavour'? It could not be 'preparation or endeavour' simultaneously. One excludes the other. That was the gravamen of the legal submissions made against the indictments by Mr. Berthan Macaulay, the 12th accused, but was overruled by the learned Acting Chief Justice Okoro-Cole. And so we won our appeals.

Twelve hours before judgment was delivered, we were served with notices by the prison authorities, in which the Government detained us with effect from the date on which the judgment was given. And so we were re-arrested in Court after the judgment of the Appeal Court, and detained as published in the Notice above.

That Justices Tambiah, Bridges and Beccles Davies were able to resist the alleged pressure and/or bribery by President Stevens, they saved the lives of ten innocent men, Suppose the allegations were true and these honorable gentlemen had succumbed to filthy lucre, how rich they would have been today, yet how miserable in conscience.

The hero in these sordid allegations is Dr. Raymon Sarif Easmon for daring to challenge President Siaka Stevens to wit, as alleged, that he was attempting to bribe these Justices to reject our appeals. That he should have been detained almost immediately, thereafter, having published the contents of the above interview with President Siaka Stevens, leaves many questions unanswered by President Siaka Stevens. We hope the allegations were only allegations. But if they were only allegations, why was Dr. Raymon Sarif Easmon detained after he had challenged President Siaka Stevens with these allegations. And why was he not prosecuted for public mischief?

Dr. Raymon Sarif Easmon is one of the few great Africans alive. He defied the colonial government of Sierra Leone during the Second World War over the medical report he wrote about I.T.A. Wallace-Johnson who was then a political prisoner. Because of this defiance, he was terminated from the colonial medical service. As a member of the Scholarship Advisory Committee, he wrote a threatening letter to Governor Beresford Stookes, that he would publish all the recommendations of the Committee awarding a scholarship to me for three years in a row, but which were always alleged to have been sabotaged by an expatriate officer in my Department. I was immediately awarded a scholarship to the London School of Economics and Political Science in 1948.

When the Sierra Leone Peoples Party announced their intention to introduce a one-party republican system of government, Dr. Raymon Sarif Easmon led a vicious attack in the press against Sir Albert Margai, the Prime Minister. As soon as Sir Albert announced that his party had abandoned the idea, Dr. Easmon stopped attacking him and the Sierra Leone Peoples Party. Some stalwarts of the Sierra Leone Peoples Party could not readily appreciate his academic stand on constitutional matters, while the All Peoples Congress Party crowned him as their hero. When the APC began violating the constitution, he was once again on the war path, this time, against President Siaka Stevens. Unlike Sir Albert, President Stevens arrested him and detained him at Pademba Road Prison.

His house has been attacked a couple of times and the furniture destroyed by APC gangsters, to silence him, He is indeed a great African. Africa is in dire need of a few Easmons.

The foregoing account is only a drop in the ocean of perversion of justice and abuse of executive authority, by the All Peoples Congress Party since they came to power. We shall now consider other decisions of the Appeal Court in the famous treason trial.

BRIGADIER DAVID LANSANA'S EXTRADITION

When Siaka Stevens became Prime Minister, he applied to the Liberian Government to extradite Brigadier David Lansana to stand trial for alleged unlawful imprisonment of the then Governor-General. President Tubman refused to extradite him to be tried for a political offence, as that would be contrary to international law. The emissaries who were led by Luseni Briwah, the then Attorney General, assured the President, falsely, that he would not be charged with any political offence.

As soon as Brigadier David Lansana arrived in Sierra Leone, he was charged with false imprisonment of the Governor-General, and Justice Sam Forster found him guilty and sentenced him to five years' imprisonment, with hard labor. That was the prelude to the APC vendetta. Contrary to their promise to President Tubman, and against international law, he was charged with treason, the first treason trial in the annals of Sierra Leone, convicted and sentenced to death. He won his appeal, but was re-arrested and detained, together with his colleagues, including the author, for a further period of six months. After his release, he was implicated in another treason trial, convicted and hanged. The trial of Brigadier Lansana for a political of fence contrary to the promises made to the Liberian Government is repugnant in international law, and therefore, illegal.

After our acquittal by the Appeal Court, we were re-arrested and gaoled. The All Peoples Congress Party Government then embarked on a systematic campaign of mental torture by instigating vicious rumours that they were determined to indict us again. The Government's controlled paper, "*Unity*" carried the following headline on the 17th May, 1971:

> Treason: After that Appeal Court ruling CAN LANSANA BE TRIED?

> Ex-Brigadier David Lansana may never face trial for treason again, inspite of an official statement last week that Government has decided that all the accused persons in the treason trial which was nullified by the Appeal Court last week, will be charged again.

In the 117 page judgment, Justice H.W. Tambia, Chairman, ruled that

> ...the first accused/appellant (Brigadier Lansana-mine) could have been prosecuted in this case by the simple devise of obtaining the consent of the Liberian Government.

> This was not done and the prosecution in indicting the first accused/appellant without obtaining the consent of the Liberian Government acted in undue haste.

> I would agree with my learned brothers that the joinder of the first accused/appellant on the fact of the case was illegal and the proceedings against him a nullity.

In his 15 page addition to the judgment, Justice Phillip Bridges, concurred that:

> ...under the terms of Article VII (of the Extradition Treaty) the first accused cannot be tried for any 'crime or on account of any other matters' than those for which the extradition shall have taken place - namely in this case False Imprisonment...

In layman's language, Luseni Briwah deceived President Tubman that Brigadier David Lansana would be prosecuted for falsely imprisoning the Governor-General, nothing more and nothing less. As soon as Brigadier Lansana arrived in Sierra Leone, he was charged with the said alleged offence and convicted by Justice Sam Forster. He was imprisoned for five years, with hard labor. Then followed the historic treason trial in which Brigadier Lansana was accused number one, from which conviction he and his colleagues now appealed.

Justice S. Beccles Davies also concurred with his learned brothers, as follows:

> ...the appellant (he concluded) was brought here for the offence of False Imprisonment and it is my considered view that he ought not to have been tried for treason without the consent of the Liberian Government.

EXTRADITION CRIME

The law governing extradition was debated at length during the treason trial. It is the Extradition Act, 1870 as amended by 36 and 37 Vict., c. 60 and 7 Edw. 7, C. 15. which was applicable in Sierra Leone. It covers cases in which an extradition agreement exists between Sierra Leone and another state. In this case, such agreement did exist between Sierra Leone and the Republic of Liberia. Therefore, the 1870 Act applied. The salient sections read as follows:

> 3.   Restrictions on surrender of criminals.
>
> The following restrictions shall be observed with respect to the surrender of fugitive criminals:-
>
> (1)   A fugitive criminal shall not be surrendered if the offence in respect of which his surrender is demanded is one of a political character, or if he prove to the satisfaction of the police magistrate or the court before whom he is brought on habeas corpus, or to the Secretary of State, that the requisition for his surrender has in fact been made with a view to try or punish him for an offence of a political character.
>
> 9.   Hearing of case and evidence of political character of crime.

...The police magistrate shall receive any evidence which may be tendered to show that the crime of which the prisoner is accused or alleged to have been convicted is an offence of a political character or is not an extradition crime.

10. Committal or discharge of prisoner.

In the case of a fugitive criminal accused of an extradition crime, if the foreign warrant authorizing the arrest of such criminal is duly authenticated, and such evidence is produced as (subject to this Act) would, according to the law of England, justify the committal for trial of the prisoner if the crime of which he is accused had been committed in England, the police magistrate shall commit him to prison, but otherwise shall order him to be discharged. (Parenthesis supplied).

First, Section 3 says that Brigadier David Lansana "shall not be surrendered if the offence in respect of which his surrender is demanded is one of a political character." To circumvent this hurdle, the All Peoples Congress Government submitted fabricated evidence to the Liberian Government that he would not be indicted for an offence of a political character.

Second, when he arrived in Freetown and was charged with false imprisonment of his Excellency Sir Henry Lightfoot Boston, Justice Foster should have determined whether that was a political offence before trying the case and convicting him to 5 years' gaol with hard labor. One does not have to be a lawyer to know that the imprisonment of a Governor-General in the prevailing circumstances of the 21st March 1967, was of a political character, that is of course, if at all he was imprisoned, Brigadier David Lansana testified that he was not imprisoned. Yet the learned Justice Forster must have satisfied himself that it was not a political offence.

Third, when he was again arraigned before Senior Police Magistrate Donald Macaulay on charges of treason, treason felony or misprision of treason, he too should have carried out similar exercise before committing him to the Supreme Court for trial.

Fourth, at the Supreme Court, Brigadier David Lansana's lawyer pleaded that under the Extradition Act 1870, his client could not be tried for "an offence of a political character." The learned Acting Chief Justice

Okoro-Cole should have ordered forthwith, that the accused "be discharged," and returned to Liberia.

Although this is an Act of the British Parliament, yet it applies to the colonies, of which Sierra Leone was one and after independence, it formed part of the Sierra Leone legal system, unless otherwise so stipulated. The relevant Section as applied to colonies reads as follows:

Fugitive Criminals in British Possessions

17. Proceedings as to fugitive criminals in British Possessions.

This Act, when applied by Order-in-Council, shall, unless it is otherwise provided by such order, extend to every British Possession in the same manner as if throughout this Act the British Possession were substituted for the United Kingdom or England, as the case may require...

Extradition law is an elementary legal principle in international law.

That Cyril Rogers-Wright and those associated with the prosecution were ignorant of this principle would be an uncharitable interpretation of their actions. The 'learned' Cyril Rogers-Wright was known for his astute and acute legal alacrity. My impression was and still is, that, President Siaka Stevens chose to ignore the law and President William Tubman in his inordinate desire to set an example of a few of us by the gallows, particularly, Brigadier David Lansana.

A leading trade unionist from Liberia informed me at Howard University, in 1980, that President William Tubman was distressed by the deceitful way in which he had been hood-winked to surrender Brigadier David Lansana to what might well turn out to be his doom, as indeed it turned out to be. The realization that posterity might judge him as an accomplice in this sordid conspiracy so angered him, that the President was going to sever diplomatic relations with Sierra Leone and recall his ambassador. He was advised not to.

The All Peoples Congress Party's example has been emulated by the governments of Kenya and Tanzania:

Last fall, the governments of Kenya and Tanzania swapped political exiles, with Kenya returning three Tanzanians alleged to have plotted against Tanzanian President Julius Nyerere in exchange for two Kenyan airmen later sentenced to death for organizing the unsuccessful 1982 coup against President Daniel arap Moi.[2]

The alleged offences of the refugees were clearly political in content. Exchange of these refugees was motivated by political considerations and therefore, contrary to international law which forbids the extradition of political refugees.

The Vice President of Kenya Mwai Kibaki, said that, "those who create mischief in one country and run into another country will have nowhere to go."[3] The government of Kenya and others which feel likewise would have to exclude political crimes from their definition of "mischief." To lump all offences in an omnibus and indiscriminate bag called "mischief," would be objectionable in international law.

We shall close the Brigadier David Lansana and seventeen others treason trial, by paying special tribute to the three gallant Appeal Court Judges: Tambia (Ceylonese), Bridges (English), Beccles-Davies (Sierra Leonean), with a quotation from Liversidge Vs. Anderson (1942) A.C. 206 at p. 244; when Lord Atkin delivered his remarkable dissenting judgment:

> ...Amidst the clash of arms the Laws of England are not silent. They speak the same language in times of peace and in times of war. I view with apprehension the attitude of judges who on a mere construction when face to face with claims involving the liberty of the subject show themselves more executive minded than the executive.

Our gallant Appeal Court Judges proved abundantly clearly, that they would not be intimidated by any executive, nor bribed by any president.

While Brigadier David Lansana's treason case was grinding slowly to a halt in the Supreme Court, and it was quite clear that the Government had lost the momentum and initiative to secure convictions, the All Peoples Congress Party Government arrested their Brigadier, John Bangura, who trained the guerrillas in Guinea, and charged him together with some senior army officers, with treason.

(v)   R. V. BRIGADIER JOHN BANGURA AND 3 OTHERS

It was alleged by the Government, that Brigadier John Bangura attempted a coup on the 23rd of March, 1971 which floundered. Four soldiers, Brigadier John Bangura, Colonel Farrah Jawara, Captains Korlu Gbonda and D.D.K. Vandi, were charged with treason and were found guilty. Three of them, Brigadier John Bangura, Colonel Farrah Jawara, and Captain Korlu Gbonda were hanged.

After three years of increasing unpopularity of the All Peoples Congress Party Government, Brigadier Bangura became disenchanted with Siaka Stevens' regime. The Prime Minister was not slow in smelling the rat. He reacted swiftly by appointing his henchmen to key strategic positions, and according to Amnesty International,

> ...building up his personal guard and increasing the strength of the newly-created second battalion, which is in the process of being equipped with sophisticated radio and telecommunication devices. Bangura was ousted by a group of his fellow officers under Colonel Sam King, a Creole, who swung his own people behind the government and immediately recognized it as the 'only legally constituted authority in the country...'[4]

This alleged coup gave President Stevens the impression that the soldiers were "thoroughly untrustworthy. This led him to the extreme step of inviting Guinean troops in to keep the peace and act as a personal bodyguard."

When Siaka Stevens realized that his government was becoming unpopular and there were rumours of instability in the Army, he appealed to President Sekou Toure of Guinea for military assistance. Amnesty International published in March 17, 1972, that of the original 300 soldiers sent, about 50 were still in the country. They were President Stevens' personal bodyguards, and were also at the State House, at Pademba Road Prison and at the Sierra Leone Broadcasting Station.

Having been installed as Prime Minister by the guerrilla army which Sekou Toure helped to train in Guinea, whenever he suspected an insurrection, he quickly appealed to Sekou Toure. The framed up charges against Brigadier John Bangura is a case in point. As Sir Banja Tejansie revealed in his interview by *West Africa*, referred to earlier on, that when

Dr. John Karefa-Smart visited Sierra Leone, he was so frightened of him that he immediately appealed to Sekou Toure for military aid. In the words of Sir Banja,

> ...Stevens was worried, so he once again went to Guinea to see Sekou Toure. On that trip he took with him Captain Jawara, the chap who was hanged with Brigadier Bangura. In Guinea, Jawara overheard Sekou Toure saying to Stevens: 'If you do not get rid of Bangura and Sir Banja, I cannot help you. Sir Banja is a lawyer and would insist on the constitutional procedures and so he cannot very much help you if you want a republic and he is likely to oppose it.' He told him, Bangura cannot be trusted.
>
> Of course two years previously I had repeatedly refused the Republican business because they wanted to achieve it in a way I thought was unconstitutional. Some people like the half-baked communist chaps like S.I. Koroma, had put pressure on me that they wanted a Republic. I said, 'no, I wouldn't do it, you have first to go to the country in an election; it is in the constitution'.
>
> So when he came back to Freetown, Jawara told Bangura what Sekou Toure had told Stevens in Guinea. Bangura went and reported the matter to me. I asked Stevens but he denied it. So this was how enmity started.[5]

This enmity culminated in the executions of Brigadier John Bangura and Colonel Farrah Jawara, two outstanding army officers, one of whom, Brigadier Bangura, was Sandhurst trained.

The President stepped up the training of a selected number of the guerrillas trained in Guinea in para-military duties. The Government recruited Chinese and Cubans to train these men who were designated the Internal Security Unit, and lived in barracks contiguous to the regular police barracks. According to Amnesty International,

> ...The aim is presumably to provide another counter-balancing element to the army... One concrete development was a sizeable shipment of arms (from Peking-mine). We believe this amounted to about 80 tons, mainly of small arms, grenades, light automatic weapons and ammunition.[6]

The All Peoples Congress Party became increasingly unpopular when Siaka Stevens introduced the Republican Constitution and made himself

President. Some of his cabinet ministers, Dr. Mohamed Forna (Minister of Finance), M.O. Bash-Taqui (Minister of Works), Ibrahim Taqui (Minister of Information and Broadcasting) resigned from his cabinet. Two of them were later charged with treason, bringing the number of treason trials to six since the APC came to power.

(vi)　R. V. MOHAMED FORNA AND 14 OTHERS

On the 10th of September, 1974, fifteen persons were arraigned in the High Court of Sierra Leone before Justice Marcus Cole on charges of treason, contrary to Section 3(1) of the Treason and State Offences Act No. 10 of 1963.

The indictment charged that on the 1st of June, 1973, and on diverse dates, to the 30th of July, 1974:

1. Dr. Mohamed Sorie Forna, (MD) - former Minister of Finance;

2. Lieutenant Habib Lansana Kamara - Sierra Leone Military Forces;

3. Ibrahim Taqui - former APC Minister of Information and Broadcasting;

4. Abdulai Bai Kamara (Bai Bai) - former APC Electoral Commissioner;

5. Ex-Brigadier David Lansana - former Force Commander;

6. Abu Mohamed Kanu - former APC Counsellor, Freetown Municipal Council;

7. Albert Tot-Thomas - Ex-Police Officer and Ex-Serviceman;

8. Alusaine Bedor Kamara - Tanker Driver;

9. Ahmed Bundu Kamara - Businessman;

10. George Thompson - Storekeeper;

11. Issa Jalloh - Businessman;

12. Bai Makari N'Silk - Ex-Paramount Chief;

13.   Sub-Inspector Mohamed Mansaray - Internal Security Unit;

14.   Sergeant Mohamed Turay - Internal Security Unit;

15.   Unfa Mansaray - Cook for P.Z. Co.;

prepared and endeavoured to overthrow the Government of Sierra Leone by unlawful means; to kill the then Acting President, Honorable S.I. Koroma, the then Acting Vice President, Honorable C.A. Kamara-Taylor and the Force Commander, Brigadier J.S. Momoh

> by attacking their official residences through means of explosives.

> To attack, seize and take control of the magazine at Tower Hill Freetown, and the Sierra Leone External Telecommunications (SLET) establishment in Wilberforce.

They were all found guilty of all the charges by the jurors. On the 16th of November, 1974, they were sentenced to death by firing squad. Before pronouncing the death sentence, the accused made the following statements, as reported in the Daily Mail of Monday 18, 1974.

1.   Dr. Forna - "I am not guilty of any offence"

2.   Lieutenant Habib Lansana Kamara - Pleaded not guilty

3.   Mr. Ibrahim Taqui said,

> ...that despite everything, (he) wished to thank the Trial Judge for the patience and industry shown in bringing the trial to a speedy end.

> He said that whatever the sentence one would once more be permitted those basic human facilities.

> He thanked the Defence Counsels, whom he said labored to defend them so admirably. To the prosecution officers, he said they had a duty to perform which they had done earnestly and personately (sic).

> Ibrahim Taqui said he bore no man any ill-will for what had transpired in the Trial not even those who bore false testimonies. Taqi reiterated his non-violent nature and said that he did not look upon violence as an instrument for

achieving political power. He admitted being a fighter but said that his weapons had always been words and ideas.

He maintained that he was innocent for (sic) all the crime for which he stood convicted.

4.   All the other accused persons maintained of the crime (sic) for which they were convicted.

Mr. Marcus Cole...pronouncing the sentence said:

'You have been found guilty of the two count charge of Treason by the twelve man jury.

The sentence of this Court upon you each accused persons is that you be taken from this place to a lawful prison, and then to a place of execution and there you shall be shot dead by a firing squad.

May your souls rest in peace.' He indicated to them of their rights to appeal within twenty-one days.

The following proceedings, like the extracts above, were notes extracted by the author from published Reports of the case by the Government Information Services, Ministry of Information and Broadcasting.

At the trial, the Government was represented by N.A.P. Buck, Attorney General; C.S. Davies, Solicitor General; M.O. Adophy, Principal State Council; R.J. Bankole-Thompson, Senior State Council; Dr. A.D. Conteh, State Law Officer; T.S. Johnson and N.D. Tejan-Cole,

They appealed to the Appeal Court.

HELD

The Appeal Court, presided over by Justice Livesey Luke, upheld one appeal and dismissed fourteen others. Those who lost their appeals sought leave to appeal to the Supreme Court, but the Appeal Court rejected their applications.

COURT MARTIAL

Warrant Officer Class 1 Kalogoh and eight others were charged with two count charges of Treason. The Court acquitted and discharged two of the soldiers and convicted the other seven of treason. They were sentenced to death. One of them was recommended for mercy. In accordance with the Royal Sierra Leone Military Forces Act, the sentences were reviewed by the Reviewing Officer and confirmed as follows:

(a)   The sentence on a soldier with recommendation for mercy by the Court Martial commuted to Life Imprisonment.

(b)   The sentence on the remaining six to receive the full penalty of the law.

All the sentences and recommendations were submitted to the Committee on the Prerogative of Mercy who unanimously advised the President as follows:

In the case of the State vs. Mohamed Fornah and fourteen others,

six should suffer death by hanging

six sentences of civilians...commuted to Life Imprisonment.

Of the six soldiers sentenced to death:

three should hang

three commuted to Life Imprisonment.

The President, Dr. Siaka Stevens directed that the following civilians:
1.   Dr. Mohamed Forna
2.   Ibrahim Taqi
3.   Paramount Chief N'Silk
4.   Habib Lansana Kamara
5.   Brigadier David Lansana
6.   Abdul Bai Kamara

and two soldiers should suffer death by hanging, while the death sentences of eight civilians and four soldiers were commuted to Life Imprisonment. The six civilians and two soldiers were executed at the Central Prisons, Pademba Road in Freetown on the 19th of July, 1975. It was reported in *West Africa*[7] that after the executions, five bodies were laid out in front of the gates of Pendembu (sic Pademba) Road Prison - dead from hanging but (according to eyewitness reports) - their bodies showing the marks of torture,... (Parenthesis supplied).

Chapter 6 Notes

1. *Washington Post*, Washington, D.C., U.S.A., May 29, 1976.

2. *Ibid.*, October 2, 1984.

3, *Ibid.*, October 2, 1984.

4. *Amnesty International*, Vol. II No. 7, April I, 1971.

5. *West Africa*, Holborn Viaduct, London, April 30, 1984, p. 925.

6. *Amnesty International*, Vol. 13 No, 6, March 17, 1972.

7. Barrell Bond, Barbara, An article entitled, *When Lifelines Are Cut, in West Africa, ibid.*, May 28, 1984, p. 1117.

PART II

NOW AND FOREVER

INTRODUCTION

When the National Reformation Council was formed in March, 1967, Siaka Stevens went to Guinea for assistance, and President Sekou Toure gave him facilities to train guerrillas under the Command of Colonel John Bangura. The guerrillas infiltrated the Sierra Leone Army and Police Force. The soldiers forced the warrant officers to lead them, and they staged a counter-coup. They arrested all Army and Police Officers and detained them at Pademba Road Prison. Colonel John Bangura convened a meeting of elected members of Parliament under the Chairmanship of the Acting Governor-General the Honorable, Chief Justice Banja Tejansie, and addressed the meeting. After he left, the members 'agreed' to form a coalition government, to be led by Siaka Stevens as Prime Minister. It was also specifically agreed that the cabinet should consist of APC and SLPP members. It is worthy of note, that this was precisely what Sir Henry envisaged when he proposed the formation of a coalition government, because the elections had been fought on tribal grounds. So that after all the machinations, Siaka Stevens and Sir Albert were back to Sir Henry's original plan which he was pressurized by some influential persons to cancel and instead, to appointment Siaka Stevens as Prime Minister.

Once again, Siaka Stevens' engineers set to work. He repudiated all the terms of the agreement reached at the meeting presided over by the Acting Governor-General and the APC unleashed a reign of terror on the people of Sierra Leone, comparable only to Hitler Germany's planned extermination of the Jews. He formed an Internal Security Unit comprising the most vicious elements of his guerrillas. The remainder were absorbed into the Army and the Police Force. They were supplied with the most sophisticated weapons, while the regular soldiers were deprived of all automatic weapons and had only simple First World War rifles.

The main functions of the Internal Security Unit are alleged to include the assassination of political opponents, terrorize the populace from day to day to a point where people suspect even their brothers and sisters as police informants. They are alleged to have been given carte blanche by the President, who is alleged to have assured them that they are above the law, and may shoot to kill, and that they would not be liable criminally.

The record of the All Peoples Congress Party Government shows quite clearly that they were not qualified to govern Sierra Leone in 1967. This record is a compendium of mercenary scares designed to create panic and hysteria, as an excuse for the declarations of states of emergency, arbitrary arrests, trumped-up charges of treason, treason felony and misprision of treason, fabricated evidence of criminal offences, or of complicity in crimes, assassinations, arson. The allegations by Dr. Raymon Sarif Easmon (MD) that it was rumored that President Siaka Stevens attempted to pervert the Appeal Court Judges to reject our appeals in the first treason trial, as a result of which he had an interview with the President and which he published in the Daily Mail, underscores the breed of politicians we are considering. Incidentally, Dr. Easmon was arrested because of the publication, and detained at Pademba Road Prison. That he did not issue a public denial of the allegations as advised and subsequently published in the Daily Mail, by Dr. Easmon leads to only one inference. Alternatively, why was Dr. Easmon not charged in a court of law for slander or public mischief or any crime which the President's legal advisors could think of?

Furthermore, according to Sir Banja Tejansie, who was then Acting Governor-General:

He got Luke to do all the dirty work for him.[1]

The Honorable Justice Luke was Speaker of parliament when the Sierra Leone Peoples Party members were unseated as a result of elections petitions, when Siaka Stevens became Prime Minister in April 1968. Siaka Stevens held a press conference immediately after Sir Banja's revelations of the sordid manner in which "He got Luke to do all the dirty work for him," His reply was that "the only thing I have to say is that the wicked flee when no man pursueth."[2]

The cavalier manner in which he avoided the core of Sir Banja's charge is characteristic of Stevens. Nevertheless, we have the evidence of two highly respected citizens of Sierra Leone about the way in which Siaka Stevens perverted the judicial system of Sierra Leone (Dr. Easmon and Sir Banja).

As far as Siaka Stevens was concerned these were petty matters. His main goals were more hair-raising, as they affected the constitution of Sierra Leone, which he had planned to pervert systematically. We shall begin with the first rape of the 1961 Independence Constitution.

CHAPTER 7

SIERRA LEONE BECOMES A REPUBLIC - 1971

After 150 years as a Crown Colony under the British Government, Sierra Leone became independent on the 27th of April, 1961 under the Sierra Leone Independence Act, 1961. Ten years later, in order to satiate his delusions of grandeur, Siaka Stevens' insatiable ambition for fame led him to impose a presidential constitution on the people of Sierra Leone. Section 26 of the 1961 Constitution provided that

> There shall be a Governor-General and Commander-in-Chief of Sierra Leone, who shall be appointed by Her Majesty and shall hold office during Her Majesty's pleasure and who shall be Her Majesty's representative in Sierra Leone.

Section 29 established a monarchical form of Government: "There shall be a Parliament of Sierra Leone which shall consist of Her Majesty and a House of Representative."

Although Parliament is the supreme legislative organ, certain clauses of the Constitution were entrenched. That is to say, an amendment of any of the entrenched clauses should be in accordance with the provisions of Section 43 - Alteration of the Constitution.

This Section stipulated that in order to amend an entrenched clause, such as Section 29,

> a bill for an Act of Parliament under this section shall not be submitted to the Governor-General for his assent unless the

bill has been passed by the House of Representatives in two successive sessions, there having been a dissolution of Parliament between the first and second of those sessions.

(2)   For the purposes of Section (1) of this section, a bill passed by the House of Representatives in one session shall be deemed to be the same bill as a bill passed by the House in the preceding session if it is identical with that bill, or contains only such alterations as are certified by the Speaker to be necessary owing to the time that has elapsed since that bill was passed in the preceding session.

(3)   A bill for an Act of Parliament under this section shall not be passed by the House of Representative in any session unless at the final vote thereon in that session it is supported by the votes of not less than two-thirds of all the members of the House.

(4)   The provisions of this Constitution or (insofar as it forms part of the law of Sierra Leone) the Sierra Leone Independence Act, 1961, shall not be altered except in accordance with the provisions of this section. (parenthesis supplied)

Politics is the art of the possible, and it is the mark of a statesman to surrender like former President Nixon of the United States of America did, when the odds are overwhelming. This lesson was wasted on the All Peoples Congress Party of Sierra Leone. The attempt by the Sierra Leone Peoples Party to introduce a one-party system in Sierra Leone was resisted by people in the Western Area. Although the bulk of the population which lives in the Provinces were in favour of it, yet Sir Albert abandoned the idea.

When the All Peoples Congress Party came to power in 1968, they began to lay the foundation for the introduction of a republican constitution which the APC had opposed when proposed by the SLPP. 'It was reported by *Africa Confidential* that,

Now Stevens, faced with declining popularity of his government, has reached for the same panacea. He first adopted the old Sierra Leone People's Party republic which he had earlier rejected. He repeated his intentions frequently in 1969 and 1970. In the latter half of 1970, a constitutional commission started to inquire into the whole republican issue. But the opposition refused to participate and at one stage the commissioners were so afraid of violence in up-country areas that they desisted from travelling and taking evidence.[3]

Again, there was universal condemnation of the move to introduce a republican constitution. The All Peoples Congress Party ignored these protests. They re-submitted the Sierra Leone Peoples Party Republican Bill with some amendments which are explained in the Certificate of Compliance at page 52 of the Act No. 6 of 1971 as follows: "52 No. 6 Constitution of Sierra Leone 1971."

CERTIFICATE OF COMPLIANCE

I, SILLA DURAMANI KOROMA, Deputy Speaker of the House of Representatives, hereby certify that a Bill entitled 'THE CONSTITUTION OF SIERRA LEONE' was first introduced by the Honorable Prime Minister, Sir Albert Margai, in the Second Parliament of Sierra Leone on the 24th day of January, 1967, then passed the First Reading, the Second Reading and Committee stage when a number of amendments were made thereto, and that on the 25th day of January, 1967, the then Prime Minister reported to the House that the said Bill, 'THE CONSTITUTION OF SIERRA LEONE' Bill passed the House with certain amendments. It then passed its Third Reading with the majority required under Section 51 of the 1961 Constitution.

I further certify that a Bill entitled "THE CONSTITUTION OF SIERRA LEONE" was again introduced by the Honorable Prime Minister, Dr. Siaka Stevens, in the Third Parliament of Sierra Leone on the 19th day of April, 1971, then again passed the First Reading, the Second Reading, the Committee stage, and then passed its Third Reading with the majority required under Section 51 of the 1961 Constitution (as amended).

I am satisfied that the Bill introduced on the 19th day of April, 1971, is the same Bill as was passed on the 25th day of January, 1967, with only such alterations as are necessary owing to the time that has elapsed since 1967.

I further certify that the Bill entitled "THE CONSTITUTION OF SIERRA LEONE" has been this day duly passed by Parliament and has become law.

GIVEN under my hand this 19th day of April, 1971.

S.D. KOROMA,
Deputy Speaker

Section 16 of the APC Act No, 6 of 1971 reads as follows:

(1)   There shall be a President of the State of Sierra Leone who shall be Head of State, Commander-in-Chief of the Armed Forces and the Fountain of Honor.

(2)   The President shall be appointed by the Cabinet and hold office during the pleasure of the Cabinet.

19.   There shall be a Parliament of Sierra Leone which shall consist of the President, the Speaker and Members of Parliament.

In April 1971, Siaka Stevens became the Second President under the Republican Constitution. Second, because by the process of transition from the 1961 to the 1971 Constitution, the Acting Chief Justice Okoro-Cole was sworn in as first care-taker President, only to hand over quickly to Siaka Stevens.

The Certificate of Compliance signed by S.D. Koroma, Deputy Speaker of the House of Representatives confirms that

'the Constitution of Sierra Leone' was first introduced by the Honorable Prime Minister, Sir Albert Margai, in the Second Parliament of Sierra Leone on the 24th day of January, 1967... It then passed its Third Reading with the majority required under Section 51 of the 1961 Constitution.

The Certificate makes it appear as if the amendment to the entrenched clause provision had been complied with.

Assuming that the APC Bill was in fact

identical with that Bill (the SLPP), or contains only such alterations as are certified by the Speaker to be necessary owing to the time that has elapsed since that bill was passed in the preceding session. (parenthesis mine)

(See 43 of 1961 Act.) Most critics feel that it was immoral for the APC to have introduced a republican system of government which they had vigorously opposed only four years earlier.

The illegal manner in which the Republican Constitution was introduced in Sierra Leone by the All Peoples Congress under the Constitution of Sierra Leone Act No. 6 of 1971 was the forerunner of yet more startling erosions of the fundamental principles of democracy for which the people of this country shed their blood during the First World War in defeating the Germans in the Cameroons, and for which they similarly lost their lives and some maimed in the jungles of South East Asia during the Second World War to defeat the Japanese.

(a)   INDEPENDENT JUDICIARY

One of the bastions of democracy is an independent judiciary. When judges can be hired and fired by the head of state in his executive capacity, then the judicial system loses its aura and independence.

Under Section 85 of the 1961 Constitution, the Judicial Service Commission consisted of:

> (2)   (a)   The Chief Justice, who shall be Chairman;
>
> (b)   such other judge of the Supreme Court as may be designated by the Governor-General, acting in accordance with the advice of the Prime Minister;
>
> (c)   the Chairman of the Public Service Commission; and
>
> (d)   one other member, who shall be appointed by the Governor-General, acting in accordance with the advice of the Prime Minister.

The member appointed at (d) shall be a judge and shall hold office for five years. In fact, with the exception of the Chairman of the Public Service Commission, the other three members of the Judicial Service Commission shall be judges of the Supreme Court.

The Judicial Service Commission shall have the power "to dismiss or exercise disciplinary control" over members of the Judicial Service Commission.

The Republican Constitution increased the number of the Judicial Service Commission to five as follows:

(2)   (a)   The Chief Justice who shall be Chairman;

       (b)   The Chairman of the Public Service Commission;

       (c)   A Justice of Appeal or a Justice of the Supreme Court;

       (d)   ...judge...;

       (e)   one other member.

and shall with the exception of the Chief Justice and the Chairman of the Public Service Commission be appointed by the President acting in accordance with the advice of the Prime Minister.

With the exception of (a) and (b), the other three members "(3) (a) shall vacate office at the expiration of three years

(b) any such member may be removed from office by the President,"

for infirmity or for misbehavior. The power of the Judicial Service Commission to "dismiss or exercise disciplinary control" over members of the Judicial Service Commission, was removed and such power vested in the President.

Two of the four members of the Judicial Service Commission in the 1961 Constitution appointed by the Governor-General were judges, whereas, one of the three appointees of the President under the 1971 Republican Constitution does not have to be a judge. Since he has a majority of appointees on the Judicial Service Commission, they could always outvote the other two members, viz., the Chief Justice and the Chairman of the Public Service Commission.

Chapter 7 Notes

1. *West Africa*, Holborn Viaduct, London, April 30, 1984.

2. *Ibid.*, May 14, 1984.

3. *Africa Confidential*.

CHAPTER 8

CHANGES INTRODUCED BY THE CONSTITUTION OF SIERRA LEONE ACT NO. 6 OF 1971

(1) PRESIDENT

Section 16 substituted a President as Head of State and "the Fountain of Honour," for Governor-General, who, under the Independence Constitution of 1961, was "appointed by Her Majesty and shall hold office during Her Majesty's pleasure and who shall be Her Majesty's representative in Sierra Leone."

Unlike Nigeria (which copied the United States Constitution) where the President is elected by the people and is therefore, responsible and answerable to them, in Sierra Leone, the 1971 Republican Constitution provided that the President "shall be appointed by the Cabinet and hold office during the pleasure of the Cabinet." Since it is the prerogative of the President to appoint a Prime Minister and Ministers under section 50, who constitute the Cabinet, his reappointment is assured.

(2) APPOINTMENT OF PRIME MINISTER

The controversy surrounding the appointment of Siaka Stevens as Prime Minister on the 21st of March, 1967, when the elections were in progress was quite wisely resolved by Section 50 (1) (c), of the APC Republican Constitution, 1971, namely,

No person shall be appointed Prime Minister during a dissolution and before all the results of the general election held under section 48 have been declared except that, if the Prime Minister dies during the said period, the President shall appoint any person who was a member of Parliament immediately before the dissolution as Prime Minister.

(3)   ABOLITION OF APPEALS TO THE PRIVY COUNCIL

While the treason trials were floundering, the Government hastily introduced the aforesaid Republican Constitution, and abolished appeals to the Privy Council as provided by Section 84 (1) of the 1961 Constitution, that

> An appeal shall lie from decisions of the Court of Appeal to Her Majesty in Council as of right....

> (3) Nothing in this section shall affect any right of Her Majesty to grant special leave to appeal from decisions of the Court of Appeal to Her Majesty in Council in any civil or criminal matter.

(4)   PARAMOUNT CHIEFTAINCY

Cabinet was supreme under the 1961 Constitution and the Governor-General acted at all times on the advice of the Prime Minister who derived his authority from Cabinet. This supremacy was transferred to the President under the 1971 Act. For instance, Section 44 of the 1961 Act, which recognised and protected the institution of Paramount Chieftaincy "as existing by customary law and usage", was re-enacted by Section 35 of the 1971 Act. Immediately, at sub-section (2), the latter Constitution provided that

> (2) A Paramount Chief may be removed from office by the President if, after a public enquiry conducted under the chairmanship of a judge of the High Court or a Justice of Appeal, the President is of the opinion that it is in the public interest that the Paramount Chief should be removed,...

The usual "inaccordance with the advice of Cabinet...conveyed to him by the Prime Minister", is omitted.

(5)   ABOLITION OF APPEALS TO HER MAJESTY IN COUNCIL

The 1961 Constitution as amended from time to time and reprinted as Act No. 1 of 1966, gave an aggrieved person the privilege to appeal to Her Majesty in Council. With leave of the Court of Appeal, such appeals lay in

> Section 84 2. (a) Where in the opinion of the Court of Appeal the question involved in the appeal is one that, by reason of its great general or public importance or otherwise, ought to be submitted to Her Majesty in Council....
>
> (3) Nothing in this section shall affect any right of Her Majesty to grant special leave to appeal from decisions of the Court of Appeal to Her Majesty in Council in any civil or criminal matter.

During the colonial days, appeals lay from the four West African colonies of Nigeria, Gold Coast, Gambia and Sierra Leone, to the West African Court of Appeal, and then to Her Majesty in Council, i.e., the Judicial Committee of the Privy Council. In East Africa, there was the East African Court of Appeal. When they became independent, the constitutional instruments contained the aforementioned sections. When Ghana became a republic, Kwame Nkrumah abolished appeals to the Privy Council, and so did Idi Amin Dada of Uganda.

By and large, as sovereign states, it is arguable that they should reorganise their legal systems to reflect their new status among the comity of nations, including final courts of appeal. When however, Kwame Nkrumah sacked the Chief Justice, because he did not convict persons accused of plotting to assassinate him, or when Idi Amin Dada's soldiers dragged the Chief Justice of Uganda from his Chambers in his robes, and has never been heard of since, or when it is alleged that Siaka Stevens attempted to bribe the Judges of the Appeal Court in our treason trial, and got Justice Luke to do his dirty job, as alleged by Sir Banja Tejansie, it might be advisable to re-establish regional appeal courts, on the colonial model.

In line with his colleagues, by his 1971 constitution, President Siaka Stevens abolished appeals to the Privy Council by Section 95 (7) which "provided that no fresh appeals shall lie to the said Privy Council." By his alleged attempt to interfere with the result of the appeal in the treason trial in which I was involved, it is a matter of grave concern as to what extent Sierra Leone can justifiably boast of an independent judiciary; particularly also when it is alleged that he used Justice Luke, then Speaker of Parliament to "do all the dirty work for him."

President Siaka Stevens disillusioned his various admirers. The first treason trial was resented by some, as they interpreted it as the beginning of a reign of government by victimisation and revenge against opponents. By his unconstitutional establishment of a republic he became extremely unpopular. Those of his admirers, like Ambassador John Akar who had any lingering doubts about him, now critised him openly.

The Republican idea did not receive unanimous support within the All Peoples Congress Party hierarchy. Dr. Fornah (MD) and the two Taquis were opposed to it, on the grounds that it might lead to dictatorship. They resigned from his Cabinet. Dr. Fornah and Ibrahim Taqui were subsequently hanged by Siaka Stevens. The manner in which the APC Government substituted a President for the Governor-General, so as to facilitate Siaka Stevens' dictatorial proclivities was one of the other startling constitutional illegalities committed by him. Other staunch supporters were similarly horrified.

The intellectuals who supported him to come to power were now scared of the turn of events, as they could visualise the road to serfdom. With the solitary exceptions of Dr. Raymond Sarif Easmon (MD) and Professor Awunor Renner of Fourah Bay College, the elite who were vociferous in denouncing the SLPP republican proposals, now recoiled quietly into their shells for fear of being detained at Pademba Road Prison. Some SLPP members, sought sanctuary in America and England from where we continued sniping at the APC from time to time.

His Excellency, John Akar, Sierra Leone's Ambassador to the United States of America sent a cablegram immediately to President Stevens when he declared a republic. He also issued a press release which summarised the salient points enumerated in his cablegram and letter. He added that:

> ...Dr. Stevens is in sole command in that West African country including hiring and firing the Vice President, Cabinet Ministers, Judges, Electoral Commissioners, Public Service

Commissioners, Permanent Secretaries and top Civil Servants. He can summon and dissolve Parliament when he chooses. He has installed himself as Executive President for five years even though General Elections are constitutionally due in about two years.

Sierra Leone is still under a State of Emergency declared by President Stevens in September last year. Many political opponents, including his former Ministers of Finance and Information are still in detention; all opposition papers were banned and the opposition United Democratic Party headed by American-educated Dr. John Karefa-Smart, was also banned.

The Ministers referred to by John Akar were later executed. His Excellency John Akar's cablegram and letter showed quite clearly, that even his ardent supporters, and one time admirers of his predecessor, were horrified that in their precipitate reactions, they had misled themselves and created a Frankenstein monster of prodigious dimensions in lamb's clothing.

In the Kansas City Times of May 22, 1971 Robert Dye, Staff Reporter wrote that

An invitation by armed forces will be necessary to topple the government of Sierra Leone and restore democracy, says the former ambassador to the United States from the tiny West African nation. He terms the current government a Communist dictatorship.

Dr. John J. Akar resigned as ambassador last month in response to Dr. Siaka Stevens promoting himself from Sierra Leone prime minister to 'supreme chief of state.' 'Our leader has gone Communist, dictatorial.' Akar said. 'I would never believe it could have happened in Sierra Leone. I refuse to serve with a Communist.'...

Akar said President Stevens had strengthened his regime by bringing in troops from neighbouring Guinea and disarming the 1,500 man Sierra Leone army. The army had only rifles and submachine guns, he said, but the Guinean troops have brought in bazookas, helicopters and MIG fighters. Sierra Leone itself has no air force.

'I can't go back,' Akar said. 'In order to consolidate his power, he (Stevens) may eliminate the opposition. His only reaction is to lock up people.'

Having made himself President against external as well as internal opposition of his APC, Siaka Stevens began to strengthen the Internal Security Unit in preparation for the General Elections.

CHAPTER 9

GENERAL 'SELECTIONS' OF 1973

After two and a half years in office, the All Peoples Congress Party removed all doubts about their insatiable capacity to misgovern, their inexhaustible repertoire of falsifications, their penchant to harass friends and foes, if they disagreed with the undemocratic methods they were introducing into the country.

Africa Confidential of 15th January, 1971 reported that

> Few African leaders now face as many hazards as Siaka Stevens. His All People's Congress (APC) Party has just declared that in spite of last year's clamour it will not, after all, stage Sierra Leone's General Elections this year nor introduce a republic, but Parliament will run its course until 1973. Why the change?

The facts are that if the APC had begun their term in 1967, as they alleged that they won the elections, their five years' term would have expired in 1972. But since the army intervened for twelve months, they rationalised the *volte face* to 1973. But why indeed as African Confidential enquired, the change of dates? The reasons are:

FEARS OF EXECUTIVE PRESIDENCY

> Freetown Creoles and smaller groups supported Mr. Stevens and in Parliament he had a safe majority. He still has: but it could now disappear in a general election.

> ...political volatile Creoles, led by Dr. Sarif Easmon, were soon critical of a style of government...of Mr. Stevens' intention of initiating a republic...and make himself 'executive' president with full powers.
>
> Mr. Stevens' argument for a republic ('Africans now don't understand where power lies') also apply to a 'constitutional presidency'.[1]

For obvious reasons, like all African states, Sierra Leoneans prefer a republican state to having the Queen of England as head of an African state. Yet, they are afraid of substituting a despot in the process. Therefore, the opposition to Siaka Stevens was due to well founded apprehensions that he might introduce an 'executive' and not merely a 'ceremonial' presidency.

RESIGNATIONS

The resignations of Mohamed Bash Taqui and his brother, and Dr. Mohammed Forna (M.D.) former cabinet ministers of the APC Party with port folios, were a bombshell for the Party. While the President was on a state visit in Zambia these three cabinet members resigned. They formed the United Democratic Party, and invited Dr. John Karefa-Smart, then Deputy Director of the World Health Organisation in Geneva, to lead their Party. Dr. Karefa-Smart's arrival complicated matters for Siaka Stevens, who as soon as he returned home, declared a state of emergency and detained the leaders of the UDP, including Dr. John Karefa-Smart (MD).

MARGAI-PHOBIA

Although thousands of miles away from Sierra Leone, the charismatic personality of Sir Albert Margai cast a spell over Sierra Leone and became a spectre that haunted Siaka Stevens in particular, the APC, who felt the numbing chill of his presence in their homes. This phenomenon was aptly described by Africa Confidential as Margai-phobia.

> The Government has alleged that Sierra Leone is threatened by 'mercenaries' a far-fetched, notion, springing from the belief that Sir Albert will stop at nothing to over-throw the APC. Ten thousand Ghanaian fishermen who have for years suppled Sierra Leone with cheap fish, have been expelled because the Government believes that their presence

on Sierra Leone's beaches would facilitate an invasion-again by Sir Albert.

SAGGING INTERNATIONAL IMAGE

The international image of the APC sagged as its relationship with other West African states worsened due to the attempted recognition of Biafra, by the APC Government

> Mr. Stevens has complained to President Tubman about Liberians readiness to harbour Sierra Leonean political exiles. Guinean accusations of Sierra Leonean complicity in the Portuguese invasion embarrassed him because financial support for Guinean political exiles does come from Foulah traders in Freetown.

Mr. Salia Jusu Sheriff, leader of the SLPP was convinced that the Sierra Leone people are not "keen on the republican idea," which they identify with hunger and serfdom.

INDISCIPLINE AND DIVISION IN THE ARMED FORCES

The problems in the armed forces were indiscipline and polarisation. Morale dropped as indiscipline increased. As Africa Confidential put it, "Even now privates, led by Morlai Kamara, may still run the army." Mr. Siaka Stevens was faced with an impossible situation. The junior soldiers feared that if their officers returned to the army they would naturally victimise them, while they also saw in their absence, opportunities for being pitch-forked into positions for which they could not qualify. By APC subversion, warrant officers down to privates both in the army and in the police rounded up their officers and detained them in Pademba Road Prison. The President had to bulldoze them into accepting the reality of releasing their officers and reinstating them.

A second problem emerged. It was humiliating enough for Sandhurst trained officers to have been rounded up and detained at Pademba Road Prison. It was asking the impossible for them to tolerate guerrillas as officers. The problem of the absorbtion of the over two thousand guerrillas trained in Guinea fitted into Siaka Stevens' schemes of creating a countervailing force against regular disciplined police and soldiers. The

Internal Security Unit was therefore, carved out of the guerrillas with preferential treatments, and responsible direct to the President.

For administrative purposes, they were an arm of the Police Force, but the Commissioner of Police exercised only nominal control over them. They received their orders direct from President Siaka Stevens. They had the most sophisticated weapons.

> Then there is a special police security force trained by a free lance British officer. And, finally, there are 20 to 30 Cubans who have been training militia at Jui Camp at Hastings and at Kasserie Kychom in the Kambia district near the Guinea frontier.[2]

As a privileged class, they looked down upon regular soldiers who were virtually disarmed and left with First World War repeater rifles. This discrimination led to polarisation in the armed forces between the "haves" and the "have not".

THE OLD BRIGADE AND THE NEW

When the army staged the first coup d'etat and formed a government in March, 1967, Siaka Stevens and his lieutenants, S.I. Koroma, Kamara Taylor, Mohamed Bash Taqui, Ibrahim Taqui, Barthes Wilson, Shears, S.A.T. Koroma, Nancy Steele, went into the wilderness to train guerrillas. In the meantime, new blood was added to their ranks-Dr. Mohamed Forna, a medical practitioner, Sembu Forna and some dormant members who could not openly identify themselves with the APC.

The presence of new intellectuals, Dr. Forna, S.A.J. Pratt was viewed as a threat to the old brigade. A second confrontation was in the making as S.I. Koroma and Kamara-Taylor watched each other while both kept the "opportunists" under surveillance. These simmering conflicts gave rise to rumours that Siaka Stevens "is prisoner of those he himself calls the 'boys'." The internecine vendetta was deep-rooted.

While in opposition, the APC throve on fabrications, slander and false accusations of its opponents. It contained a conglomeration of misfits and opportunists. Even when new intellectuals were attracted to the Party, their presence was resented by the old fogies who saw in them, a threat to their status within the Party.

Shortly after they came to power, a bomb blast ripped open part of Dr. Forna's residence. He escaped being killed as it is believed that he had been warned of the assassination attempt, and so never slept in his house that night. The next victim was Kamara-Taylor, General Secretary of the Party. His house too was bombed and he also escaped assassination under identical circumstances as Dr. Forna. Once more it was suspected that both bombs were exploded by rival supporters in the APC.

The vendetta in the APC, was substantiated by Africa Confidential, as follows:

> Political interest in Sierra Leone, indeed, is concerned as much with the internal politics of the ruling party as with the prospects of its opponents. At the center is the well-known rivalry between S.I. Koroma, and Kamara-Taylor. In November Kamara-Taylor was badly injured in a road accident...

It was rumoured that agents of Koroma had a hand in the incident. Similarly, when Koroma had a serious accident which subsequently led to stroke, Kamara-Taylor's agents were suspected. While Kamara-Taylor was recovering in London, S.I. Koroma "went there for undisclosed reasons; it was said that he had gone to suggest to his rival that in view of the coming election the party should close its ranks." The first flush of power so drunk the APC members that they rode rough-shod through the country as monarchs of the wilderness. "The formidable Alderman Nancy Steele, leader of the APC's women's wing" was so infatuated with power that she once attacked barrister Barlatt while in the performance of his legal duties, in the Supreme Court Building and slapped him in the face. She went a stage further. There was an altercation between her and the wife of President Siaka Stevens at Lungi Airport. In full view of passengers and well-wishers, she attacked her and hit her in the face. President Siaka Stevens never forgave her for this affront. Africa Confidential underlined the internal strife in the APC aptly that, "His (Siaka Stevens) problem, therefore, may be less his opponent's than his own party."

Because of insecurity within his own Party, Siaka Stevens asked Sekou Toure for help. He received over 300 Guinean soldiers in April, 1971, to protect him from his own army whom he had little or no confidence in. This distrust was accelerated after Brigadier John Bangura and three officers were hanged on the 29th of June 1971 for alleged coup d'etat.

LADIES OF THE PARTY

While S.I. Koroma and Kamara-Taylor were fighting it out, the ladies were also having a side show. They were divided into two factions, (i) The National Congress of Sierra Leone Women under the leadership of Nancy Steele and (ii) the APC Women's Wing under the leadership or aegis of Mrs. S.I. Koroma. It was rumoured that Nancy Steele supported Kamara-Taylor and would challenge Koroma in his constituency, Freetown Central One. Mr. Koroma's decision to go to Port Loko instead, lent credence to this story. Then there was speculation that she would send "a number of her ladies in the election including possibly one up in Port Loko against Vice-President Koroma."[3]

These simmering hostilities and occasional overt confrontations seemed to have haunted the APC even as lately as 1982, as we shall see in due course. For example, Akibo-Betts leader of the Youth Branch of the APC and his sabre rattlers attacked and beat up Nancy Steele's old women's rally. It was rumoured that this attack was inspired by the President in revenge for Steele's attack on his wife, Rebecca.

ECONOMIC PROBLEMS

When they came to power, the APC alleged that they had inherited a bankrupt treasury and the "Kitty is empty", became the slogan against the SLPP, by Siaka Stevens. Yet, after two and a half years, Amnesty International reported that

> The position of the big diamond company, SLST, is far less satisfactory since illicit digging on its leases, to protect which the government is solemnly committed, is on an unprecedented scale, suggesting a total inability of the government to enforce its will and supporting charges that

government supporters condone or encourage this lawlessness....

like the infamous Henneh Shameh diamond hold up at Lungi Airstrip, as alleged.

It is not proposed in this study to examine the economic performance of the All Peoples Congress Party Government, since they came to power in April, 1968. This aspect of the consequences of the APC Government would be considered at a later date, as it calls for special treatment. Suffice it to say for the present that by 1981, thirteen years after his "Kitty is empty" slogan to discredit the SLPP, President Siaka Stevens personally unearthened the first major financial scandal of all times, the "Voucher Gate" scandal, in which the President informed the people of Sierra Leone, that preliminary inquiries revealed that Le30m ($30m) of government funds were alleged to have been misappropriated. Within six months, the "Squander Gate" was unearthed, in which over Le40m ($40m) of government funds were again, alleged to have been stolen. President Siaka Stevens appointed three commissions of inquiry following the arrest of hundreds of public officers and businessmen, the interdiction of a lot of the public officers. This has led to serious allegations of financial impropriety and the acquisition of properties by the establishment, in and out of Sierra Leone, including hotels in the West Indies. Now the kitty must be over-flowing to cope with such an avalanche of leakages. With the confirmed discovery of kimberlite deposits in 1960, which the SLPP Government initiated in 1964, coupled with the rediscovery of tons of gold, Sierra Leone must be flowing with milk and honey. So perhaps President Siaka Stevens' revelations of millions of dollars (leones) that have been allegedly misappropriated are only the tip of the ice-berg that the commissions might disclose.

Since the All Peoples Congress Party came to power, the APC caucus have invented mercenary invasions as an excuse to increase the army, the police and a para-military force, the Internal Security Unit as a counterpoise to the army cum police. They use these forces to harass, molest, intimidate, hound, arrest people without warrant, in accordance with their new motto: Vigilance is the prize we should pay to protect our liberty. As a result, the meagre resources of the country are dissipated on armaments. What is left over, filters sluggishly to the peasants who cannot now cope with shortages that have become endemic. A thorough study of how Siaka Stevens replenished the kitty is the subject of our next inquiry.

It is in the wake of these colossal administrative, executive and financial mismanagement of the country, that Africa Confidential summarized the plight of the APC Government as follows:

> The keynote in Sierra Leone politics is uncertainty: uncertainty about when the forthcoming general elections will take place, what form they will take, or even whether they will take place at all.

The basic factors are:

> (1)   President Siaka Stevens' ruling APC has lost much of its popular support (though it has strengthened its representation in Parliament by various means).

> (2)   The APC lacks cohesiveness and is riven by rivalries, the most important of which is that between Vice-President and Prime Minister S. I. Koroma and Finance Minister and Party Secretary General C. Kamara-Taylor.

> (3)   The opposition forces are also, however, in disarray with UDP leaders Dr. Mohammed Forna and Ibrahim Bash Taqui detained under emergency powers and the SLPP weakened partly by government harassment and partly by rivalry between Salia Jusu Sheriff and M.S. Mustapha.

> (4)   President Stevens, who does not himself have to face election now, retains some prestige and considerable power, having done much to guarantee his own personal security.

> (5)   Whatever political events take place will do so against an economic background which is fairly sombre.[4]

THE KAILAHUN MURDER TRIAL

The All Peoples Congress Party made no attempts, nor did they even pretend to protect the judiciary from any suspicions of executive encroachment into their domain. By overt and not only alleged covert acts of the Government and its arms, the law enforcement agencies, made accused persons apprehensive, not without justification, that the All Peoples Congress

Party would stop at nothing to obstruct the course of justice, and what is more, to secure convictions of Sierra Leone Peoples Party executive members and their followers. By so doing they hoped to fragment the Opposition Party in the country, thereby adding further lies to their fabrications that the Opposition Party had disintegrated or lapsed by inanition.

Early in 1972, the Honorable Salia Jusu Sheriff, leader 'of the Opposition Party, Honorable Mohammed Sanusi Mustapha, SLPP member of Parliament for Bo north-east and Kande Bure a leading SLPP member, went to Kailahun to secure the nomination of their candidate for the by-election. They, together with 7 other SLPP members and supporters were charged with the murder of an APC activist. In his plea of not guilty, the Honourable Salia Jusu Sheriff addressed the Magistrate that

> I impugn the good faith of the prosecution; thirdly, I say that the charge against me is a sordid and disgusting fabrication--that it is a political charge is clear and transparent.

> I had not until this case been confronted with the naked fact that the processes of our law could be so grossly abused for party political reasons. Of course my Lord I prefer to believe that the learned and Honourable Attorney General has had no hand in this fabrication; but in the light of the evidence adduced so far, particularly the police evidence, I am finding it difficult to sustain that preference.[5]

Again, with these introductory remarks about how responsible people were losing faith in the judicial processes of Sierra Leone under the APC, the Honourable Salia Jusu Sheriff then went on to describe how they were hounded by APC hooligans in Kailahun.

> One of the APC thug took up a big stone larger than his own head and attempted to smash my head with it. How I escaped death is one of the miracles of providence. All these things happened in the presence of the Police and Assistant Commissioner of Police Mr. A. J. Brown who simply stood by and watched with resignation doing hardly anything....

> 8. We made several reports to the Police and at the Police Station in Kailahun but all we got from Assistant Commissioner A. J. Brown was that he would refer the matter to Mr. C. A. Kamara-Taylor, General Secretary of the All

Peoples Congress and Minister of Finance who was in Kailahun at the time and in whose hands the decision whether or not to allow the SLPP to nominate appeared to rest.[6]

Honourable Salia Jusu Sheriff went on to bemoan the serious danger to democracy when the General Secretary of the opposing political party and minister of finance has to be consulted,

> before his opponents are allowed to file nomination papers for a parliamentary election. Whatever the outcome of that consultation was, the fact remains that after it, we were not allowed to nominate.[7]

The All Peoples Congress Party has perverted the law to such an extent, as Honourable Sheriff put it; that "experience has taught us that whenever the APC cause trouble it is their innocent victims who are arrested charged or detained for the consequences of APC lawlessness." During the murder trial against him, El Hadj M.S. Mustapha and Kandeh Bureh, he gave a historical account of the record of the APC since they came to power in 1968, from his personal knowledge.

> 14. My Lord the APC has an outrageous predilection for violence and an appalling record of thuggery and vandalism. In 1968 they caused three persons to be shot and killed in my constituency and had another beaten to death. At that time I was in detention in Mafanta Prison at Magburaka. Since then they have shot and killed an innocent school boy during their gunning of the offices of an Opposition Press in Freetown. They have dynamited houses in Freetown and burnt to death two innocent children and an adult. These are only some of the more serious cases of a general record of violence. None of these cases have been prosecuted.[8]

An APC activist was struck and killed by a land rover in the Kailahun area. The Honourable Salia Jusu Sheriff, the Honourable El Hadj Sanusi Mustapha and Kandeh Bure, all of them leaders of the SLPP who had fled from Kailahun before the incident, were arrested together with seven SLPP members and charged with the murder. The irony of their case was brilliantly portrayed by Honourable Sheriff in his statement to the Magistrate:

I was charged with murder before the police even tried to find out who the driver of the land rover was that was involved in the accident. And in evidence here a police officer said that at the time we were charged with murder, he knew that none of us was the driver of the land rover.[9]

The most startling revelation of this disgraceful perversion of justice was the fact, as the Honourable Salia Jusu Sheriff stated, that

In the Demand Note which the Police presented to me long after I had been charged with murder, and in which I was required to name the driver, the offences the Police alleged against the driver were manslaughter, failure to report an accident. My Lord how can the allegation against the driver be manslaughter and I am charged with murder in respect of the same accident? Why should I be charged at all in respect of a motor vehicle accident in which I was neither driver nor passenger and at the scene of which I was not present?

18. My Lord since I became Leader of the Opposition in this country this is the third time this Government is bringing me before the courts on serious charges which are fabricated and entirely political.[10]

He reminded the court that he had been detained in the prisons at Kenema, Mafanta, Pademba Road, various police cells in the country. These were part of the APC plan to stifle and then wipe out all opposition to the APC, "NOW AND FOREVER". They were determined, in the words of Salia, to restrict, eliminate and weaken constitutional opposition to the APC.

He went on,

In two of the three cases Mr. N.A.P. Buck who is now acting as Attorney General has been my prosecutor.

For challenging the legality of the republican constitution, Buck

brought a motion before Parliament (a couple of months ago) to consider withdrawing recognition from me as Leader of the Opposition.

My Lord---the APC are determined to wreck the very foundations of this society....Events (before) this trial have shown that even the dignity and inviolability of the Courts, bench and bar are threatened. I NEED SAY NO MORE -- THE PROSPECT FOR LIBERTY AND FREEDOM ARE

OMINOUS BUT I AM CONFIDENT THAT GOD WILL DELIVER THIS NATION."[11] (caps mine)

Speaking about the inordinate power of the House of Commons, an eminent British jurist once wrote that the British Parliament is so powerful that it could legislate to convert a man into a woman. Since, not even the mother of Anglo-Saxon Parliaments would like to see such a woman, they would not enact such a law. That the APC Government could entertain a motion in Parliament to divest the leader of the Opposition of his leadership, is explicable only in the All Peoples Congress Party's ideology. Nevertheless, it was a forerunner of the repugnant one-party republican oligarchy which the APC imposed on the people of Sierra Leone six years later.

The Honourable El Hadj Mohammed Sanusi Mustapha, the other leader of the SLPP in the dock, substantiated the address of Honourable Salia to the Court. Honourable El Hadj Mohammed Sanusi Mustapha was one time Minister of Finance and acted several times as Prime Minister in the Sierra Leone Peoples Party Government. He is one of the leading politicians in Sierra Leone. He is a brilliant Islamic scholar and ardent Muslim. His magnanimity is proverbial and his energy for work, prodigious.

In his statement he told the Magistrate that

> You have abundant evidence before you sir to show that the Police whose duty it is to investigate alleged commission of crimes and take statements from alleged wrong-doers were not given the chance to do so. Instead the Acting Attorney General of all persons, caused us to be charged by the Police with a capital crime, after which, he got certain persons Bunting John and others to make oral statements to him. Well, this strange procedure in handling such a serious charge-murder by no less a person than the Acting Attorney General of Sierra Leone leaves much to be desired.

> The Acting Attorney General is a politician, a staunch member of the All Peoples Congress and a Minister of the present APC Government of Sierra Leone.[12]

This is another example of a serious breach of one of the cardinal principles of Anglo-Saxon law which we inherited after Independence, and which the learned Acting Attorney General should be the leading exponent of in the country, at least, to the police, namely, that justice should not only be done, but must be manifestly and palpably be seen to have been done.

While election campaigning in March, 1969, about 60 APC thugs attacked Honourable Mustapha and his supporters at Ngalu near Bo. Later he said that, "I was kidnapped, beaten and wounded."[13] Three of them were huddled in a van and the thugs told them they were taking them away to Magburaka "to kill us." They took away his gold wrist watch, gold parker fountain pen, cash, all valued at Le474 ($474). When they reached near Koyeima School, "Some of them alighted and said they were going to kill us in the bush near the village."[14] Fortunately, they did not kill them, but beat them brutally and abandoned them to die in the bush. They were rescued.

Even during the worst periods of colonialism, at no time did the colonialist Attorney General direct the Commissioner of Police as to how he shall or shall not interrogate witnesses, nor did he interview witnesses himself. The only time he saw witnesses was in court. There was at least some semblance of separation of the executive from the administrative and the judiciary. What happened behind the scenes, if any, was left to speculation.

In the Kailahun murder case, the leaders of the SLPP, the Honourable Salia Jusu Sheriff, the Honourable El Hadj Mohammed Sanusi Mustapha and Kandeh Bure were flabbergasted by what they genuinely believed were startling interference in the work of the police by the Acting Attorney General. This fact, coupled with the other fact that the Assistant Commissioner of Police was under the direction of the General Secretary of the All Peoples Congress Party, and Minister of Finance in the APC Government, as to the conduct of the election at Kailahun, gives clear credence to the suspicions of the Mendes who were predominantly of the Sierra Leone Peoples Party, that the legal system of Sierra Leone was in danger of becoming an integral part of the political party in power.

When the Attorney General of a country descends from his ivory tower to conduct preliminary investigations in the Central Investigation Department then there is not much aura left in the job. And when the judicial system of a country becomes the by-product of the political system, it is a sure sign that the country is heading for disaster. When Berthan

Macaulay was Attorney General of Sierra Leone (under the Sierra Leone Peoples Party Government) he was notorious for his aloofness. It would have been inconceivable for anyone, not even the Prime Minister, to suggest to him as to how he shall or when he should prosecute, nay more for him to confer with the Police. As Financial Secretary, I negotiated many loans with Berthan Macaulay with the International Bank for Reconstruction and Development and private financiers.

He had a superstitious belief in legal processes. Any interference with the office of Attorney General would have been resisted by him with the utmost resentment, punctuated by threats to resign immediately. With all their automatic weapons, not even the National Reformation Council, the first military government in Sierra Leone could push him around. It was for his meticulous industry and superstitious adherence to the rule of law that Peter Tucker, then Secretary to the Prime Minister and I, literally begged him to take up the post of Attorney General. We were confident, as indeed it turned out, that Berthan Macaulay would ensure that politicians did not politicise the legal system.

Weeks before the General Elections in March 1973, the Government erected check points all over the country. Opposition candidates were prevented from proceeding to their respective constituencies to file their nomination papers. Howard University Radio in the United States of America, broadcast the following news item on the 10th of February:

> In 1973, more than 60 people were killed during elections in Sierra Leone, there were reliable reports of candidates being threatened when they tried to hand in nomination papers. A Government Minister was seen waving a gun at a candidate, and four opposition party helpers were burned alive. Political opponents of the Government have been arrested and some have died under mysterious circumstances or have gone blind.

El Hadj Magba-Kamara, General Secretary of the Ex-Servicemen's Association, was detained at mile 47 on his way to Kabala, to file his nomination papers. After rigorous examination, punctuated by abuses and rude innuendoes, he was dumped into a land rover by Internal Security Unit, and taken to Port Loko under the spurious excuse that, because he had a shot gun, it was necessary for him to be further interrogated by Senior Officers at Port Loko.

When they arrived, they locked him up in a cell like a prisoner. While there, they brought Lamin Sidique in for "interrogation". Mr. Lamin Sidique was retired Provincial Secretary, and former Secretary to the National Reformation Council and head of the civil service. He was on his way to file his nomination papers for the elections, when he was arrested by the ISU and taken to Port Loko prison. They dragged Sidique into the prison covered with blood, and pushed him into the worst cell that was in the most insanitary condition. The El Hadj pleaded with the ISU to let them transfer Sidique into his cell, which was relatively clean.

Sierra Leone Peoples Party candidates were hounded like vermins, arrested, beaten to death while their wives and children were defiled. The leaders of the Opposition Party, El Hadj Sanusi Mustapha, Salia Jusu Sheriff, Kandeh Bureh were arrested and charged with murder. Before his arrest, Kandeh Bureh was kidnapped between the Law Courts and the Headquarters of the Police Department, dragged along Westmoreland Street in broad day-light, while he was being kicked and brutalised. He was dragged into Victoria Park and dumped into a taxi which drove off to an unknown destination. All these atrocities happened in full view of police officers who nodded their acquiescence.

Harassment, victimization, assassination and a state verging on declaration of war against the Sierra Leone Peoples Party would be an understatement of the APC policy for the 1973 general elections, as they realised that they could not win fair elections.

> Their representation (SLPP) in the recent election (1977) contrasted with their performance in the May 1973 polls when their candidates were prevented from registering their nominations. The opposition boycotted the elections permitting the APC to gain all 85 contested seats.

After this rigged so-called general elections, the Government issued a Press Release:

> Landslide Victory for the All Peoples Congress Party (APC).

All the results of the General Elections were declared on 15th May, 1973.

Twelve Paramount Chiefs were returned unopposed in all the twelve districts.

Out of 85 seats for Ordinary members, the All Peoples Congress Party (APC) secured 84 seats, the Sierra Leone Peoples Party (SLPP) did not *Repeat* did not secure any seat. Only one Independent Candidate, Hon. Desmond Luke secured a seat.

Parliament was convened on Thursday, 17th May, 1973, when a new Speaker and Deputy Speaker were appointed and all Members of Parliament sworn-in.

The newly elected Speaker is Mr. Justice Percy Richmond Davies and Deputy Speaker Mr. A.B.M. Jah.

The State of the Parties
A.P.C.	84 seats
S.L.P.P.	nil
Independent	1 seat[15]

In the light of these atrocities and more, a delegation of both Christian and Muslim leaders saw the President on the 19th of October, 1972, to express their grave concern about the rapid deterioration of law and order in the country, as follows;

Human rights

Some seem intent on setting aside a multiparty system of government. It is our conviction that to embark upon a one-party system of government would greatly endanger the citizen's rights to offer constructive criticism to any government of the future and would not be in the best interests of our national development.[16]

Economic situation

We have been appalled at the serious breakdown in the distribution and sale of rice to the ordinary consumer...

Chapter 9 Notes

1.　　*Africa Confidential*, 15th January, 1971.

2.　　*Africa Confidential*, 30th March, 1973.

3.　　*Ibid.*

4.　　*Ibid.*

5.　　The People, Printed and Published by the Proprietor Editor, Julius Cole, 9 Regent Road, Freetown. October 26th, 1972. Mr. Julius Cole was General Secretary of the Sierra Leone Peoples Party.

6.　　*Ibid.*

7.　　*Ibid.*

8.　　*Ibid.*

9.　　*Ibid.*

10.　　*Ibid.*

11.　　*Ibid.*

12.　　*Ibid.*

13.　　*Ibid.*

14.　　*Ibid.*

15.　　Issued by the Information Division, Embassy of the Republic of Sierra Leone, 1701-19th St. N.W., Washington, D.C. 20009.

16.　　The People, *ibid.*, October 26th 1972.

CHAPTER 10

THE PEN IS STILL MIGHTIER, AS STUDENTS DEMONSTRATE

Fourah Bay College, the Athens of West Africa, and a College of the University of Sierra Leone, held its 150th Annual Convocation on the 29th of January, 1977. After the Vice-Chancellor's Speech, His Excellency, President Siaka Stevens rose to deliver his Speech as Chancellor of the University. As soon as President Stevens stood up to address the Convocation, the students started hissing, then jeering and finally, began booing the President. They carried placards alleging corruption in high places and demanded that "Shaki and Cabinet Must Resign. We want jobs not just degrees."

The President was hurriedly rushed out of the campus while the students continued booing him and shouting his name with scurrilous remarks. In response to this challenge, an emergency meeting of Cabinet was held that evening. It is alleged that the President was so frightened that he did not press for reprisals but that his Vice President Sorie I. Koroma, and the Prime Minister C.A. Kamara-Taylor insisted that disciplinary actions should be taken against the students.

On the following day, army lorries carried soldiers to the University campus. The students explained the reasons for their protests to the soldiers in the hope that the Government would take action to remedy the deteriorating economic situation of the country. The soldiers appeared convinced that the students were not irresponsible and so they returned to their barracks.

Subsequent events showed that the Government was dissatisfied with the sympathetic attitude of the soldiers towards the students. The Government despatched a contingent of Internal Security Unit storm troopers to wreak vengeance on the students. The recklessness and ruthlessness of the ISU are proverbial. As soon as they arrived, all hell was let loose. In the words of a Roving Ambassador:

> They shot and killed indiscriminately; beat and maimed by the scores. A Nigerian student and a refugee student from Zimbabwe (then Rhodesia) were among those shot to death. Damage to property was extensive. The College itself was declared closed indefinitely by Government Order.

> ...Secondary School kids took to the streets in protest. Again the ISU was sent to restore order. It is estimated that fifteen kids were killed.

...The Sierra Leone Labour Congress

> At this point, the Sierra Leone Labour Congress threatened to join the protest. Their leadership had a series of meetings with the President and his cabinet on January 31st to discuss the situation. They withdrew their threat after the president had promised to do his best to defuse the situation in a humane manner. Humane? Just as one of these meetings was to start report came that school children were blocking the streets. The Prime Minister, C.A. Kamara-Taylor callously remarked that the soldiers should have run them over with their trucks.

> That was how far the SLLC could go. The Trade Union couldn't even back (sic) in unison. But those students did.

> Those gallant students.

ARREST OF HINDOLO TRYE

Mr. Hindolo Trye, cousin of a school boy who was shot as he was leaving the Express, S.L.P.P. newspaper office to go and sell newspaper, master-minded the students' demonstrations at Fourah Bay College. Before the demonstrations, as president of the Fourah Bay College Students Union, he had assurances from the Sierra Leone Labour Congress of the workers support. When the Congress did not follow up their promise to go on strike in support of the students, they suspected that they had been betrayed. If they had, it would have changed the course of the political history of Sierra Leone.

When the APC Government planned a counter-demonstration, the Government ordered the arrest of Hindolo Trye. His lieutenants hired a taxi-cab to smuggle him out of Freetown to a safe rendezvous from which he would direct operations. While they were speeding towards Regent, the hub-cap of the taxi flew off. They stopped to find out what had gone wrong. The ISU arrived and asked who they were. Their leader came forward and identified himself to avoid any of his lieutenants being shot. He was arrested and taken to the Criminal Investigation Department of the Sierra Leone Police Department. The students went to his aunt, Mrs. Eku Fallah to inform her of his arrest and that he was hungry. By the time she arrived at the C.I.D., it was over-crowded with school children and students of Fourah Bay College who had heard of his arrest.

The following day, school children joined the Fourah Bay Students in demonstrations for the release of Hindolo Trye, the hero of the students' discontent. They chanted various slogans; "No Hindolo, no School. Something butu, something timap." (Meaning-cowards surrender, while the valiant remain defiant). News of the students' demonstrations spread throughout Sierra Leone. School children in other parts of the country also demonstrated against the APC Government. Corroborations and additional versions of the incidents appeared in the world press and radio net work.

On the 10th February, 1977, *Howard University Radio* in Washington, D.C., United States of America, confirmed the Roving Ambassador's Report:

> Recently, thugs who have been reported as being Government agents, attacked the University of Sierra Leone, killing seven students and wounding many others. Professors, lecturers and students were thrown into jail and have not been heard from since. Students are demanding the eradication of corruption, social and economic reform and the resignation of the Sierra Leone Government headed by President Siaka Stevens. The Sierra Leone Labour Congress, the sole trade union movement in the country has denounced the attack on the University and are demanding an inquiry by the Stevens Government into the incident....

The beleaguered Stevens met with members of the student movement and promised to repair the damage done to the University. In addition, he promised to dissolve parliament this Tuesday to make way for new elections.

In 1973, more than 60 people were killed during elections in Sierra Leone....

A Government minister was seen waving a gun at a candidate, and 4 opposition party helpers were burned alive....

Political opponents of the Government have been arrested and some have died under mysterious circumstances or have gone blind....

This Radio Station further broadcast on the 8th of March 1977, that

At least 7 students were killed and many others injured in the clashes.

The University of Sierra Leone in the capital city of Freetown was extensively damaged. Professors, lecturers and students were thrown in jail and have not been heard from since. WHUR (Washington Howard University Radio) confirmed the ultimatum given to the Government by the Sierra Leone Labour Congress.

The *London Times* of 23rd. February, 1977,

...estimated that 36 people were killed in the riots in Freetown and at least 100 wounded by gunfire from the Internal Security Unit. They included students and school-children, demanding Dr. Stevens' resignation.

The security forces are accused of pursuing the injured to hospitals and interrupting the supply of blood plasma.

While in prison, Hindolo Trye was coerced by the Government to make a broadcast appealing to students and pupils to return to their colleges and schools. As soon as he was released from gaol, the students clarified the broadcast, in

A document purporting to be circulated by the Students' Union of the University of Sierra Leone declared that the broadcast, about reopening schools and colleges, made on February 9 by Mr. Hindolo Trye, President of the Fourah Bay College Students Union, was not voluntary but made under duress from armed members of the ISU.

The Students' document says that they were opposed to such reopening until 'our very reasonable demands are met.' The demands are listed as: Freedom of Speech and Press; Disbandment of the ISU; General Elections within 9 months and a money-saving 40 percent reduction in Government ministers.

In *New Africa* 23rd of March 1977 Cecil Hennessy corroborated the account of the Roving Ambassador. He added that,

...Some (of the placards-mine) called for the resignation of the president....

The business community, sensing trouble, stayed indoors. There was no school or work either.

The Youth League, aided by armed police, took over the college and arrested those students they could lay hands on.

A new self-appointed 'Vice Chancellor' announced the closure of the college. Students and lecturers were arrested and detained and foreign students were left out in the streets to find places to sleep.

The Sierra Leone Labour Congress issued a statement supporting the students and condemning the counter-protest. Congress called on government for the immediate release of all detained students....

But late in the night Congress leaders were rounded up by the police and carted off to the President's residence. Next morning it was announced over the government-owned radio that the statement had been withdrawn after consultations with government leaders and government had agreed to hold an inquiry.

Most people supported the students and praises were whispered for the students who had the courage to stand up....

During that same day the matter escalated when a bunch of police and APC supporters attacked two secondary schools at the foot of Mount Aureol on which Fourah Bay nestles.

The student leaders held a meeting and decided to take to the streets. Thousands of students converged on down-town Freetown.

In 1827 the Church Missionary Society established an institution for training teachers at Fourah Bay.

Source: Christopher Fyfe, A Short History of Sierra Leone, Longmans, Green and Co. Ltd., London 1962, pages 51 & 68.

The President went on the air and announced that he was declaring a state of emergency.

The Ministry of Education also issued a statement saying that at no time did it give orders for the college to be closed. But all schools and colleges in the country were closed for one week in a bid to keep the rebellious students off the streets.

At the same time a split occurred within the party. Some Ministers were accused of instigating the students and of passing on official secrets to them. That was the reason why the students got wind of the planned attack on the college.

According to *Encore, American and Worldwide News*, April 18, 1977:

This unexpected turn of events caught Stevens by surprise....

Following the disturbance at the university, however, the All Peoples Congress Party initiated a back lash. The party's central committee met and its youth league smashed its way onto campus and violently dispersed the students....

News of these events brought supporters of the students into the streets of Freetown, chanting, throwing stones, and attempting to storm the state house building. The police retaliated by stoning the students and Stevens was forced to declare a state of emergency the following day.

The Sierra Leone Government's account of the Students' Demonstrations as prepared and published in a *Release* by the Embassy in Washington, D.C., United States of America was, inter alia, that:

...The University authorities have today averred to Government that they themselves had no prior knowledge of the intentions and plans of the miscreant students. Immediately following the incidents last Saturday, a representative section of the community who were against at (sic) the perpetration of the students and were very much concerned at the great damage which would be done to the nation's image, at home and abroad, approached Government and sought permission to stage a peaceful and counter demonstration at Fourah Bay College and Foreign Embassies in Freetown in order to correct the bad image which the students concerned had sought to create within and outside our borders. This permission was readily granted after assurances had been sought and obtained that the counter demonstration was to be both peaceful and totally unaccompanied by violence. The fact that a sizeable number of the female population participated is further evidence that nothing of violence was contemplated. The counter demonstration, however, met with a very hostile and violent reception from students at the campus at Mount Aureol who hurled sticks, stones and chemicals. Resultant scuffles and woundings followed. The Police, as is duty bound, went to the scene, and had no alternative but to apprehend the ring-leaders and any others who were thought to be connected in any way and to bring them down to the C.I.D. Headquarters for normal interrogation.

It has come to the notice of Government that this affair is being exploited in many quarters by subversive elements, particularly in the Colleges and Schools.

Since the notorious subversive elements broadcast of May 28, 1968 by the Prime Minister Siaka Stevens, which preceded the first wave of mass arrests, every short-coming of the Government, is attributed to subversive elements.

The Government *Release* lied that

The police had no directive or intention of organising any large scale detention of students or others. In point of fact, the legislation providing for detention was revoked in September, 1976.

So that by the Government's admission, Sierra Leone had been in perpetual State of Emergency since they took the reins of government, eight and a half years earlier. In the wake of wide-spread demonstrations by students all over Sierra Leone in sympathy with their colleagues at Fourah Bay College, the Government invited the students' leaders to a round-table conference to iron-out their grievances.

Incensed by the murders, beatings, woundings, mass destruction of properties, raping of students by the Internal Security Unit who led the All Peoples Congress Party's organised thugs, criminals and vandals to counter-demonstrate against the students at the College, the students submitted a petition to the President, Dr. Siaka Stevens. The Senior Staff Association of the University of Sierra Leone also sent a letter of protest to the President dated 8th January, 1977. Thirteen members of the Freetown City Council condemned the Government's handling of the students' demonstrations in a letter addressed to the public.

These documents reiterate condemnations of the President and his Government for the rapid deterioration in the economic, social and political conditions in Sierra Leone since the APC Government came to power. The fundamentals of life, liberty and the pursuit of happiness, are entrenched in the 1961 Constitution of Sierra Leone. The APC Government had after 8½ years, raped the very Constitution which they relied upon to assume the role of government. It is universal knowledge that, these fundamental liberties have been violated with regular consistency by the APC Government. The Resolutions quoted above enumerate in clear English the fact, that the fundamental liberties of the people, have gone with the wind. It is also abundantly clear that 8½ years of APC Government, led by His Excellency Dr. Siaka Stevens have ushered into Sierra Leone, the worst forms of despotism, heading a disreputable oligarchy.

The Sierra Leone Council of Churches who played such a prominent part in political agitation and organised a mammoth meeting at the Queen Elizabeth II Playing Fields to protest the introduction of a one-party system of government in Sierra Leone by the Sierra Leone Peoples Party, were once again on the war-path, this time against the All Peoples Congress Party for the rapid deterioration of law and order.

The so-called counter-demonstration against the students of Fourah Bay College was the last straw in the catalogue of wanton, calculated and brutal atrocities of defenceless Sierra Leoneans, which also led to protests by Sierra Leoneans all over the world. Sierra Leoneans in the United States of America assembled under the umbrella of "Citizens for a better Sierra Leone", (whose pro-tem chairman is Samuel Tucker) and expressed sincere condolences to the families and friends of the bereaved who lost their lives at the hands of the APC Government. They commended the students of Fourah Bay College for their courage in challenging the citadel of inhumanity in Sierra Leone.

Sierra Leoneans in other parts of the world also protested the ruthless massacre of students by the APC Government. The Students Union of the

United States of America and Canada sent the following cablegram to the President:

```
SZCZC AWA772 GXB229 ORC0044 2-007274E034
SLPX HL URNX 190
LT TDMT LANDOVER MD 190 03 0911A EST VIA RCA
```

LT
PRESIDENT SIAKA STEVENS
STATE HOUSE
FREETOWN (SIERRA LEONE)

WE THE SIERRA LEONE STUDENTS AND NATIONALS IN THE UNITED STATES AND CANADA VIEW WITH SHOCK AND UTMOST CONCERN THE RUTHLESS AND WILLFULL (sic) KILLING OF SIERRA LEONE CITIZENS THAT HAVE MUSTERED THE COURAGE AND CAUGHT THE CONSCIENCE OF OUR PEOPLE DESPITE YOUR PERSISTANT (sic) REPRESSION TO PROTEST THEIR ABHORRENCE OF THESE ATROCITIES STOP WE IN NO UNCERTAIN TERMS CONDEMN YOUR BRUTISH, BARBAROUS AND EXPLOITATIVE RULE THAT HAVE HUNG OVER SIERRA LEONE FOR THE LAST 9 YEARS STOP WE DENOUNCE YOU AS A LIAR, THIEF, EMBEZZLER, SQUANDER (sic) OF PUBLIC FUNDS AND WORST OF A SPINELESS MURDERER OF INNOCENT PEOPLE WHO DARE TO EXPOSE YOUR TRUE NATURE STOP WE CALL UPON YOU NOW TO RESIGN UNCONDITIONALLY MAKING WAY FOR A MORE MEANINGFUL LEADERSHIP IN SIERRA LEONE STOP YOU ARE NEITHER A SOCIALIST NOR A DEMOCRAT NOR A RULER OF ANY MERIT STOP YOUR IMAGE OF SOCIALIST, DEMOCRAT ARE ALL DECEPTIVE YOURSELF IN POWER. (sic) THE SPIRITS OF THOSE YOU MURDERED WILL HAUNT YOU UNTIL WE BURY YOU IN THE HISTORY OF OUR COUNTRY.

PRESIDENT SIERRA LEONE STUDENT UNION UNITED STATES AND CANADA

COL 9 (capitals supplied)

It is in the light of these deteriorations in Sierra Leone that the All Peoples Congress Party announced another General 'Selections'.

PART III

FOREVER AND EVER

CHAPTER 11

ANOTHER GENERAL 'SELECTIONS' OF 1977

The All Peoples Congress Party was shaken by the repercussions of the students' demonstrations which galvanized the whole nation. But the students' parents were frightened stiff to follow the light which the students and school-children had sparked. President Stevens wrangled General Selections, euphemistically called, General Elections immediately, although Parliament still had a year to go. General Elections had, since the APC took office, become selections of APC candidates only.

Fortunately, the Executive Committee of the SLPP was apprehensive of the hooliganism, vandalism and brutal attacks on its members. The leaders of the Party, the Honorable Salia Jusu-Sheriff, the Honorable Dr. H.M. Conteh (MD), the Honorable El Hadj Mohammed Sanusi Mustapha, appealed to the Commissioner of Police to protect members of the Party, since they were always the immediate targets of the APC thugs. They no doubt realized that their entreaties would fall on deaf ears, since the Commissioner of Police could not possibly order the apprehension of any APC malefactors.

The People published a letter written to the Commissioner of Police by the leaders of the SLPP - Appendix 1.

After attending the British Commonwealth Parliamentary Association Conference in Ottawa, Canada, where he spoke on the subject of Commonwealth Human Rights Commission, the Honorable Salia Jusu

Sheriff, leader of the Sierra Leone Peoples Party members of Parliament, visited the United States of America in October 1977. Mr. Mohamed Bash Taqui joined him in the States. It will be recalled that Taqui was one of the three prominent cabinet ministers who resigned from the APC in protest over the dictatorial powers that their leader Siaka Stevens was rapidly assuming.

They addressed various meetings of Sierra Leoneans, established branches of the Sierra Leone Peoples Party, and revitalized existing ones in the USA. These activities were a follow-up of agreement reached by Sir Albert Margai, Sir Banja Tejansie and Dr. John Karefa-Smart in London, to consolidate their political activities and pursue a united front, against the All Peoples Congress Party. As candidates, eye-witnesses, victims of the APC obstructions during the elections, we shall let them give us their accounts of the General Elections. On the 26th September, 1977, Sheriff and Taqui addressed Sierra Leoneans in Washington, D.C. They informed us that there were about 100 persons in gaol who had not had baths since May 1977. With the exception of 1976, since the APC formed a Government in 1968, there had been a perpetual state of emergency.

In 1969, the APC raped the constitution because of the "vanity of one man," and in 1971 Sierra Leone was declared a republic. There have never been fair elections in Sierra Leone since they assumed the reins of government in 1968. The APC has been kept in office by sheer brute force. Internal Security Unit directed thugs beat up people and loot houses. The APC "buys yamba and omole" (marijuana and illicit gin) and distributes them to boys and girls, who they instigate, to vandalize people.

According to *West Africa*:

> In contrast to the 1972, election, however, when in all but the Freetown seats it was virtually impossible for any opponent of the ruling APC to secure nomination, much less to be elected, this time the opposition Sierra Leone Peoples Party will contest 48 seats and could win a number of them...

> The election has already been more violent than at one time was hoped and the number of deaths has been high. It was alleged that in some constituencies candidates have been prevented from registering. Freetown itself has seen

considerable violence, some of it alleged to be the work of party supporters from outside the city; but the worst reports of violence come from Makeni in the centre of the country. There are also reports that some SLPP candidates have been detained in Pademba Road. (Prison, mine)[1]

With this background, we shall now hear Mohamed Bash Taqui and Salia Jusu Sheriff. The following are the notes which I took down at the meeting. I shall endeavor to reproduce their accounts as closely as possible. Mr. Mohamed Bash Taqui who spoke first, substantiated the *West Africa* Report. He told his audience that they resigned from the Government in 1970, that is, he, his brother Ibrahim Taqui, and Dr. Mohammed Forna (MD), and formed the United Democratic Party. The Party was hounded, molested, and subsequently banned by Stevens. It was impossible for them to operate. In 1973, Ibrahim, his brother, then APC Minister of Information and Broadcasting, Dr. Forna APC Minister of Finance, and he were detained at Pademba Road Prison shortly after they resigned from the APC. The SLPP tried to put up candidates in 1973, but the government unleashed thugs on them. Mr. Sheriff and others withdrew from the elections to avoid fatalities, because many of their followers were brutally assaulted by the APC thugs.

In 1977 students, reflecting "the opinion of the silent majority," demonstrated. At Kabala in Koinadugu, over 20 people were killed. There was going to be mutiny in the army and ISU. The Government bribed them Le 30,000 ($30,000), according to Taqui. He then informed the audience about the brutalities in various constituencies in the country during the elections:

Makeni: They killed 4 people in Makeni. Some APC leaders carried automatic weapons. Many people were wounded. *Tonkolili*: There were combats between their candidates and the APC. Two lorries full of ISU were sent to Tonkolili and some people were wounded. *Port Loko*: On the 13th April, S.I. Koroma (Vice President) imposed a curfew in Port Loko. No vehicles were allowed to enter or leave Port Loko. Mr. Bangali Mansaray and Taqui's cousin were taken to S.I. Koroma. He requested them to withdraw their nominations. When they refused, he imprisoned them until the nominations were over, and so returned themselves unopposed.

Kambia: Mr. Kamara-Taylor, (Second Vice President), and S.I. Koroma (First Vice President) are inveterate enemies. They are so afraid of each other that, Kamara-Taylor feared to travel to Kambia through Port Loko. He therefore, went by way of Kamakwie. Each of them has his private army. Paramount Chief Yumkella and Thorlu went to register their nomination papers. Mr. Kamara-Taylor instructed the returning officer to carry the nomination boxes to the Government District Office. They killed five of the SLPP men. Paramount Chief Yumkella was almost killed. The ISU looted all his property. *Kenema*: In Kenema, the SLPP did not get the kind of opposition they had in 1973, when they burned all their nomination papers. *Kono*: Thugs invaded Kono District. The SLPP ran away and the thugs collected all the marbles and put them in the APC boxes. *Kailahun*: The SLPP won five seats. *Pujehun*: The SLPP won two seats, Bo: Government had no opportunity to intimidate the people, so they cancelled the elections before voting ended.

On the 18th of September, El Hadj M.S. Mustapha was arrested and gaoled. After nominations, he was released. The ISU arrested all SLPP candidates and took them to Freetown, locked them up in gaol, and the Government declared the APC candidates returned unopposed. They then began arresting members of Parliament: Gombu, Margai, Ngobeh, Manna Kpaka, Dr. Conteh, Dr. Dauda. The power base is the ISU, the police and the army and not the people. The two doctors took legal action against the APC and so they were arrested. They now have at least 100 political prisoners. The Executive Committee of the SLPP lodged 52 elections petitions against their candidates and had paid Le 45,000 ($45,000) to lawyers.

Freetown: Mr. Taqui informed the audience that he stood against Mr. Akibo Betts. The latter had two guns and threatened to shoot him and his supporters. The ISU and thugs beat up their men. Mr. S.I. Koroma specially selected returning officers in his constituency. He complained about the atrocities to the authorities. The APC Executive directed their thugs to open their ballot boxes and remove all their marbles and put them in Akibo's boxes, Dr. Lahai Taylor's house and drugs were destroyed. In 1973 and 1977 elections, over 500 people were killed by the APC, and the ISU, according to Taqui.

In these circumstances, he advised the audience that it was unwise to have splinter groups. "Why not join the SLPP?" Taqui enquired. The only channel left of challenging the APC is the SLPP who have 15 members in parliament, and 4 detained in gaol. On the one-party, he said that in 1973, when they withdrew from the elections, the APC said that they then had one-party. "Now the Speaker of the House, the Honourable Singer Betts", he went on, "ruled that because we did not exceed 15 members elected therefore, we did not constitute an opposition. But the APC had only 10 in 1967 and yet the then Speaker regarded them as the opposition, in the same manner in which the UPP who had 7 and Bankole Bright who had 5 were regarded as oppositions."

Mr. Mohammed Taqui concluded that,

> The APC have proved that whatever the SLPP, and the army (the National Reformation Council) did, they were chicken feed. The APC cannot impose a one-party. They have made overtures to us several times to form a one-party government. Each time we referred them to the Constitution. This is the time for national solidarity. Excessive expenditure for security should be stopped. The government spends Le8m, ($8m) on the army each year. What right have we to condemn infractions of human rights in other parts of the world when we have not got it at home?

The Honourable Jusu Sheriff endorsed Bash Taqui's account of the events in Sierra Leone. The Government misconstrued the meeting in London between him, Sir Albert Margai, Sir Banja Tejansie and Dr. Karefa-Smart as a conspiracy to overthrow the Government. It was reported in *West Africa* that:

> The APC party *We Yone* has alledged that Ex-Prime Minister Sir Albert Margai is involved in a plot to overthrow the Government. According to *We Yone* Sir Albert has offered to raise $300,000 to finance the plot and suggests American involvement.
>
> ...The newspaper also claims that the Opposition Leader, Salia Jusu Sheriff, the ex SLPP Minister, Dr. John Karefa-Smart, and the former MP, Mohammed Bash-Taqui, are linked with the plot which is said to have the coda name 'Operation Apple-Jack.'[2]

Refuting these allegations, Salia Jusu Sheriff, parliamentary leader of the Opposition SLPP, wrote that:

> My attention has been drawn to a publication in the All Peoples Congress Party Sunday *We Yone* of 27th November, 1977, reporting an alleged plot involving Sir Albert Margai, Dr. John Karefa-Smart, Mr. M.O. Bash Taqui and myself to seize power in Sierra Leone.
>
> I wish to take this opportunity to state at once that I have no knowledge whatsoever of any such plot if there was one. I did deliver legitimate political speeches, as I was entitled to do, during my recent visit to the United Kingdom and the United States of America; but I cannot see the connection between such open activity and subversion.[3]

By the Autumn of 1976 Siaka Stevens had ensconced himself so firmly in the saddle that after the International Monetary Fund pressured the Government, it was rumoured that he planned to reduce the constituencies from 100 to 60 and hold elections in October. While the party caucus were deliberating the next general elections for 1978, students were planning the course of action which precipitated the general elections 12 months earlier.

The Sierra Leone Council of Churches appealed to the President on the 30th of April, 1977,

> ...to launch an immediate inquiry into pre-election violence in which at least 7 people have been reportedly killed.
>
> A statement urged President Stevens to defend the Constitution and electoral law, and ensure that law breakers be dealt with 'irrespective of rank, social position or political affiliation.'
>
> It expressed 'sadness and much concern' at President Stevens' announcement on election nomination day on April 15 that at least 7 people had been killed and property damaged.
>
> General elections for the House of Representatives are to be held on May 6.
>
> The council quoted reports that an entire village in the Koinadugu District had been almost completely burned down and that there had been sporadic shooting in the Waterloo area near Freetown.

'The Council feels that if these acts of violence are allowed to continue they will damage the image of Sierra Leone as a peaceful country where law and order have prevailed,' it said.

Meanwhile, the newly formed United Alliance of Opposition Parties announced that it intends taking action over the 34 seats in which candidates of the ruling All Peoples Congress Party, headed by President Stevens, were declared unopposed.

The Alliance, which groups the Sierra Leone Peoples's Party, the Democratic National Party and Independents,....[4]

The prestigious *London Times* carried a report on the Elections.

It stated that:

...a free and fair election would almost certainly have unseated President Stevens' Government. He made sure of its victory of his All Peoples Congress by methods akin to those alleged against President Bhutto in Pakistan...indeed, taking scale into consideration, what happened in Sierra Leone was arguably far worse.

The Sierra Leone Christian Council and the Trade Union Council are demanding an inquiry into violence intimidation, illegalities and corruption while it is reported that the Solicitor-General is under pressure to prosecute four ministers on charges of murder committed during the last days of the campaign. The election of thirteen of the Sierra Leone Peoples Party candidates in the conditions that have prevailed for weeks is itself noteworthy and a testimony to the country's anger. It is typical that, because the APC realizes that it might lose three more seats in Bo (which threw the APC strong arm out of town) the elections there have been deferred by decree.

President Stevens's APC won 76 seats, of which 50 were unopposed, despite every effort by the SLPP to put up candidates...several of those who tried were jailed...President Stevens's doubts about his party's chances may be judged from such instances as the use of tear gas at polling stations where the SLPP in Freetown...did manage to get candidates on the ballot paper. The toll of death and injury will be heavy, and follows the bloodshed that occurred before the campaign, which was forced on the President by widespread protests that began with his humiliation in the university under a hail of accusations of corruption....

But by 1973 he was under severe criticism, He began to surround himself with bodyguards from Guinee, as well as local undesirables, turned on his former supporters, and won the elections in 1975 by methods which were a foretaste of those used in recent weeks. At present he rules not by the results of the polls, but by grace of his Internal Service Unit and riot police. The elections, however, were not in vain: they have publicly demonstrated that he cannot and does not rule by consent. That in itself is a lesson to some of his peers in Africa.[5]

The *London Times* story was corroborated by Amnesty International.

The Director wrote that:

Violence surrounding the general election in May 1977...24 people died...The Internal Security Unit and the police were particularly active...directed primarily against the SLPP. More than 650 people were detained without charge or trial during 1977 at the order of...president Siaka Stevens....The charges against all appear to be quite false.... Detention without trial continues to be used all too often as a means of suppressing opposition in Sierra Leone.... Many of those detained last year have still not been released.... April 15, 1977, nominations began...pre-election violence some members of the Opposition were killed and others detained.... 120 people were killed in Bo District, and in a northern village 26 people were killed when the village was burnt down by a government candidate. Available reports indicated that hundreds of people had been arrested and detained especially during the election period, without being charged and brought to trial.[6]

Despite these inhumanities and obstacles to free and fair elections, the Sierra Leone Peoples Party won 15 seats in an 88 member Parliament. The tide turned swiftly against the Government as the people were determined to oust the All Peoples Congress Party from office. As the peoples' determination to rid themselves of the APC Government increased, so did the latter resort to wholesale and indiscriminate detentions. According to the Government's publications in the *Gazette*, from 17th February, 1977 to 2nd June, 1977, (4 months) over 400 persons were detained by the All Peoples Congress Party Government. It is a corroboration of Amnesty International's figure of "More than 650 people were detained without charge or trial during 1977," as recorded above. The "Public Notices - Supplement" to the Sierra Leone Gazette Vol. CVIII No. 28 dated 14th April, 1977 contain the names.

In its report for 1977, *Amnesty International* high-lighted violations of human rights, and the *Washington Post* underscored Sierra Leone as one of the worst violators thus:

> The African section also details numerous assassinations and mass arrests of various political figures following military coups. One person in Sierra Leone, was for example, beaten and raped by supporters of the new government before she was placed in goal.[7]

Africa Publication No. 70 dated June 1977 reported that:

> In a broadcast on Nomination Day, President Stevens admitted that seven deaths arising from political incidents had been officially reported.

> A Delegation of the United Christian Council of Sierra Leone met the President to voice concern and sadness at the way thuggery coupled with the connivance of some officials had turned the electioneering into a spectacle of wide scale disturbance. The Council, called on the President to order an inquiry and was joined in the call by the Sierra Leone Labour Congress, some of whose officials, however, did not enhance their neutrality by seeking opposition party nomination.[8]

On the General Elections in Sierra Leone, *Howard University Radio* broadcast the following news:

> Reports from Freetown, say Sierra Leone's ruling All People's Congress (APC) had all of its candidates for eight parliamentary seats in the Southern Province District of Bo, returned unopposed on a no-contest basis.

> Observers believe that the opposition Sierra Leone People's Party (SLPP) was unable to field candidates as nominations closed yesterday because they were detained by security forces. The by-election, initially scheduled for last May as part of the general elections, was postponed because of campaign violence. Polling was to have taken place October 7th and the SLPP was widely favored to have won the eight seats.

> But speaking on nomination day yesterday, acting President Sorie Koroma, disclosed alleged plans by a 'certain political party to use violence' on nomination and election days in Bo.

> Koroma, said that he therefore put all security forces on the alert since there was evidence that people were being recruited

from neighboring districts to cause violence on what he said, the 'force of evil' had declared 'D-Day'.

Meanwhile, opposition parliamentary leader Salia Jusu-Sheriff is at present attending the Commonwealth Inter-Parliamentary Conference in Ottawa, Canada, AFP BBE 14H29.[9]

West Africa reported that Amnesty International reported that several members of the SLPP were physically beaten and at least 158 members of the party were detained.

> ....in June and again in August, Amnesty International had asked the Government of Sierra Leone either to release all the detainees ...or to charge them and bring them to trial. Amnesty International also asked for medical treatment for sick prisoners, some of whom it said were being held in *solitary confinement* (italics mine) and Mrs. Regina James and Dr. Hadj Conteh.[10]

In presenting *Public Notice*, No. 11 of 1977, which was ratified by Parliament, the Vice President, S.I. Koroma informed members of Parliament that after the President had declared a State of Emergency under Public Order Act No. 46 of 1965, there had been a wave of vandalism. Houses of prominent persons had been burnt down; in Bo, the houses of the Minister of Labor, Mr. George Gobio-Lamin, and the Resident Minister Southern Province, Mr. N.M. Moriba. "The offices included the District Office, Court Barrie and Ministry of Works, all in Bo, and the Income Tax Department, Government Sub-Treasury, Bata Shoe Company and Aureol Tobacco Office in Makeni. At Mattru Jong, the house of the member for Bonthe North Mr. Sam Goba, was destroyed. Other buildings destroyed include the new IDA buildings and the Police Station. In Pujehun, the houses of the Foreign Minister, Mr. Francis Minah and Dr. Jaja (sic) Kai-Kai were also destroyed."[11]

In an address to Paramount Chiefs and Chiefdom Councillors, the Resident Minister advised that "the people should have an early warning system to alert the authorities about lawlessness.[12]

A former Minister of Finance in the Sierra Leone Peoples Party Government who contested one of the seats in Bo, and who was believed to be extremely popular and undoubtedly was from all accounts, breaking all records by the overwhelming turn out of his supporters, El Hadj M.S. Mustapha, was arrested in Bo and taken to Pademba Road gaol. It was alleged in SLPP circles that he was arrested because, while the votes were being counted in his constituency, the indications were, that he was leading by an overwhelming margin, when the Government was alerted that the SLPP were winning by a landslide margin. The Government cancelled the elections for the 8 seats in Parliament. It was then that other candidates were arrested, namely, Frank Anthony, a former APC Resident Minister for the Eastern Province.

The inhabitants of Bo resisted intimidations and violence against them. The Resident Minister, Southern Province, Mr. A.J. Sandy,

> ...told Paramount Chiefs to get rid of all strangers... Mr. Sandy told them that some of them had proved disloyal, inspite of the fact that they are an arm of the Government...

We shall now compare and contrast the results of General Selections (Elections) and Referendum in Sierra Leone: (a) the General Elections of 1973; (b) the General Elections of 1977; (c) the Referendum of 1978.

The results show glaring inconsistencies with the reality of the existing situations, which vitiate the statistical value of the results.

"The newly elected Speaker is Mr. Justice Percy Richmond Davies and Deputy Speaker Mr. A.B.M. Jah.

"The State of the Parties:

APC	84 SEATS
SLPP	NIL
INDEPENDENT	1 SEAT."

TABLE 1
GENERAL ELECTIONS AND REFERENDUM
IN SIERRA LEONE

| Constituency | 1 9 7 7 General Elections | | | 1 9 7 8 | |
	Votes Cast	Winners' Votes	Political Party	Referendum For	Against
Western Area					
Freetown					
East 1	13,556	7,312	APC		
East 11	18,828	14,601	APC	22,908	101
East 111	15,540	8,636	APC		nil
Central 1	14,539	8,339	APC	30,920	nil
Central 11	5,598	2,400	SLPP	13,723	nil
West 1	Unopposed		APC	11,135	nil
West 11	13,356	10,308	APC	16,935	nil
West 111	Unopposed		APC	11,900	nil
Mountain R.D.	1,274	543	APC	2,618	nil
York R.A.	Unopposed		APC	15,717	27
Waterloo R.D.	3,974	2,716	APC	7,575	nil
Koya R.D.	11,211	10,757	APC	12,160	nil
Totals	97,876	65,612		145,591	128
Northern Province					
Port Loko					
P.C. Bai					
Sama					
Lamina Sama					
III	Unopposed		APC		
Central	"		")		
South	"		")		
South East	"		")		
North East	"		")	249,278	nil
North	"		")		
South West	"		")		
West 1	"		")		
West 2	"		")		
East	"		")		

Constituency	1 9 7 7 General Elections Votes Cast	Winners' Votes	Political Party	1 9 7 8 Referendum For	Against
Tonkolili					
P.C. Bai Kurr					
Kanasaky III	Unopposed		APC		
East	Unopposed		APC)		
North	Unopposed		APC)		
Central	Unopposed		APC)	208,731	nil
West 1	Unopposed		APC)		
West 11	Unopposed		APC)		
South	Unopposed		APC)		
Bombali					
P.C. Kande					
Saio III	Unopposed		APC		
West	Unopposed		APC)		
Central	Unopposed		APC)		
South-East	Unopposed		APC)	171,995	nil
South-West	Unopposed		APC)		
North	Unopposed		APC)		
East	Unopposed		APC)		
Konadugu					
P.C. Manga					
Salifu	Unopposed		APC)		
South	Unopposed		APC)		
North	14,287	11,170	APC)	122,953	nil
North-East	Unopposed		APC)		
West	8,564	8,111	APC)		
East	18,498	18,082	APC)		
Totals	41,349	37,363			

Constituency	1 9 7 7 General Elections Votes Cast	Winners' Votes	Political Party	1 9 7 8 Referendum For	Against
Kambia					
P.C. Kande Saidu	Unopposed		APC		
East	Unopposed		APC)		
West	Unopposed		APC)		
Central	Unopposed		APC)	135,433	nil
South	Unopposed		APC)		
North-West	Unopposed		APC)		
Southern Province					
Moyamba					
P.C.F.N. Kangaju III	Unopposed		APC		
North	11,908	9,997	SLPP)		
Central	11,520	7,078	SLPP)		
West 1	19,613	17,750	APC)	149,349	nil
West 11	23,376	21,947	APC)		
South 1	19,899	14,184	APC)		
South 11	12,019	11,620	SLPP)		
Totals	98,335	82,578			
Bonthe					
P.C. Prince Wornie Bio III	Unopposed		APC		
Sherbro U.N.	Unopposed		APC)		
Sherbro U.S.	Unopposed		APC)	66,319	nil
Bonth N.	Unopposed		APC)		
Bonth S.	Unopposed		APC)		

Constituency	1 9 7 7 General Votes Cast	Elections Winners' Votes	Political Party	1 9 7 8 Referendum For	Against
Pujehun					
P.C. Alhaji					
Dr. Jai Kai-Kai	Unopposed		APC		
West	13,816	8,466	APC		
North	18,149	11,956	SLPP	116,652	nil
East	14,826	8,067	SLPP		
Totals	46,791	28,489	_____		
Bo				166,782	7,040
Eastern					
Province					
Kenema					
P.C.V.A. Dassama	Unopposed		APC		
West	14,500	10,853	SLPP)		
North	10,435	6,158	APC)		
North-West	15,663	7,915	APC)		
East	16,869	6,359	SLPP)		
Central	14,535	10,996	SLPP)	174,489	51,007
Kenema Town	10,487	8,738	SLPP)		
South-East	15,902	8,262	APC)		
South	13,883	8,797	SLPP)		
Totals	112,274	68,078	_____		
Kailahun					
P.C. Fayia Morlm					
Jabba III	Unopposed		APC		
Central	15,776	11,430	SLPP)		
South	16,377	10,123	SLPP)		
East	18,495	12,547	APC)	155,597	1,152
West	18,143	10,628	SLPP)		
North	15,837	11,451	SLPP)		
Totals	84,628	56,179	_____		

216

| Constituency | 1 9 7 7 General Elections | | | 1 9 7 8 | |
| | Votes Cast | Winners' Votes | Political Party | Referendum | |
				For	Against
Kono					
P.C.S.S. Briwa	Unopposed		APC		
West	49,441	46,737	APC)		
North-East	18,812	16,253	APC)		
Central	27,816	25,308	APC)		
North	34,963	26,438	APC)	239,746	1,013
East	28,294	20,811	APC)		
North-West	33,090	25,717	APC)		
South	13,751	12,174	APC)		
Totals	206,167	173,438			

Sources: (1) Sierra Leone Gazette (Extraordinary) Vol. CVIII, No. 8, 9th May, 1977.

(2) Newsletter of the Republic of Sierra Leone Volume II, No. 2, Dated 31/5/73: Issued by the Information Division--Embassy of the Republic of Sierra Leone, 1701 19th Street, N.W., Washington, D.C. 20009: "Landslide Victory for the All Peoples Congress Party (APC).

"All the results of the General Elections were declared on 15th May, 1973. Twelve Paramount Chiefs were returned unopposed in all the twelve districts.

"Out of 85 seats for Ordinary members, the All Peoples Congress Party (APC) secured 84 seats, the Sierra Leone Peoples Party (SLPP) did not Repeat did not secure any seat. Only one Independent Candidate, Honorable Desmond Luke secured a seat.

"Parliament was convened on Thursday, 17th May, 1973, when a New Speaker and Deputy Speaker were appointed and all members of Parliament sworn in.

REMARKS

(1) Following widespread hooliganism perpetrated by the Internal Security Unit, and the APC thugs and activists, on the orders of the All Peoples Congress Government, the Sierra Leone Peoples Party withdrew from the General Elections in 1973. The APC Government declared its candidates, "returned unopposed in all the 12 districts." Thus, Parliament continued to consist of only APC members for 9 years, from 1968-1977. By 1977, the fortunes of the APC had eroded so drastically by their excesses, that the country was ripe for a change.

(2) Hard-core Sierra Leone Peoples Party members were determined to contest the 1977 general elections, regardless of the odds which they knew were enormous. The Government alleged that the SLPP had imported arms and ammunition. This allegation cannot be ruled out as being entirely false, in view of the casualties inflicted on the ISU at Bo.

In the Northern Province where the APC ordered the ISU to terrorize the people, and for tribal loyalties, as the APC was a predominantly Temne-Limba Party, the Government sealed off the area, and imprisoned opposition candidates. They then declared their candidates unopposed in Port Loko, Tonkolili, Bombali, Kambia Districts and, in the Bonthe District. In two constituencies in the Western Area and in Koinadugu District, the SLPP were able to field candidates. But for the corrupt practices of the APC Government, the whole of the Western Area and Koinadugu would have been swept away by the SLPP.

In the Western Area, the Government managed to get away with three "unopposed" APC members in Freetown West I and III, York Rural Area. The other eight constituencies were hotly contested. Of the votes cast, the APC won 67.07 percent. It is ludicrous that in the Mountain Rural District, the votes cast were 1,274 and the winning APC candidate won 543. It is a miniscule constituency which should be abolished and perhaps merged with York, as its representation is grossly below any reasonable figure for parliamentary representation in other constituencies. The fact that they burnt down a whole village in Koinadugu District, showed that the APC had lost its grip over the Foulahs, Yalunkas, Kurankos, Maninkas.

All the districts of the Southern and Eastern Provinces, with the exception of Bonthe and Kono Districts, were solidly for the SLPP, as the Mendes had had it for too long and would tolerate humiliation no longer. They fought back and were prepared to die to prevent any thugs being sent to harass them, as the APC did in 1968/9, and in 1973.

The following excerpts from the above table highlight Mende determination in the Southern Province:

District	Votes Cast	Winning Votes	Winners' APC	Votes SLPP
Pujehun	46,791	28,489	8,466	20,023
Kenema	112,274	68,078	22,335	45,743
Kailahun	84,628	56,179	12,547	43,632
Moyamba	98,335	82,578	53,883	28,695
Total	342,028	235,324	97,231	138,093

Of the votes cast 58 percent were cast for the SLPP. This figure does not include the Kono District, which although predominantly Kono, yet were saturated with APC activists from the Northern Province.

Bo is a classic example of Mende determination. As the returns indicated, they were one hundred percent for the SLPP. Realizing that the eight SLPP candidates would win by overwhelming margins, the Government stopped the counting of the votes, and despatched contingents of the commando raiders of the ISU to Bo District.

(3) Although Paramount Chiefs are traditionally above politics, in the sense that they do not contest elections on any particular political platform, once elected, they support the government party in parliament. This convention of the constitution was unacceptable to the APC when in opposition and was criticized by the Dove Edwin Report. Yet, in the 1977 elections, there was a dramatic *volte face* on the part of the APC. The Government Gazette published that all eleven Paramount Chiefs were unopposed APC candidates. Furthermore, this was contrary to the Dove Edwin Report which the APC had accepted.

This is in sharp contrast to the political status of Paramount Chiefs during the 1973 general elections. The press release from the Sierra Leone Embassy in Washington, D.C., United States of America, showed the Paramount Chiefs as, "Elected Paramount Chief Members of Parliament," even though they were all returned as unopposed.

The then Secretary-General of the All Peoples Congress Party, E.T. Kamara made the position crystal clear when he warned Paramount Chiefs that their survival as chiefs depended on their unflinching support and loyalty to the APC and government.[13] Furthermore, the results showed the following "unopposed" APC candidates.

TABLE 2
DISTRIBUTION OF SEATS BETWEEN THE APC & THE SLPP

Constituency	Members Elected	Results APC	SLPP	Remarks		
Paramount Chiefs	12	12		12	APC	Unopposed
Western Area	12	11	1	3	"	"
Northern Province						
Port Loko	9	9		9	"	"
Tonkolili	6	6		6	"	"
Bombali	6	6		6	"	"
Koinadugu	5	5		2	"	"
Kambia	5	5		5	"	"
Southern Province						
Moyamba	6	3	3			
Bonthe	4	4		4	"	"
Pujehun	3	1	2			
Bo	8	8		8	"	"
Eastern Province						
Kenema	8	3	5			
Kailahun	5	1	4			
Kono	7	7		7	"	"
Total	96	81	15	62	"	"

Sixty-two of the 96 members were declared unopposed APC candidates by the Government.

After the 1973 general elections, President Siaka Stevens began a policy of big government out of all proportion to the population or economic realities of Sierra Leone. The Ministry of Lands, Mines and Labor was divided into three ministries, namely, Lands, Mines, and Labor.

1978 Cabinet

President Stevens (centre) with his Cabinet after it met recently at Makeni.

After the 1973 general elections, President Siaka Stevens began a policy of big government out of all proportion to the population or economic realities of Sierra Leone. The Ministry of Lands, Mines and Labor was divided into three ministries. namely, Lands, Mines, and Labor. Thereby creating two additional ministries. A new Ministry of Tourism and Cultural Affairs was created. These subjects were previously handled by the Ministries of Trade and Industry, and Social Welfare, respectively. Another post of Minister of State III was created. In all, three ministries and one cabinet post were created.

Ten new posts of Deputy Ministers were created. So that, out of a total of 96 members of Parliament, there were twenty-six cabinet ministers and fifteen deputy ministers; total forty-one. That is to say, in 1973, one out of every 2.4 members of parliament was either a cabinet minister or deputy. The Deputy Ministerial Posts created were:

> Defence I, Defence II, Finance I, Finance II, Works, Interior, Mines, Transport & Communications, Health, Trade & Industry, External Affairs, Special Assignment President's Office, Agriculture & Natural Resources, Vice President's Office, Development and Economic Planning.

In November, 1984, the government created a new Ministry of Establishment.

The previous government of the Sierra Leone Peoples Party had fifteen Ministers and 3 Deputy Ministers in the Ministry of the Interior, Prime Minister's Office, and External Affairs. For a population of 4 million, 96 member parliament supervised by 26 cabinet ministers and 15 deputy ministers, is the height of reckless extravagance.

(4) Realizing that the APC might stay in power only at the point of a gun, and in order to entrench his executive presidency, President Siaka Stevens had a new constitution drafted. A sham referendum was held, and the Government declared that the results showed that an overwhelming majority of Sierra Leoneans had voted in favor of his one-party APC Constitution. The results of the 1978 referedum as compared with the rigged elections of 1977 are as follows:

TABLE 3
THE GENERAL ELECTIONS VERSUS THE REFERENDUM

| Constituency | Votes Cast in 1977 | | | 1978 Referendum | | |
	Total	APC	SLPP	For	% of Votes Cast in 1977	Against
Western Area	97,876	63,212	2,400	145,591	148	129
Northern Province						
Port Loko	All APC Unopposed			249,278		nil
Tonkolili	"			208,731		nil
Bombali	"			171,995		nil
Koinadugu	41,349	37,363		122,953	297	nil
Kambia	All APC Unopposed			135,433		nil
Southern Province						
Moyamba	98,335	53,883	28,695	149,349	151	nil
Bonthe	All APC Unopposed			116,652		nil
Bo				166,782		7,040
Eastern Province						
Kenema	112,274	22,335	45,743	174,489	155	51,007
Kailahun	84,628	12,547	43,632	155,597	183	1,152
Total	434,462	189,340	120,470	1,796,850	413	59,328
Kono	206,167	173,438		239,746		1,013

One significant difficulty which these figures poses, is that no meaningful comparison can be made between the grand total of votes cast in 1977 and the results of the Referendum in 1978. This limitation is due to the fact that the APC candidates in 5 Districts, namely, Port Loko, Tonkolili, Bombali, Kambia, Bonthe, were declared unopposed. This lacuna vitiates the statistical value of the referendum.

The results of the referendum reveal some curious demographic patterns:

(1) Over 2,000,000 Sierra Leoneans voted at the referendum. Given an approximate population of 4,000,000, over 50 percent of the population are of voting age.

(2) The percentages of voters at the referendum were far in excess of those people who voted at the general elections. The figures range from an increase of 48 percent in the Western Area to 97 percent in Koinadugu District, despite the fact also, that a whole village was completely burnt down by APC thugs in Koinadugu District.

(3) The figures show other startling results. Whereas votes cast for the SLPP in Kailahun District were 43,632 against 12,547 for the APC in the General Elections of 1977, 155,597 voted "for" the referendum. Similar figures for Kenema District are SLPP 45,743, APC 22,335 (General Elections, 1977), the referendum being 174,489 in 1978. These figures lend support to the preposterous results issued by the Government in the Gazette, That the electorate who showed their preference for the SLPP over the APC by 5 to 3 candidates elected in Kenema and 4 to 1 elected in Kailahun in 1977, could within twelve months in 1978, endorse a policy which would nullify their yeoman's service to their party, defies political analysis.

(4) Finally, the Temnes are renowned for their penchant for controversy. Yet the APC government referendum showed that no votes were cast against the referendum in the Northern Province and in particular, in Port Loko, the heart of Temnedom.

In spite of these glaring statistical revelations, the Government issued a *Press Release* that,

> The results of the Referendum, nationwide, reaffirm the long-expressed desire of the majority of the population to have a

cohesive political system which will harness all possible resources to put the country firmly on the road to uninterrupted development.

...If the Dictum: 'The voice of the people is the voice of God', is anything to go by, then the All People's Congress Government of Sierra Leone, according to the results, has not only heard the voice of God, but implicitly received his blessing to eliminate the virus of devisiveness which has plagued many a society, always with dire consequences. As President Siaka Stevens once mentioned: 'We are a nation in a hurry'-in a hurry for unity, in a hurry for development, in a hurry for absolute stability, in a hurry to enjoy, in peace, the bounties which Sierra Leone has to offer. This is our chance.[14]

Chapter 11 Notes

1. *West Africa*, May 2, 1977.

2. *West Africa*, December 12, 1977.

3. *West Africa*, December 19, 1977.

4. AFP BRN 1836 Freetown.

5. *Times*, May 10, 1977.

6. *West Africa*, May 29, 1978.

7. *West Africa*, May 29, 1978.

8. *Africa*, No. 70, June 1977.

9. WHUR (Howard University Radio, Washington) AFP/BBE 14H29.

10. *West Africa*, October 31, 1977.

11. *West Africa*, March 7, 1977.

12. *West Africa*, March 14, 1977.

13. *West Africa*, January 29, 1979.

14. Press Release by the Embassy of the Republic of Sierra Leone, Washington, D.C., June 14, 1978.

...In a certain number of underdeveloped countries the parliamentary game is faked from the beginning. Powerless economically, unable to bring about the existence of coherent social relations, and standing on the principle of its domination as a class, the bourgeoisie chooses the solution that seems to it the easiest, that of the SINGLE PARTY. It does not yet have the quiet conscience and the calm that economic power and the control of the state machine alone can give. It does not create a state that reassures the ordinary citizen, but rather one that rouses his anxiety.

The state, which by its strength and discretion ought to inspire confidence and disarm and lull everybody to sleep, on the contrary seeks to impose itself in spectacular fashion. It makes a display, it jostles people and bullies them thus intimating to the citizen that he is in continual danger. The SINGLE PARTY is the modern form of the dictatorship of the bourgeoisie, unmasked, unpainted, inscrupulous and cynical. (Capitals mine).

FRANZ FANON
The Wretched of the Earth, 1961

CHAPTER 12

THE ONE-PARTY REPUBLICAN CONSTITUTION, ACT NO. 12 OF 1978

It will be recalled that one of the main campaign slogans against the Sierra Leone Peoples Party in the 1967 General Elections was, that the latter were planning to introduce a one-party state, as a prelude to dictatorship. When the SLPP introduced the Republican Bill in Parliament, the All Peoples Congress Party also opposed it. Yet, the APC adopted the SLPP Republican Act and passed it into law a second time, in 1971, in apparent conformity with the entrenched clause provision of the 1961 Constitution.

Six years thereafter, in 1977, the APC Government now embarked on the One-Party Republican Constitution. In May, 1977, in an address at an APC Convention, as reported in the Party Newspaper *We Yone*, the President Dr. Siaka Stevens said:

> It has been his view in the past that if we are to become a one-party state this would be by evolution.
>
> But he was now convinced, particularly in the absence of a responsible, organized opposition, that the country should now legalize the already existing *de-facto* one-party state.
>
> This, he said, was necessary in order to maintain economic, political as well as social stability.[1]

This *volte face* contrasts sharply with the following answer given to a Staff Correspondent of Africa who interviewed the President as reported in the June 1977 issue; a month after *We Yone's* report:

Q. Do you still propose to introduce a one-party system here?

A. We want to evolve. As we see it we may be very near it now. But we do not want to bring in legislation to achieve it. At any rate we've been in office now for about four years virtually without opposition. So we do have a gradual progress cowards the one-party state.[2]

The May 1977 Convention was attended by "about 10,000 delegates." At the Convention:

President Stevens recalled that several APC supporters were killed during the electioneering campaign, as a result of acts of vandalism and evil machinations of SLPP agents.

If the APC had retaliated, he said, there would have been chaos, and anarchy throughout the country...[3]

He blamed the foreign press for erroneous comments in the *Times*, and *West Africa* magazine.

...It was immoral of them, on the face of it, to suggest that the APC was trying to obstruct the opposition, President Stevens said.

He said until seven months ago, the unions were scattered like lost sheep and the Government had to take steps to amalgamate them. (He) cautioned the students that whenever they want to demonstrate they should think twice about the consequences.[4]

One of Dr. Stevens' arguments for a one-party is "the absence of a responsible, organized opposition, that the country should now legalize the already existing de-facto one-party state." What a fraudulent and deceitful argument. As Dr. Raymon Sarif Easmon wrote at the time, what has a disorganized opposition party got to do with the president? One would have thought that he would be happy that the opposition party was disorganized.

According to the Howard University Radio broadcast:

One-Party rule was introduced by the APC in 1970, and opposing parties were banned, their leaders exiled and in some instances worst. After the banning of the United Democratic Party in 1970, former Commander Brigadier General John Amadu Bangura and three senior members of the Army were executed on charges of belonging to the out-lawed party.

In July of 1975, two former senior Cabinet Ministers together with eight party colleagues were also executed as potential threats to the All Peoples Congress, headed by President Siaka Stevens.

At the APC Convention in May 1977, Dr. Stevens said that "the country should now legalize the already existing *de-facto* one-party state." In June 1977, only 30 days after the Convention, he was telling the Staff Correspondent of Africa that, "we want to evolve... But we do not want to bring in legislation to achieve it..."[5] (the one-party system). This lamentable sleight of hand and double-talk is hardly consonant with the shrewdness for which Siaka Stevens is known, at least not so blatantly, and within so short a time.

To give some semblance of legality to the one-party constitution, a sham referendum was held. The great majority of voters boycotted the referendum, since the people were opposed to a one-party system of government as they were to the Republican Constitution of 1971. The economic situation had deteriorated since 1971 and the political system had become more acrimonious and violent.

In an interview with Matchet Diary, President Stevens disclosed his plans for a New Constitution.

> 'Public opinion in general is in favor of a one-party state,' he said. 'They have shown it with many requests. The country nearly erupted in serious trouble at the last election because of the activities of the SLPP. We cannot allow that.' He also said that it should be remembered that 'Britain started with a one-party system', without making clear what period of history he was referring to.[6]

When interviewed for the Opposition Party's reaction to the proposal for a one-party, Salia Jusu Sheriff:

> ...rejected as illegitimate the government plan to call a referendum on a new constitution, claiming that inspite of the 1971 Amendment providing for a referendum, any change in fundamental constitutional rights still had to be passed, by a two-thirds majority at two sessions of Parliament with a General Election between them. However, he indicated that he would probably fight the referendum.

> Mr. Jusu Sheriff was indignant that this 'major event for every one' should be introduced without any sort of consultation with any one from his party: they had not even been informed, he said.[7]

As far as individual parliamentarians were concerned Matchet of *West Africa* reported that:

> ...Some MPs relied on their parliamentary income to live and anyway he could understand people becoming tired of the difficulties and harassment an opposition MP faced.[8]

The Citizens for a Better Sierra Leone, an Association of Sierra Leoneans resident in the United States of America with headquarters in Maryland, addressed a letter dated July 13, 1977, under the leadership of Samuel E.G. Tucker, to His Excellency Dr. Siaka Stevens, President of Sierra Leone, protesting the proposal to introduce a one-party system in Sierra Leone. They recounted the fundamental rights provisions, Section 34 of the 1961 Independence Constitution and the entrenched clause of the said Constitution. The latter was spelled out in detail. The letter concluded with the "hope that your Excellency, as defender of the Constitution will see to it that proper and constitutional steps are taken to amend or alter the Constitution the Supreme law of the nation."

Copies of the letter were addressed to the Leader of the Opposition, all Members of Parliament, the Sierra Leone Labor Congress, Sierra Leone Council of Churches, Fourah Bay College Senior Staff Association, Fourah Bay College Students' Union. An Association for the Restoration and Maintenance of Democracy in Sierra Leone, which was formed by Sierra Leoneans in the United Kingdom, with Headquarters in London, under the Chairmanship of Sir Banja Tejansie, former Chief Justice and Acting Governor-General of Sierra Leone, and General Secretary, Colonel (retired) Ambrose Genda, former Sierra Leone's Ambassador to Moscow and High Commissioner in London, petitioned President Stevens to take steps to correct the deteriorating conditions at home and to safeguard the constitutional rights of the people.

In the last chapter, we examined the 1973 and 1977 General Elections and compared the results with the referendum. The anomalies in the referendum results as compared with the rigged elections are very glaring. Despite severe opposition by the Sierra Leone Peoples Party members in Parliament, the One Party Republican Constitution was enacted on the 14th of June 1978. The Resolution introducing the Bill in Parliament was moved by William Conteh, the Member for Bombali South East:

> Be it resolved that this House hereby agrees to implement the wishes of the people of Sierra Leone to transform this country into a one-party state and for this purpose calls upon Government to introduce a new one-party Republican Constitution for Sierra Leone under Section 42 of the 1971 Constitution.

Section 42 empowers Parliament to make laws by "Bills passed by Parliament and signed by the President."

The House approved the Resolution by the positive votes of the 74 members present as there were 17 absentees. The latter were the Sierra Leone Peoples Party Members. Mr. Conteh's argument for the motion was that the advantages of the multi-party democratic system introduced by Europeans were doubtful.

So that in the teeth of opposition by Sierra Leoneans and the world press, the A.P.C. introduced a one-party system of government in Sierra Leone; a system which, led by Siaka Stevens when he was leader of the opposition party, they opposed vigorously, both in Parliament as well as through the medium of their newspaper, *We Yone*. We shall now examine the changes introduced by the one-party republican constitution.

CHANGES INTRODUCED BY THE 1978 ONE-PARTY REPUBLICAN CONSTITUTION ACT NO. 12 OF 1978

The 1978 One-Party Republican Constitution introduced more startling changes in the political system of Sierra Leone - freedom to hold different political views from those of the All Peoples Congress Party was proscribed; fundamental rights and freedoms of the individual were curtailed; executive presidency was introduced, as opposed to the ceremonial Governor General; the president exercises all major executive powers without the "advice of the Prime Minister" as heretofore; key civil service posts are to be held only by members of the APC; primary elections to Parliament and selection of a prospective candidate for president are controlled by the Central Committee of the All Peoples Congress Party; the president may appoint up to seven members to Parliament.

We shall now examine in depth, these repugnant provisions of the Constitution:

(1)   One-Party State.

By Section 1 of the One-Party Republican Constitution of 1978.

> Sierra Leone is a Sovereign Republic...and recognizes a One-Party form of Government.

(2)   The All Peoples Congress Party may have a para-military force.

Although Section 140 of the Act prohibits the raising of an armed force,

> ...this Section shall not apply to the organization of unarmed and voluntary community and customary defense arrangements and voluntary and customary training arrangements of the Recongized Party.

The dividing line between unarmed and armed Internal Security Unit intervention is so thin, that the provision is meaningless.

(3)   Qualified Protection of fundamental rights and freedoms of the individual.

The fundamental rights and freedoms of the individual were unqualified and inviolate under the 1961 Constitution.   The One party Constitution made these rights and freedoms subject to certain conditions:

(a)   they are subject to the rights of the   Recognized Party, the All Peoples Congress Party - Section 5;

(b)   laws may be enacted for "safeguarding the proper functioning of the Recognized Party..." Section 15(2) (a) (ii)

(c)   freedom of assembly and association shall be subject to "the interest of the proper functioning of the Recognized Party". Section 16(2) (a) (i)

(d)   laws may be passed under Section 16 (2) (c)

...which imposes restrictions on the establishment of political parties other than the Recognized Party, which regulates the organization, functioning, and registration of the Recognized Party; and except insofar as that provision, or as the case may be, the thing done under the authority thereof, is shown not to be reasonably justifiable in a democratic society.

How a one-party can be justified in a democratic society raises fundamental questions about what democracy is, or is not. The fundamental rights and freedoms of Sierra Leoneans are now subject to the rights of the A.P.C: A glaring legal semantic or quibble is manifest in Section 16.

Sub-section (1) states that

...no person shall be hindered in the enjoyment of his freedom of assembly and association...and in particular to form or belong to trade unions...

But sub-section (2) states that

Nothing contained in or done under the authority of any law shall be held to be inconsistent with or in contravention of this Section to the extent that the law in question makes provision

(a)   which is reasonably required

(i)   in the interest of the proper functions of the Recognized Party...which is the All Peoples Congress Party.

Section (16) Sub-section (1) clearly contradicts Sub-section (2). One such law referred to in Sub-section (2) is Section 44 (b) requiring membership of the APC as condition precedent to membership of Parliament. Therefore, that "no person shall be hindered in the enjoyment of his freedom of assembly and association..." Under Section 16(1) is absolutely meaningless, because it contradicts the requirement that all persons in Sierra Leone shall now belong to the APC. There is no "freedom of assembly and association" in Sierra Leone, because it is a One-Party State. To say that "no person shall be hindered in the enjoyment of his freedom of assembly and association" is undisguised fraud.

How can there be "freedom of assembly and association" in a One-Party State? The APC recognized this contradiction as far back as 1966 when it declared that:

> The Executives of the APC and DPC have found that party members as well as non-Party members are totally opposed to the One-Party system of Government especially when they observe the happenings in other parts of West Africa where the system obtains.
>
> The Parties also feel that the introduction of the One-Party system of government in the present form of the Constitution would be a violation of one of the entrenched clauses of the Constitution which guarantees the right of FREEDOM OF ASSOCIATION. (Capitals supplied).[9]

How did they proceed to overcome this formidable hurdle? They did not attempt to overcome it. But in their dictatorial powers they chose to bury their heads in the sand pretending that their feet were safe. In other words, they ignored it completely, by reneging on their promises on a matter of the most sacred constitutional importance.

(4) Qualification for membership of Parliament

Section 44 (b) stipulates that to be a member of Parliament a candidate shall be "(a) a member of the Recognized Party..." Section 164 (2) and (3) state that;

Sub-section (2)	"All existing members of Parliament shall make a declaration that they are members of the Recognized Party";
Sub-Section (3)	"Members of Parliament, not members of the Recognized Party who do not within 24 days"

become members of the Recognized Party in writing to the Speaker "shall be presumed to have vacated their seats in Parliament..." Under this Section the IS SLPP members were COMPELLED to join the APC. And yet Section 16 (1) can pretend that "no person shall be hindered in the enjoyment of his freedom of assembly and association..." The exception made for trade unions is, again, meaningless, because it applies to other associations like the Porro,

Wonde, Lodge, Sande, benevolent societies. Therefore, so long as an association is non-political, it shall not be an illegal association under the APC One-Party Republican Constitution. The apparent exclusion of trade unions from the obnoxious Section is, therefore, superfluous and could only have been enacted to pacify trade unions into thinking that they are a privileged class. Subsequent events in early 1980 proved that the APC does not in fact think that they are privileged.

(5)   Executive President Substituted for Governor-General who was Responsible to the People

There was no specific provision in the 1961 Constitution as to how the Governor-General shall be appointed. His appointment followed the British convention by which Her Majesty appointed the Governor-General on the advice of the Prime Minister.

By Section 57 (1) of the 1961 Constitution "The executive authority of Sierra Leone is vested in Her Majesty." This authority "may be exercised on behalf of Her Majesty by the Governor-General..." (Section 57(2); the "Cabinet of Ministers whose functions shall be to advise the Governor-General in the Government of Sierra Leone and which shall consist of the Prime Minister and such other persons, being Ministers, as the Governor-General acting in accordance with the advice of the Prime Minister, may from time to time appoint."

The difference between an Executive President and a Governor-General is in the exercise of their functions as provided by the clause, "acting in accordance with the advice of the Prime Minister." The cases in which the Governor-General acted "in accordance with his own deliberate judgement" were outlined by Section 64 as follows:

(a)   dissolution of Parliament - Section 55 (4)

(b)   appointment of Prime Minister - Section 58 (2) and (5)

(c)   his personal staff shall be approved by him - Section 95

In all other cases, the Governor-General acted in "accordance with the advice of the Prime Minister."

The President under the 1978 Act is elected by the following process:

(a) He shall be a member of the Recognized Party - Section 22(b)

(b) The National Delegates Conference of the Recognized Party

...shall elect a person to be the Leader of the Party, and such person shall be the sole candidate in an election to the office of President..." - Section 23 (I).

Obviously, by no stretch of any imagination, not even the imagination of the most rabid fanatic of the APC can anyone conceive, that by the declaration of the one-party state, they have even 10% support of the SLPP. So that, so long as this Constitution remains in force, the President shall be elected by the caucus of only the APC. We therefore, now have a

one man,
one vote,
one party,
one candidate constitution.

Mrs. Nancy Sumner, sister of Sir Albert Margai, calls it "one country, one person." By imposing the one-party constitution on the people of Sierra Leone, the APC has succeeded in polarizing the parties into sharply divided camps, which only the Internal Security Unit can prevent from open confrontation. Meanwhile, the SLPP will pretend to have joined the APC.

The candidate selected by the APC Conference shall be President. The Returning Officer shall be the Chief Justice, whose decision shall be final. Hence it was also expedient to abolish appeals to the Privy Council in 1971, so as to clear the way for any embarrassment which an appeal to the Privy Council might create.

(6) Primary Elections

For elections to the House of Representatives, there were political parties which selected candidates to contest the elections. The 1961 Constitution did not contain any provision with regard to political parties. Therefore, persons who did not belong to any political party, or who were not nominated by or sponsored by their parties, were free to stand as independent candidates. In some cases, party members challenged the party nominee and stood as independent candidates. That is the essence of democracy; freedom to challenge constituted authority, so long as it is done constitutionally.

Since the 1971 APC Constitution did not make any provision about political parties, certain APC stalwarts who were not supported by their party contested as independent candidates in the 1973 general elections. This freedom of association or dissociation was removed by the 1978 One Party Constitution. To become a candidate for election to the House of Representatives, the

> Central Committee of the Recognized Party shall hold a primary election in that constituency - Section 38(1).

It is the Committee that now selects candidates for election to the House of Representatives.

> In any constituency only the two persons who have received the greatest number of votes at the primary election shall be qualified for nomination as candidates for election to Parliament from that constituency, unless the Central Committee disapproves the nomination of any such person on the ground that his nomination would be inimical to the interests of the state...Section 38(5).

The last general elections in Sierra Leone in 1982 showed clearly the corruption to which this section is prone. It was alleged that some committees were bribed by influential candidates to disqualify opposing candidates. A pluralist political system discourages corruption because potential candidates know before hand that they have a constitutional protection to challenge the executive committee that sponsors candidates and allocates party symbols, by contesting as independent candidates. The APC one-party state does not tolerate independent candidates.

By and large, the 1982 general elections were so violent in character, principally by APC candidates, that 13 elections were cancelled and it was alleged that President Siaka Stevens' son captured ballot boxes and walked away with them when he realized that he was losing. When President Siaka

Stevens was interrogated by the foreign press about the whereabouts of his son, who was hiding from the police, he replied, "I am not my son's keeper." Having disowned his son, he will soon disown the one-party. More about this matter anon.

(7)   Member of Parliament

In 1961 the House of Representatives consisted of

(a)   Paramount Chief Members
(b)   Ordinary Members - Section 30

The One Party Constitution added a third category of

(c)   such other members not exceeding seven as may be appointed by the President...- Section 43(c).

(8)   Qualifications for Membership of Parliament

One additional qualification for contesting election to Parliament is, membership of the Recognized Party - Section 44(b).

(9)   Retroactive Membership of All Peoples Congress Party

Section 164 (2) and (3) state that

All existing members of Parliament shall make a declaration that they are members of the Recognized Party. Sub-section (2).

Members of Parliament, not members of the Recognized Party who do not within 24 days, Sub-section (3)

become members of the Recognized Party in writing to the Speaker,

shall be presumed to have vacated their seats in Parliament...(Sub-section (3).

In the event, the 15 members of the Sierra Leone Peoples Party joined the APC, one after the other. The last two to do so were, the indomitable Manna Kpaka of Pujehun, and his calm, cool, and unflappable leader, Salia Jusu Sheriff. With tears in his eyes, Salia delivered a moving speech in Parliament before 'joining' the one-party system.

(10)   Advice of the Prime Minister Abolished

Again, in the 1961 Constitution, the Governor-General acted on the advice of the Prime Minister, who was responsible to the Cabinet, who in turn were elected members of Parliament in the first instance. He was therefore, by implication, answerable to the people, via the Prime Minister, the Cabinet and Parliament, elected by the people, in free and unfettered general elections.

In his executive capacity, the 1978 Constitution abolished all reference to the "advice" of anyone. For example, contrary to the powers of the Governor-General, the 1978 executive President has the following powers:

(a)   Chief Justice

The "Chief Justice shall be appointed by the President, by warrant under his hand" - Section 113(1).

In 1961, he was appointed by the Governor-General "acting in accordance with the advice of the Prime Minister" - Section 76, that is to say, the Cabinet of persons elected by the people.

(b)   Public Service Commission

"Members of the Public Service Commission shall be appointed by the President," and removed under Sections 135(2) and (6), respectively.

In 1961, they were appointed and removed by the Governor-General "acting in accordance with the advice of the Prime Minister." Sections 94(2) and (6) - again the Cabinet.

(c)   Electoral Commission

Members of the Electoral Commission shall be appointed and removed by the President - Section 34(3);

whereas in 1961 such appointments and removal were made by the Governor-General "on the advice of the Prime Minister" - Sections 37(3) and (6).

(d)   Representatives Abroad

Sierra Leone's high commissioners and ambassadors are appointed, promoted, transferred and removed from office by the President. This power applies to the Force Commander and the Commissioner of Police - Sections 138(1), (2). These powers were exercised by the Governor-General, "in accordance with the advice of the Prime Minister" under the 1961 Constitution - Sections 96(1) and (3).

Furthermore, such advice was given in consultation with the Public Service Commission.

(e)   Presidential Awards

The President is empowered by Section 155 to make and confer national awards, titles, and decorations. These functions were performed by the Governor-General "on the advice of the Prime Minister."

(11)   Only APC Members Appointed as Permanent Secretaries and Certain Other Officers

To be appointed a permanent secretary, the appointee shall be a member of the Recognized Party. The posts are, Secretaries to the President, Vice Presidents; Secretary to the Cabinet, Financial Secretary, Secretary to the Foreign Minister, Establishment Secretary, Development Secretary, Director of Public Prosecution, Solicitor General, Administrator and Registrar-General - Section 139 (1) and (2).

Under the 1961 Constitution, the civil service was sheltered from politics. Civil servants were free to join any political party of their choice, and never took active part in politics. Appointments to the posts of Secretary to the Cabinet, Financial Secretary, Secretary to the Prime Minister, Establishment Secretary, Permanent Secretaries were made by the Governor-General acting "on the advice of the Prime Minister," who consulted the Public Service Commission - Sections 97 (1), (2) and (3).

The reason for the active involvement of civil servants in politics under the APC One Party Constitution, was given in an interview by President Stevens, when he replied that

> ...A system, for example, which precludes the whole of the civil service from engaging in politics openly which deprive (sic) us of their abilities, needs very serious study."[10]

In *We Yone*, the APC newspaper of June 9, 1977, it was reported that S.A.J. Pratt, one of the leading advocates of the one-party, defended the system during the debate on the "Speech from the Throne."

The theory of opposition in Parliament is foreign to us, he went on, even in the days of the Legislative Council and the Protectorate Assembly.

'What we need is a unifying factor' he declared, Mr. Pratt said that the All Peoples Congress and the SLPP have...ideology and philosophy and it is only left with the SLPP to forego its identity by fusing into 'the greater whole' for the benefit of the nation.'[11]

To hear Solomon Pratt, a qualified legal practitioner fabricate such blatant untruth that there was no opposition "even in the days of the Legislative Council," would make the late Bankole Bright, Reffell, Lamina Sankoh (Reverend Jones), I.T.A. Wallace Johnson, turn in their graves.

The evidence shows that the Executive Committee of the All Peoples Congress Party apparently support President Siaka Stevens' one-party system. In his contribution to the debate on the one-party resolution, Vice President Sorie Koroma is reported as having supported the Motion, when he said that

...of all nations in the U.N. only about fifteen still practiced the multi-party system. Of OAU states, he said just four retained the two-party system and two of those were monarchies - Morocco and Swaziland. The Vice President suggested that in any case OAU states tended to evolve into effective one-party systems in time.

The Prime Minister C.A. Kamara-Taylor made this reflection...

'if we look around this House, we see people who have in the past been politically opposed, sitting around the despatch box in friendly and meaningful deliberations for the good and progress of this nation.' He went on to complain against the Westminster model saying that 'whole sections of the national community have been completely unrepresented in the Government machinery because of a post-colonial system which assigns them to nothing but the job of opposing.'[12]

The journal *Africa* added that

It would be easy to say that, having eliminated or suppressed opposition, Dr. Stevens' APC is an unchallengeable force. That would be too cynical. As was pointed out in an editorial by Clarence Labor of the Daily Mail, 'in some East African states with one party constitutions large numbers of parliamentarians have lost their seats in elections. In

> supporting this motion...I will urge that this country adopts the Tanzanian or KENYAN CONSTITUTION, with the necessary modifications to suit Sierra Leone's requirements.' (Capitals mine).

The Government had apparently 'succeeded' in eliminating all opposition. Sierra Leoneans who could not stay home for fear of being arrested and hanged, or imprisoned, or deprived of employment opportunities, chose exile.

REACTIONS TO THE ONE-PARTY CONSTITUTION OF 1978.

Local as well as international condemnation of the one-party constitution were swift and unequivocal. Like other parts of the continent south of the Sahara Desert, the peoples of Sierra Leone are by no means homogeneous in character, temperament and disposition. They however, have certain basic traits in common; their sophistication, their built in capacity for endurance, their resilience, their love of freedom and the right to disagree, their uncompromising belief in the Almighty God who "moves in a mysterious way, His wonders to perform."

President Siaka Stevens is ostensibly quite a religious man, like the great majority of Sierra Leoneans. The above Biblical quotation is the bedrock of Siaka Stevens' faith. It is also true, as he was reminded by Maccoi, that "Siaka Stevens moves in a mysterious way, God's wonders to perform." Mysteriously, he cajoled the people into believing that he was more God-fearing than Sir Albert. Mysteriously, they rebelled and took up arms against the Mendes, whom they molested, hounded and slaughtered into submission by splitting their votes among the Mendes on the one hand, and the Temnes and their followers on the other hand.

Having put their trust in the hands of the All Peoples Congress, the APC bull-dozed the people into a republican state, and finally into a one-party republican state. In both cases, the whole country suffered irreparable harm; Mendes, Temnes, Yalunkas, Fullahs, Maninkas, were victims of APC thugs and the Internal Security Unit.

It has been an uphill task for President Siaka Stevens and his APC. Some of his Party stalwarts and sympathizers; Brigadier John Bangura, Dr.

Mohamed Forna, M.D., Ibrahim Taqui, were together with non-party citizens, hanged for treason by the APC, after they protested the APC's rough-shod methods. The people of Sierra Leone did not take these atrocities meekly. In the teeth of threats by the Internal Security Unit, Dr. Raymon Sarif Easmon, a medical practitioner, had the courage to challenge President Siaka Stevens' alleged attempts to pervert the Judges of the Appeal Court to reject our Appeals against convictions in the treason trials. Similarly, other eminent Sierra Leoneans attacked the one-party constitution. Professor Awunor Renner is another gallant fighter for freedom in Sierra Leone. He wrote an open letter to the President while he, like Dr. Sarif Easmon were and are still in the country. Another gallant freedom fighter has been Reverend M.G.M. Cole, who while in exile in London, continued to challenge President Siaka Stevens and his APC Executive Committee for raping the constitutional and other legal processes of Sierra Leone. In the next chapter, these Sierra Leoneans will represent a cross-section of the Sierra Leone peoples' indignation for the betrayal of the peoples' aspirations to enjoy the fruits of their hard earned independence from colonialism.

In the next chapter, we shall let the prominent Sierra Leoneans summarize the points we have labored to prove in this book, before we conclude with an examination of the one-party system in practice in Sierra Leone. At this juncture, the author would request the reader to compare his hypothesis and variables together with his research to substantiate his variables with the accounts narrated in the next chapter.

Chapter 12 Notes

1. *We Yone*, May 1977.

2. *Africa*, June 1977.

3. *We Yone*, May 1977.

4. *Ibid.*

5. *Africa*, June 1977.

6. *West Africa*, May 22, 1978.

7. *Ibid.*

8. *Ibid.*

9. *Africa,* No. 50, October 1975.

10. *Africa,* No. 7, June 1977.

11. *We Yone*, June 9, 1977.

12. *Africa,* No. 5, October 1975.

CHAPTER 13

THE BETRAYAL OF A NATION

Through his astute political strategy, Sir Milton Margai led a national front of all political parties in Sierra Leone to the constitutional conference in 1960, and negotiated successfully, the independence constitution of Sierra Leone. After the first post-in-dependence general elections, the Sierra Leone Peoples Party emerged with a landslide majority, while the All Peoples Congress Party became the opposition party.

By the next general elections in 1967, the APC had mounted the most acrimonious propaganda against the SLPP. Their slanderous strategy was so effective that they were able to split the electorate equally between the two political parties. The APC swore to oust the SLPP "NOW OR NEVER." When by hook and by crook they captured the government of Sierra Leone, they determined to rule Sierra Leone "NOW AND FOREVER." Once firmly ensconced in power, the APC Executive Committee decided it was going to be in power "FOREVER AND EVER."

We set out to explore the performance of the first opposition party government in Sierra Leone. We have proved that

(a) the All Peoples Congress Party Government introduced a reign of terror as soon as they came to power;

(b) the APC abused the executive powers of government by malicious and illegal use of the Treason and State Offences Act No. 10 of 1963;

(c) the APC perverted the legislative powers of government by enacting legislation to re-enroll a disbarred lawyer, to wit, the said Cyril Rogers-Wright;

(d) the APC interfered with the judicial processes, e.g. the interview between Dr. Raymon Sarif Easmon and President Siaka Stevens about the allegations that the said President Siaka Stevens was threatening to pervert Appeal Court Judges to reject our appeals, and the *West Africa* interview in which Sir Banja Tejansie said that Siaka Stevens "got Luke to do all the dirty work for him;"

(e) the APC illegally abolished the Independence Constitution Act of 1961, and illegally introduced the Republican Constitution Act No. 6 of 1971;

(f) the APC rigged the referendum as preliminary step to the introduction of a one-party system of government;

(g) the APC introduced the 1978 Republican One-Party Constitution illegally;

(h) the APC breached international law by illegally indicting Brigadier David Lansana.

The perversions of the 1961 Independence Constitution, the electoral frauds, the wholesale illegal arrests and detentions (sometime without trial), the perversions of the judicial processes, were all designed to lay the foundation for the introduction of a one-party system of government.

In this deplorable episode of man's brutality to man, the people of Sierra Leone resisted consistently. A representative sample of their collective indignation is the Fourah Bay College Students and school children's demonstrations. Since the British Government declared Sierra Leone a Crown Colony in 1808 to the date of their abdication of power in 1961, the people always resented taxation without representation, for example, the 1898 hut tax war and the 1954 Pitierre Kamara insurrection. Having wrested the government by the guerrilla army they trained in Guinea, the APC resorted to the most repugnant form of government imaginable. They introduced a form of government that was intolerable to the people who resolved that they were not going to substitute an oligarchy for British colonialism; and so opposed the despotic rule which President Siaka Stevens and his APC Executive Committee and advisors sought to impose on them. This was a betrayal of the people's trust.

We shall now select a physician, a university professor and a priest as a cross-section of the peoples' will to resist despotism - Dr. Raymon Sarif Easmon, Professor Awunor Renner and Reverend M.G.M. Cole. They will summarize and substantiate our findings. The last straw to break President Siaka Stevens' camel was his fraudulent plans to introduce a one-party system. At that point, these gallant gentlemen once more took to the breech and gave a brilliant resume of the variable factors we laboriously tried to prove. Since they symbolize the eloquent testimony of the people's abhorrence of the APC Government, we shall briefly summarize their views.

DR. RAYMON SARIF EASMON

Dr. Raymon Sarif Easmon, one of the leading politico-medical practitioners on the continent wrote an article in 1977 on the one-party government. It was published in *The People*.[1] The APC formed their illegal government in April 1968. By 1977, when Dr. Easmon assessed their performance, he revealed abundant evidence of their betrayal of the trust reposed in them by the electorate whom they had surreptitiously hood-winked. Dr. Easmon is an academic politician who did not ally himself actively with the Sierra Leone Peoples Party or the All Peoples Congress Party. He is an African nationalist who, like Jomo Kenyatta, Nnamdi Azikiwe, Lamina Sankoh (Alias Rev. Jones), Sir Milton Margai, was opposed to British imperialism. The linchpin of his philosophy was democratic government, which was the direct antithesis of colonialism.

By 1977 Dr. Easmon once again declared war on the APC for daring to introduce a one-party system of government, which he had strenuously opposed when it was proposed by the SLPP government. The one-party system of government which has become an endemic disease in the body politic of Africa is, like colonialism, the direct and incontrovertible opposite of democratic government. By some mysterious twist of logic, some well-meaning African politicians have fallen prey to this pernicious evil. They fabricate all sorts of specious and spurious arguments in support of it. Even erudite thinkers like President Nyerere, one of Africa's luminaries, is discovering to his regret that the one-party system of government is the road to serfdom.

It is in this context that Dr. Easmon challenged President Siaka Stevens. In his Article, he gave historical development of the one-party system in Sierra Leone which Sir Albert was forced to abandon. At the time he was also

> vigorously opposed by Mr. Siaka Stevens and the APC.., The fight against one-party government was at the time conducted by Mr. Siaka Stevens and his APC. It is, therefore most puzzling that the very Dr. Stevens and the very APC should now be advocating the very same one-party system of government which a decade ago they held to be so evil, tyrannical and obnoxious to the people of this country.

The one-party was a usurpation of the people's sovereignty which could not be legislated away. If this view was valid in 1966, as Siaka Stevens maintained, why was it not valid in 1977 when the APC were pressing their claim to the one-party?

Dr. Easmon recounted how in 1965-66 he "was so closely involved with Dr. Stevens and the APC IN THE STRUGGLE AGAINST THE SLPP (capitals supplied) government," for wanting to introduce the one-party system. He could not "conceive how, if they had any regard for public morality the APC...should have swallowed all their principles to be advocating one-party government now..." Mr. Siaka Stevens was quoted by Dr. Easmon as opposing the SLPP one-party proposal in parliament because

> 'We do not think that it would be in the interest of the people of this country...the establishment of a one-party form of government will be contrary to the entrenched clauses of the Constitution.'

The reasons given for extensive quotations of Stevens' opposition to the one-party were to highlight the fact that under the Sierra Leone Peoples Party, "There was absolute freedom of the Press...Sir Albert never declared a state of emergency to imprison his...opponents. He never had any of his friends or enemies hanged."

Dr. Easmon recounted the evils of the one-party; namely, it is "a tyranny imposed on people; it is a self-perpetuating oligarchy..." He accused the APC of rigging the last elections disgracefully, by falsification and inflation of voters' lists, sharing voting marbles among thousands of APC supporters who voted "more than once." A woman in Freetown Central I was quoted as boasting that 'On the last occasion they did not even ask my name when I said I was voting for Akibo Betts.'

The violence and atrocities committed by the APC were legion. They burned down Krubola village in the Koinadugu District and killed about 80 villagers. Opposition candidates who refused Le.2,000 bribe each, were locked up in gaol for 24 hours by armed thugs to allow APC candidates to file their nomination papers in Port Loko. In York, a man's "hands (were) nailed to a board." Dr. Lahai Taylor's surgery in Freetown was attacked and looted. The four SLPP candidates in Bonthe were imprisoned, while Dr. Hadj Contech was "forcibly prevented from entering his nomination papers," and later imprisoned. Successful SLPP candidates were gaoled. "The worst excesses of the APC were in Kabala, Kenema and Bo." The APC glued the openings of SLPP boxes with chewing gum in Kono. Thuggery was so rampant that at Waterloo even the APC controlled Internal Security Unit were shocked and had to rescue Falkner by threatening to shoot APC thugs. According to Dr. Easmon "...it is not easy to define what kind of government Dr. Stevens and the APC are seeking to inflict on this country." In 1973

> Sixty SLPP and independent candidates were detained in prison to prevent them submitting their nomination papers. And according to one English newspaper, more than two hundred people were killed...

After the general elections, 50 election petitions were instituted against APC members, Dr. Easmon exhorted the people to

> pray that the moral fibre of our nation has not been so eroded and corrupted that our judges play the auctioneers selling this country into slavery, If the judges fail us, then assuredly Sierra Leone will be well set on a course to become another Uganda.

Writing in 1984, the people of Sierra Leone are assured that their lot was not better than Uganda. If anything, it was worse.

The reader will recall the similarity between Dr. Raymon Sarif Easmon's account of the violence, atrocities, hooliganism perpetrated by

APC thugs and the account given by M.O, Bash Taqui and the Honourable Salia Jusu Sheriff when they addressed Sierra Leoneans in Washington, D.C. We shall now analyze Professor Awunor Renner's Open Letter to President Siaka Stevens dated May 1, 1977.

PROFESSOR AWUNOR RENNER

He began with a historical sketch of the APC record, starting with the "unconstitutional" methods employed by Dr. Stevens to stifle the opposition.

First APC led government

Professor Renner, like many Sierra Leoneans, was shocked when Stevens adopted the SLPP Constitution which he was "elected to put aside." The new APC slogan "APC Forever", sounded like "an organization of gods." The "pointers of things to come" began, when "hooligans wearing red, attacking people who criticized your actions especially if they belonged to the SLPP." At one time they killed a school boy news vendor.

The Elections of 1973 and 1977

These two elections were also accompanied by hooliganism. He reminded Stevens of how in 1967 he criticized the chiefs who declared for the Sierra Leone Peoples Party and the fact that in 1977 twelve unopposed chiefs declared for the All Peoples Congress Party. Professor Renner also drew attention to people killed in many districts and that the APC

> supporters break the law openly and with impunity. (They) invaded the law courts building...harassed lawyers and disturbed court proceedings...you have turned out to be far worse than Albert Margai in your style of operation. (Parenthesis mine).

The Professor concluded with what he described as the "disgraceful amendments" of the constitution. Finally, we shall conclude with Reverend M.G.M. Cole's Article.

REVEREND M.G.M. COLE

Reverend M.G.M. Cole's Article is entitled, The Agony of Sierra Leone. Be began with the proposition that, "Thousands of those who voted for Mr. Siaka Stevens in 1967, know this to their sorrow and agonising disappointment." In short, that it has been the betrayal of a nation. Mr. Siaka Stevens' platform at the 1967 elections was his indomitable opposition to the one-party system of government. Since assuming the reins of government, however,

> Mr. Stevens, now Dr. Stevens has done everything corrupt, deceitful, outrageously indecent and violent, in order to impose the one-party system that he opposed and for which opposition, thousands voted for him.

As freelance journalist with no party affiliation, Reverend M.G.M. Cole opposed the SLPP one-party proposal, believing Mr. Stevens "to be an honorable man, as did many others." Reverend Cole now thinks that Stevens is a "dishonorable man," and that the "APC mean All Peoples Crooks." He charged that Dr. Stevens has employed "disreputable means including ruthless and barbaric violence to maintain power." It is "plutocratic tyranny."

During the 1973 elections, the Internal Security Unit drove away opposition candidates who went to file their nomination papers. Those who filed their papers "were forced to withdraw." He saw a dead body in the street at Kissy. He was a member of the United Christian Council delegation who petitioned the President to stop the violence. Reverend Cole asked Dr. Stevens what happened to the $5m which he allegedly received for the "Star of Sierra Leone" diamond and which "has never been reflected in the revenue of Sierra Leone." Where is this money? Dr. Stevens became president "by a trick if not dishonesty," because while a referendum was in progress to sound public opinion on the introduction of presidential system in Sierra Leone, Siaka Stevens became president. "Everything in the APC Government stinks." Dr. Stevens has absolute power to detain anyone and is not answerable to parliament or to the courts. For example, all 8 opposition candidates in Bo were arrested and detained and the APC candidates returned unopposed.

We shall now let *New Africa* of July 1978 present the case for the world press. Mr. Cecil Hennessy wrote as follows:

> In May, a new constitution was approved by the APC-dominated Parliament despite heavy opposition from the token Sierra Leone Peoples Party (SLPP) representation in Parliament, led by Salia Jusu Sheriff who voted against...

> It was unthinkable that the APC would allow a defeat in the referendum after the vigorous opposition the Party has faced in recent times.

> ...By the elections of 1973 it was apparent that there could be a major swing back to the SLPP and so the APC took steps to gain the upper hand.

> A wave of violence unknown in the political history of Sierra Leone was directed against prospective SLPP candidates by members of the APC. The violence was so extensive that the SLPP finally withdrew from the elections, giving up all the seats to the APC.

> Then came the student-inspired troubles in January 1977. Internal Security Unit killed scores of people throughout the country in a bid to quell the trouble.

> Eventually common sense prevailed and general elections were held, with even more violence than in 1973. The SLPP managed to win 15 seats with their voters under constant harassment from thugs.

> When the dust finally settled the APC realized that the SLPP was still a threat... President Stevens undertook many tours in the provinces calling for a one-party state.

> Many stage-managed demonstrations and seminars in support of a one-party state have been held throughout the country, although the atmosphere in the country makes it blindingly obvious that the people including some Cabinet Ministers, do not favor a one-party state.

> ...Meanwhile internal trouble is looming round the various blocs forming around the two main right-hand men of the President, Vice President Sorie Koroma, and Prime Minister Kamara-Taylor.

> ...With the one-party system free speech and the like - although there are assurances of freedom would be impaired. Cecil Hennessy[2]

I also wrote to *West Africa*, reproduced in *West Africa* on 24th May, 1982, on the Road to Despotism. It summarizes the Sierra Leone experience with this monstrosity, as I saw it. See Appendix 2.

It is abundantly clear that apart from the APC caucus who benefit from the fruits of oligarchical government, Sierra Leoneans at home and abroad are united in their condemnation of the executive presidency and all it connotes, particularly, the one-party fraud, both of which were foisted on the people illegally. The performance of the APC under the one-party system has been a deplorable catalogue of bad government. Under the one-party constitution, every one is compelled to become a member of the APC. Hard core SLPP members who were bulldozed into the APC, are leopards who would never change their spots. President Siaka Stevens knows that, if nobody else does.

Inspite of the foregoing indictments against President Siaka Stevens and his All Peoples Congress Party, the culmination of which, is the introduction of a one-party political system of government in Sierra Leone, the APC has had one glorious opportunity to prove that, criticisms notwithstanding, the one-party system is a viable political system. That is to say, why not give the one-party a chance. In the next chapter, we shall examine the one-party system in operation in Sierra Leone.

Chapter 13 Notes

1.   *The People*, July 14, 1977.
2.   Hennessy, Cecil, *New Africa*, July 1978.

CHAPTER 14

GENERAL 'SELECTIONS' UNDER THE ONE-PARTY SYSTEM, MAY 1982

The last general elections should have been held in June 1981. The Sierra Leone Peoples Party members who were steam-rolled into the All Peoples Congress Party, were more enthusiastic about the forthcoming elections than even the foundation members of the APC. Astute as he is, President Siaka Stevens immediately became apprehensive that all was not well within the 'party'. Why should the new 'converts', former SLPP members, become more 'active' APC members, than hard-core APC members? To be more catholic than the pope is the height of blasphemous deception. And so President Siaka Stevens postponed the elections to October 1981, to give him time to appraise the situation. From their findings, the APC Executive Committee suspected that if another general elections were held, a majority of the successful candidates would be former SLPP members and sympathizers.

When eventually, the general elections were held in May 1982, the first general elections to be held under the one-party republican constitution, it was accompanied by such wholesale violence and vandalism, that it is now confirmed beyond all reasonable doubt that the one-party system cannot work in Sierra Leone. President Siaka Stevens had no alternative but to appoint the former parliamentary leader of the 'former' SLPP, the Honourable Salia Jusu-Sheriff, to become Minister of Finance, to clear the mess created by fourteen years of APC misrule.

We shall now examine the May 1982 general elections. In his address to the APC national conference in October 1981, "President Stevens said that party politics had caused 'years of strife, family feuds and tribal disputes.'"[1] Because of shortages of capital and manpower, "...it would at present be 'economic as well as political suicide' to practice a multi-party democracy."[2] Before the general elections, "It is his thesis that with the one-party the coming ballot will avoid the violence of past elections.[3]

Meeting in London in November, the Sierra Leone Alliance Movement resolved that

> ....the one-party as imposed on the country is a failure and must be dispensed with, and the country returned to a multi-party system of government... that free and fair elections could not be held under a continuing state of emergency and that the independence of the judiciary be strengthened.[4]

As we pointed out in our discussion of the One-Party Republican Constitution, selections for the primaries are conducted by the APC Secretariat which has the authority to reject a candidate's nomination paper. To be nominated, a candidate must also make good his "financial obligations to the Party plus a standing fee of Le 200 which some candidates ran to a cost of over Le 1,000."[5] This included arrears of subscriptions.

The Executive Committee of the APC in the 85 constituencies of the Party select three candidates from lists and send the names to the Central Committee, and finally to the Electoral Commission. As soon as the elections at the primaries began, there was wide-spread violence as has never occurred in the elections history of Sierra Leone. The former Minister of Foreign Affairs, Abdulai Conteh, is reported as having been physically man-handled.

> Dr. Conteh was severely beaten...Several people were reported to have been injured - and some may have died - in clashes in Sierra Leone during recent voting to select candidates for the one-party elections."[6]

In East Koinadugu "matchetes iron-bars and sticks"[7] were used; and in Freetown, "An unspecified number of people were injured by knives, sticks and stones in Freetown West One..."[8] As the primaries gathered momentum, a special correspondent from Freetown wrote that it was

> ...characterized by unprecedented violence and scores of protests over the eligibility of some of the candidates. The whole episode which has been described as a 'hotch-potch of confusion' by political analysts, makes nonsense of President Stevens' declared *raison d'etre* for the overthrow of the multiparty system in place of the One-Party system of Government. In an address to Parliament after the One-Party Referendum in June 1978, President Stevens said:

> 'Today, after some two score years in politics, it is my considered view that the multi-party system with government and opposition, contributes an open invitation to anarchy and disunity.

> ...We have banned a system which institutionalized tribal or ethnic quinquennial warfare euphemistically known as elections... We have done away with an unnecessary system.'

> Far from putting an end to the 'quinquennial warfare,' the One-Party system seems to have aggravated violence and anarchy, as experienced in several areas throughout the country during preparations for the first general elections under the One-Party system.[9]

The correspondent went on to enumerate instances of lawlessness and anarchy in the country. According to him "several trouble broke out" in Port Loko. "His (the Attorney General) house in Kasse was attacked by thugs and his two nephews shot.[10] (Parenthesis mine) Two people were reported shot dead in Bombali, where there was "open warfare." He went on, "To prevent his opponents from filing their nomination papers for the primaries, Mr. Bangura's supporters are said to have damaged several bridges leading to the area for nomination."[11] In Bombali West two people lost their lives.

> In Freetown Central I constituency supporters of Mr. Akibo-Betts are alleged to have damaged the house of his opponent, Mr. W. Morgan. In Freetown East II terror reigned...an attempt was made to set Mr. Iscandri's house on fire...

> Clashes were reported in several other constituencies throughout the country.[12]

The dismal episode of APC rule was summarized thus:

> Since the APC took over power in 1968, general elections in Sierra Leone have always been characterized by violence, intimidation, and deaths. Over 90% of APC's parliamentarians found their way into parliament unopposed.[13]

> (President Stevens was so alarmed by the level of violence that)

> ...he warned that 'hired thugs', are disrupting Sierra Leone's general election campaign and said the violence must stop. Dr. Stevens also told tribal chiefs to stay out of party politics.

> 'Some candidates are loading thugs into hired vehicles...to help them in their campaigning. Both the thugs and the vehicles engaged in such missions expose themselves to serious danger and are here warned', President Stevens said...

> 'The use of violence and resorting to other destructive measures renders you unfit for appointment, into high public office,' President Stevens told the candidates.

> He denounced paramount and local chiefs who, he said, had been openly campaigning and canvassing for certain candidates.[14] (Parenthesis mine).

The hired thugs that the President referred to were introduced into the politics of Sierra Leone during the 1967 general elections when the APC were determined that they would win the elections at all costs, NOW OR NEVER. When the army intervened, the APC caucus, under the leadership of President Siaka Stevens, trained thugs in Guinea in guerrilla war-fare to attack the National Reformation Council and wrest the government from them. Since the APC came to power in Sierra Leone in 1968, hired thuggery has become an integral and an inseparable part of politics. To say now, as the President did that 'hired thugs' are disrupting Sierra Leone's general elections, is a boomerang.

Furthermore, it was also contradictory for the President to warn "tribal chiefs to stay out of party politics." To be a member of Parliament under the 1978 One-Party Constitution, a candidate shall be "(a) a member of the Recognized Party..." Section 164(2) stipulates that "All existing members of Parliament shall make a declaration that they are members of the Recognized Party..." The Recognized Party is the APC. In the 1977 general elections, eleven Paramount Chiefs were returned unopposed APC candidates as shown in the statistical analysis in Chapter II. (Compiled from the Government Gazette). How can Paramount Chiefs be returned unopposed APC candidates and not participate in politics when it is mandatory for them to do so under the Constitution?

On polling day, for the first general elections under the one-party constitution, it was reported by a correspondent of *West Africa* that

> polling was going on peacefully when Stevens' supporters, (Alex Stevens, the President's son) smelling defeat, went on a rampage. Alex's brother, Jengo, who had been returned unopposed... led strong-armed supporters to several of the three polling stations in the constituency and forcibly took out the ballot boxes of Alex and Murado three hours before closing time while scores of people queued outside the polling booths waiting patiently to cast their votes...[15] (Parenthesis mine).

When the President was asked what he thought of his son's (Jengo Stevens) behavior on polling day, he said, "I am not responsible for the behavior of my son. My son is of age. I can advise him, I cannot direct him ..."[16]

Fighting broke out between Stevens' supporters and Murado's; several houses were badly damaged. The Temne Tribal headman was knifed on the head and shoulder. Mr. S.A. Fofana, a founder member of the APC, former propaganda and organizing secretary, APC member of parliament for twenty years, and a cabinet minister in the last APC government, was so "disgusted with the electioneering violence in the constituency that he wrote a letter to the President...to withdraw his candidature and to resign his membership of the party..."[17]

Despite these atrocious and glaring hooliganism and vandalism resulting in the cancellation of elections in thirteen constituencies, President Stevens' comments were that, "I as well as responsible citizens of Sierra Leone, are of the opinion that we have done fairly well in the conduct of elections bearing in mind the way elections go in other parts of the world... Expedient (sic) people here know that man is a brute beast all over the world."[18] He may well have concluded after Thomas Hobbes, that in Sierra Leone, also, "life is short, nasty and brutish," as in other parts of the world.

Once again, the students of Fourah Bay College, University of Sierra Leone, issued a press release in which they

> ...condemn the existing state of affairs in the country as barbaric, shameful and disgraceful...

> That Sierra Leone has been raped, seduced and debased to a state of animal level devoid of morals, values and conscience... has been glaringly substantiated by the manoeuvres of the present regime of President Siaka Stevens.

When Akibo Betts was rejected by the All Peoples Congress Party

> A State House pronouncement read over Sierra Leone radio... said that the police had been able to retrieve 450 government files and an assortment of vouchers, local purchase orders, customs invoices and other documents from the King Tom residence of Mr. Akibo Betts...[19]

The files relate to the "Vouchergate" and "Squandergate" investigations "which he removed from the Ministry of Finance (where he was Deputy Minister of Finance) and kept in large trunks at his residence to ensure their safety."[20] (Parenthesis mine).

In the elections battles, for battles indeed they became, he was man-handled and was admitted "in an intensive care unit after having been severely beaten by thugs, believed to have been politically inspired to their attack upon him."[21] As an APC stalwart, "Akibo Betts was one of the widely known, feared thugs in the capital."[22]

> At one Steele election campaign rally at the Victoria Park in Freetown under the watchful eyes of senior police officers, Akibo Betts personally led a bunch of fellow stick-toting thugs to beat up the campaigners and disperse them in broad daylight in the center of Freetown... (the capital of Sierra Leone) Akibo Betts was thrown briefly into Pademba Road prison as a result of the unprecedented merciless beating of several hundred elderly women at the Steele rally... His arrogance and taste for power sharpened... The new junior minister questioned every move in the Ministry and sometimes even clashed openly with his minister when he attempted to question certain matters.[23] (Parenthesis mine).

Mr. Akibo Betts unearthed the Vouchergate and the Squandergate scandals. According to *West Africa* correspondent, these two scandals

> involved top-ranking civil servants. If it were not in a country where only one man is everything, the two exposures would have tumbled and smashed the entire government and its civil service...the recent Squandergate scandal, which the authorities conceded had involved Le 40m (about $34.4m) diverted from the Consolidated Fund through a neatly orchestrated racket which operated within the individual ministries involving civil servants.[24] (Parenthesis mine).

It will be recalled, that President Siaka Stevens estimated the vouchergate as involving $30m. Added to the Squandergate, the overall total is in the neighborhood of Le. 70m ($60.2m). These are alarming figures for a country with an annual revenue of $250m.

After the general elections of May 1982, President Siaka Stevens appointed 28 cabinet ministers and 14 ministers of state (without cabinet rank) and 4 parliamentary special assistants. "This is the largest single number of ministerial appointments ever made in the history of Sierra Leone Government."[25]

Thus the APC now have 46 ministers, in a parliament of 103 members - 84 elected ordinary members, 12 Paramount Chief members, 7 members appointed by the President.

At Banjul Airport, President Siaka Stevens justified the size of his cabinet because in the African context, the factors to be taken into account in determining the size of the cabinet are tribal and educational. And now he is planning to "retire from an increasingly impossible situation."[26] As reported in *West Africa*, "Sierra Leone's economic situation has never been as bad in all its existence as an independent country...to the point that observers are starting to shake their heads in despair.[27] It is also reported that over 50 people were killed and 100 injured in fighting in the provinces during the general elections.[28]

In the last chapter Dr. Raymon Sarif Easmon, Rev. M.G.M. Cole and Professor Awunor Renner, three independent and erudite luminaries of Sierra Leone, summarized the scourge of the All Peoples Congress Party since they came to power in 1968 to 1977 when it became crystal clear that

President Siaka Stevens was firmly committed to the one-party system. These learned Sierra Leoneans, representing three different professions, were unanimous in their conclusion that the first opposition political party to form a government in Sierra Leone, the APC has been a dismal failure, a betrayal of Sierra Leoneans who voted for them, as it has now become a colossal incubus.

Despite these incontestable evidence, we still had to give the APC the benefit of any lingering doubts, by an examination of the first general elections under the one-party system. Once again, we are confronted with a plethora of unbelievable atrocities, malpractices, kidnappings of candidates, corruption in the primary selections of candidates, flagrant abuse of power by the son of the President, who was also alleged to have followed victims of bullet wounds into hospital and removed blood plasma that was being administered to intensive care patients during previous general elections. That President Siaka Stevens is alleged to have snapped at a pressman that he was not his son's keeper, is true. Yet it is a hollow excuse for a head of state whose son is accused of serious infractions of the electoral law.

The first decade of the APC rule was fraught with the most diabolical abuse of power. The second decade began similarly. The singular tragedy of the second decade is the allegations of wholesale corruption by civil servants, which have necessitated the appointment of three commissions of enquiry by the government. Whether the commissions exculpate them or not, the propaganda surrounding the Vouchergate and the Squandergate scandals have inflicted irreparable damage to the prestige of the civil service, the foundation of any government.

One of the propaganda tools of the APC in 1966 was that the SLPP was corrupt. By smear campaigns in the party paper, *We Yone*, and other pamphleteers, top civil servants in the SLPP Government were vilified and persecuted. When the National Reformation Council came to power, the APC and their supporters and advisors, employed subterranean methods to engineer massive commissions of enquiry into the assets of SLPP ministers, and top civil servants, including, those that Justice Forster called the "blue-eyed boys of Sir Albert," Undoubtedly, there were strictures here and there. But the integrity of the civil service remained untarnished.

In his notorious subversive elements broadcast that preceded the beginning of the mass arrests of SLPP members and civil servants who worked in the SLPP government, including persons associated with them, President Siaka Stevens warned the nation about subversive elements who refuse to accept a change of government. Vigilance, according to him, was the prize the people had to pay because the "kitty is empty." The financial situation of Sierra Leone after sixteen years of APC rule, is far from being an improvement on the empty kitty the APC inherited. Perhaps it is, otherwise how else could the government admit that about $60m of government funds have been misappropriated?

Another disturbing phenomenon of the All Peoples Congress Party rule is the perversion of the army and the police force. We have discovered many cases in which allegations have been made by responsible citizens that the army and the police have been bribed by the APC government for faithfully carrying out the party's wishes. Other allegations are by the Honorable Salia Jusu Sheriff, Reverend M.G.M. Cole, Mohamed O. Taqui and a *West Africa* correspondent in the issue of the 21st June 1982, e.g., that "under the watchful eyes of senior police officers, Akibo Betts (and) fellow stick-toting thugs...beat up...several hundred elderly women..." mercilessly.

In order to get the loyalty of the armed forces, President Siaka Stevens has also appointed the Force Commander and the Commissioner of Police as members of parliament. The army and the police have now become constituencies of the APC. This is a sad development and does not augur well for morale and discipline in the armed forces. These distressing developments when added to the low level to which the judiciary has been reduced by the perversions of the All Peoples Congress Party, mock any pretensions of the rule of law in Sierra Leone today under the All Peoples Congress Party Government.

Chapter 14 Notes

1. *West Africa*, 26th October, 1981, p. 2488.

2. *West Africa*, 29th March, 1982, p. 2488.

3. *Ibid.*, p. 2488.

4. *West Africa*, 16th November, 1981, p. 2705.

5. *West Africa*, 19th April, 1982, p. 1054.

6. *Ibid.*, p. 1054.

7. *Ibid.*, p. 1054.

8. *Ibid.*, p. 1054.

9. *West Africa*, 26th April, 1982, p. 115.

10. *Ibid.*, p. 115.

11. *Ibid.*, p. 115.

12. *Ibid.*, p. 115.

13. Africa Agenda Vol. 1, No. 1, May 1982.

14. *West Africa*, 26th April, 1982, p. 1172.

15. *West Africa*, 17th May, 1982.

16. *Ibid.*, 1982.

17. *Ibid.*, 1982.

18. *Ibid.*, p. 1298.

19. *West Africa*, 14th June, 1982, p. 1579.

20. *Ibid.*, p. 1579.

21. *West Africa*, 21st June, 1982, p. 1630.

22. *Ibid.*, p. 1630.

23. *Ibid.*, p. 1631.

24. *Ibid.*, p. 1631.

25. *West Africa*, 12th July, 1982.

26. *West Africa*, 23rd August, 1982, p. 2148.

27. *West Africa*, 10th May, 1982.

28. *West Africa*, 23rd August, 1982, p. 2148.

CHAPTER 15

QUO VADIS AFRICA ?

In his analysis of the record of the All People's Congress Party for the past nine years ended May 1977, Dr. Easmon made the point that although it is incontrovertible that people everywhere should govern themselves, "experience of Africa has by no means proved that nations are necessarily happier and more prosperous under indigenous than under colonial rule." In the preface, we also enquire whether, in the light of the upheavals that have beset the continent in two decades of independence, Africans are still of the view that self-government is better than good-government? Personally, I still hold the view I held over twenty years ago.

Under the United States Aid Program, the author attended a seminar in man-power planning in the United States, in 1961. The *Trentonian* of 11th May, 1961, reported one of our seminars in New Jersey as follows:

> The visitors who are participating in a training course in manpower problems being conducted by the State Division of Employment Security will be in Trenton all this week. The Meeting with the Commissioners include a question-and-answer session... Mayor Holland's enquiry into the Congo situation and the *African colonies readiness for independence* produced dynamic results. To his feet sprang Sheikh Batu Daramy, Deputy Labor Commissioner from Sierra Leone, the world's newest nation. DARAMY who some observers said bore a resemblance to murdered Congo Premier Patrice Lumumba, said he left it up to the people to determine their own readiness. "I don't think that it was intended that one

nation should subjugate another and decide when a country is ready for independence," Daramy said. (Emphasis mine).[1]

A couple of days earlier, at a press conference in Boston, I told the audience that there could be no question about the readiness of any country for independence. This was borne out by American history. The British never consented that the American colonies were ready for independence, but the Americans thought differently on their readiness or 'ripeness' (as some people called it) for independence.

Africans had centuries of well developed civilizations before the advent of Europeans. When they went to Africa, Europeans plundered their valuable art treasures and exported them to Europe, destroyed what could not be exported so as to remove all evidence of the pristine glory of the people, desecrated their sacred institutions, and denigrated all aspects of their cultures. By those methods they hoped to establish the supremacy of their race and culture, and to justify the enslavement of Africans to the plantations of America, Otherwise, what justification could they have had for enslaving the African other than imperialist fabrications of his inferiority.

From time immemorial, Europeans relegated Africans to the level of apes. Their intellectuals laid the foundation of what was to become Eurocentric racist doctrines about the inferiority of the Africans, William Shakespeare, one of England's greatest playwrights, referred to Indians in the *Tempest* as, "savages and men of India, whom stripes may move not kindness." Elsewhere in the *Tempest* Prospero (the white man) was chastising Caliban (the native in one of the colonies) when he said, "I taught you language, and your profit on it, is, you know how to curse me." This admonition may well apply to twentieth century Afro-Caribbean Pan-Africanists, Marcus Garvey, W.E.B.-DuBois, Sir Nnamdi Azikiwe, I.T.A. Wallace-Johnson, Jomo Kenyatta, Sir Albert Margai, Kwame Nkrumah.

A more direct attack on Africans began much earlier in the eighteenth century. This is what the English philosopher David Hume (1711-1776) wrote about Africans:

> I am apt to suspect the negroes and in general all the other species of men (for there are four or five different kinds) to be naturally inferior to the white. There was never a civilized

nation of any other complexion than white, nor even any individual eminent either in action or speculation. No ingenious manufactures among them, no arts, no sciences. On the other hand, the most rude and barbarous of the whites, such as the ancient GERMANS, the present TARTARS, have still something eminent about them... Not to mention our colonies, there are NEGRO slaves dispersed all over EUROPE, of which none ever discovered any symptoms of ingenuity, tho' low people without education will start up amongst us, and distinguish themselves in every profession. In JAMAICA indeed they talk of one negro as a man of parts and learning; but 'tis likely he is admired for very slender accomplishments like a parrot, who speaks a few words plainly.[2]

Similar racist tendencies were developing on the continent of Europe. Wilhelm Friedrich Hegel (1770-1831) a renowned philosopher, added his Germanic contribution. For Hegel, the African neither had nor belonged to world history. Among other things Hegel wrote:

The characteristic feature of the negroes is that their consciousness has not yet reached an awareness of any substantial objectivity for example, of God or the law - in which the will of man could participate and in which he could become aware of his own being...All our observations of African man show him as living in a stage of savagery and barbarism, and he remains in this state to the present day. The negro is an example of animal man in all his savagery and lawlessness, and if we wish to understand him at all, we must put aside all European attitudes.[3]

France was not to be out-done. Arthur De Gobineau (1816-1882) even likened the African to a monkey when he wrote that:

a negro from the West Coast of Africa, tall, strong-looking, with thick-set limbs and a tendency to fat... When we look for a moment at an individual of this type, we are involuntarily reminded of the structure of the monkey, and are inclined to admit that the negro races of West Africa come from a stock that has nothing in common, except the human form, with the Mongolian.[4]

African students who avidly memorize Kant, Hegel, Hume, or those who translate Skakespeare into Swahili should take a second look at them. They do not mean the African well. What is more, they are regarded as eminent scholars among their peoples, and therefore their pronouncements are taken as gospel truth and acted upon accordingly. For example, according to the *Encyclopedia Britannica*, Gobineau's "theory of racial determinism had enormous influence upon the subsequent development of racist theories and practices in Western Europe."[5]

Imperialism was founded on these racist ideologies. European colonization was justified on the grounds that the white man was to rule other races because they were inferior to the white man, as enunciated by Kant, Hegel, Hume, Shakespeare, and quite a few others like Trevor Roper of Oxford University. Those European philosophers laid the academic foundation for the justification of racism and apartheid against which Africans rebel, even today. Arising from this myth, European colonialists justified colonialism on the grounds that it was good government and that was, according to them, what the people desired.

> What people wanted, according to Lord Lloyd, British High Commissioner in Egypt, was not independence but good administration which alone can help them to live better:
>
> 'Good administration is their only desire and concern; and it is because we have allowed administration to be obscured by political issues that we have brought such heavy troubles upon the shoulders of all concerned. In all these countries the real problem has been administrative and we have chosen to regard it as political. Indeed political changes would have no more remedial effect upon the discontents than the man in the moon...[6]

Like the present one-party systems in Africa which are repugnant to Africans, the European so-called 'good government' in Africa was equally repugnant, because its raison d'etre as enunciated by Lord Lugard in the Dual Mandate was that the tropics should be

> 'the heritage of mankind,' and felt that neither, on the one hand, has the suzerain power a right to their exclusive exploitation nor, on the other hand, have the races which inherited them a right to deny their bounties to those who need them.[7]

Since "this racist and anachronistic image of Africa... a lingering Europe-centered colonial view which perceives Africa as an extension of the European sphere of influence...[8] was formulated by the early European philosophers, it has gained currency up to this day. Most Westerners still regard Africa as the dark continent and its people, like Shakespeare's "savages and men of India, whom stripes may move not kindness." And some academics still believe today that Africans have not yet reached the stage of "backwardness." Therefore, Westminster type of democracy is definitely out of the question in Africa. These smear campaigns against Africans fortified their resolve to rid themselves of their superior masters, and to manage or mismanage their affairs.

While I do not accept this colonial proposition that good government is better than self-government, the converse that self-government is better than good government may be suitably reformulated to read: self-government is the stepping stone to good government. The road has been fraught with immense obstacles, the one-party being the most obnoxious, as we have unravelled.

Although impressive progress has been made in economic development in all emergent nations in Africa since independence, formidable problems have emerged, tribalism, inter-territorial disputes, military interventions. One solution of some of these problems has been the one-party system of government, which has created serious problems in political development. It is in this connection that Dr. Easmon also drew attention to Dr. Jean Zeigler in *We Yone*, the All Peoples Congress Party paper of March 1966, with the approval of Mr. Siaka Stevens, as he noted. He quoted Dr. Zeigler as follows:

> Most African regimes show a tendency to develop as if by fate, into tyrannies. The stages are as follows: Emergency, the suppression of basic liberties, one-party system, dictatorial powers for the president, finally tyranny of one man or of a group of men who fight for survival (political or even physical) against a whole people becoming more and more discontented. (Parenthesis supplied).

In all cases where the single party has been introduced, it has been dominated by a single individual who pretends to have all the charisma and qualities of leadership. In course of time, he is identified with the party as the latter is with the state and therefore, becomes synonymous with the state. He becomes secretary-general of the party for life and also the sole candidate for presidency. Around him is a coterie of opportunists, hired thugs and professional privilege seekers. They constitute the executive caucus of the party. They make and break aspirants to executive positions in the establishment. In the course of time the party becomes more important than the state and civil servants who are trained professionals in their jobs are expected to take orders from these party functionaries who invariably are misfits. This is the genesis of the clash between the party stalwarts and top civil servants.

There is no redeeming feature in the one-party or single-party system. All the countries that have experimented with the one-party system have tended to concentrate power in the hands of the head of state who in most cases, as in Roman law, had the *jus vitae nicisque*, the power of life and death.

In the words of Frank Fanon,

> In a certain number of under-developed countries the parliamentary game is faked from the beginning. Powerless economically, unable to bring about the existence of coherent social relations, and standing on the principle of its domination as a class, the bourgeoisie chooses the solution that seems to it the easiest, that of the SINGLE PARTY. It does not yet have the quiet conscience and the calm that economic power and the control of the state machine alone can give. It does not create a state that reassures the ordinary citizen, but rather one that rouses his anxiety.
>
> The state, which by its strength and discretion ought to inspire confidence and disarm and lull everyone to sleep, on the contrary seeks to impose itself in spectacular fashion. It makes a display, it jostles people and bullies them, thus intimating to the citizen that he is in continual danger. The SINGLE PARTY is the modern form of the dictatorship of the bourgeoisis, unmasked, unpainted, inscrupulous, and cynical. (Capitals mine).[9]

The heart of the matter is, that only a multi-party system of government contains the fundamental criteria of democracy. A country is democratic, only if its rulers treat human beings as human beings, i.e., where there is "Protection of Fundamental Rights and Freedoms" of the individual as was agreed in the Sierra Leone Independence Constitution of 1961 between the British Government and the people of Sierra Leone through their leader, Sir Milton Margai, and enacted as follows:

> Protection of right to life, Protection from arbitrary arrest or detention, Protection from slavery and forced labor, Protection from inhuman treatment, Protection from deprivation of property, Protection for privacy of home and other property, Protection to secure protection of law, Protection of freedom of conscience, Protection of freedom of expression, Protection of freedom of assembly and association, Protection from discrimination on the grounds of race...

And where there is a free and impartial judiciary not subject to the whims and caprices of dictators.

Year in and year out, the abuse of individual liberties has continued unabated. Fortunately, although there is an outward appearance of tranquility, yet the peoples everywhere are seething for a second revolution. And that is where Africa is going. Africans did not fight colonialism in order to be enslaved by their kith and kin.

Since the All Peoples Congress one-party system is not institutionalized, the Westminster theory of the collective responsibility of cabinet does not apply to the one-party. Collective conscience is an essential attribute of cabinet responsibility in a democratic multi-party system, because there is equality among the members. Each member is a potential prime minister, because the latter is only *primus inter pares*, leader among equals. This automatic mechanism is lacking in a one-party system, where there is only one dominant figure that demands obedience. In this system, the members of the executive are kept in line, not by virtue of their individual and unfettered conviction, but by fear of a dominant president, to whom the members have surrendered their initiative.

Evidence of this tendency can be seen in the All Peoples Congress Party cabinet which is now in shambles. With two vice presidents, each of whom is vying for precedence, there is no clear cut line of succession. According to the President (Siaka Stevens), in the matter of the supersession of the Honorable Salia Jusu Sheriff, the post of vice president rotates. And so the two key posts next to the president are filled in accordance with the rule of "musical chairs", determinable by the unpredictable president.

While it is conceivable to rotate the post of prime minister where there is only a president and a prime minister, in the case of president and two vice presidents, (which in Sierra Leone is superfluous any way), the latter

276

should not be "for grabs" as the Americans say, unless in an acting capacity. Otherwise, the door is wide open for unwarranted and unhealthy competition as is happening in Sierra Leone today under the APC Government. It is now a government of risk and uncertainty.

Sooner or later, the fragile props collapse and the system disintegrates irreparably. That is the state of affairs today under President Siaka Stevens' one-party oligarchy. The Cabinet appointed commissions of inquiry into alleged fraudulent misappropriation of government funds. Now the Cabinet is sharply divided because they cannot agree on the action to be taken on the reports of the "Squandergate" commissions of inquiry. This deplorable impasse was reported in West Africa, in November 1984.

> But there is still one question which is being asked by well-informed people: how far can the government go to try someone for corruption and sack 95 civil servants? Well-connected sources told West Africa that a row erupted at a recent Cabinet meeting when a senior minister told his colleagues that the government had no right to try a few people for corruption when "all of us are corrupt." The senior cabinet minister was quoted as saying that the trial and conviction of the civil servants was a serious indictment on the administrative integrity of the nation. "I can challenge anyone here to stand up and deny that he has not squandered government money," the minister was quoted as threatening his colleagues.[10]

It will be recalled that President Siaka Stevens himself estimated the alleged squandering of government funds at a conservative figure of over Le60 million (then $60 million), What concerns the people of Sierra Leone is that a "senior" member of cabinet has challenged the authority of the cabinet to try accused civil servants, as reported in *West Africa* because "all of us are corrupt." What the honorable gentleman was saying is that in Anglo-Saxon jurisprudence, "He who comes to equity, must come with clean hands." In a parliamentary democracy, when a "senior member" of the cabinet accuses his colleagues that, and I again quote, "I can challenge anyone here to stand up and deny that he has not squandered government money," the only honorable course of action left, is for the government to resign and go to the polls to renew their mandate. In an uninstitutionalized oligarchy, such as a one-party system, such allegations are the accepted norm. That is what makes the one-party system of government unacceptable to democrats.

According to Tigar and Levy, the

> 'jurisprudence of insurgency' describes a certain kind of jurisprudential activity, in which a group challenging the prevailing system of social relations no longer seeks to reform it but rather to overthrow it and replace it with another.[11]

This proposition fits the one-party states for two reasons: (a) the one-party insurgents do not replace the existing system because they cannot reform it, they start off by discrediting the existing order and dislocating it for their selfish ends. Since they came to power by violence, their stay in power is by violence; (b) the contradictions in the one-party state are basically 'institutional'. Institutionalization is the capability of a system to adapt and adjust itself to its environment. This is, the *raison d'etre* of a multi-party system, which is lacking in the one-party state.

The battle for freedom has still to be won. The one-party conspiracies are on the decline because, like imperialism, they contain contradictions which are gnawing at their foundations, one of which Dr. Welfling identified as non-institutionalization, or what one may call, a lack of multi-partism. The peoples are becoming resentful of the one-party lords for the curtailment of their fundamental freedoms of speech, assembly, association, press, movement, and the freedom to challenge despotic rulers.

The African single-party or one-party systems are now basking in the twilight zone, because they never were institutionalized systems as such, but a collection of self-seeking individuals who combined to mislead the populace and seize power for personal aggrandizement. In an Essay entitled *"Political Institutionalization: Comparative Analysis on African Party Systems*, Dr. Mary B. Welfling defined institutionalization as "a process which occurs as elements continue to interact in some relatively stable pattern..." In the African context, she stressed that, "unless a party system can accommodate existing parties or adapt to new articulated interests, it will be unable to persist and function effectively as a system and hence become institutionalized."[12]

As time goes on, "African party systems are becoming increasingly indistinct from the government,"[13] and therefore ceasing to be institutions in their own right. Adaptability is the fourth criteria of a viable institutionalized political system. She goes on:

> An institutionalized party system demonstrates the ability to adjust to both internal and external strains (intrasystem and extrasystem aspect) unless a party system can accommodate existing parties or adapt to new articulated interests, it will be unable to persist and function effectively as a system, and hence become institutionalized. (Parenthesis supplied).[14]

Furthermore, "The more years that a party is the only legal one, the less adaptable the system is."[15]

One or single-party systems are a passing phase in Africa, because they are not institutionalized. Since they owe their existence to violence they would require force to remain in power. The more pressure they exert on the people, the more unpopular they become. Sooner or later, the people rise in revolt. This is the logical outcome of the jurisprudence of insurgency we referred to earlier on in this Chapter. Without exception, all the countries in Africa that have experimented the one-party system have practiced the most inhuman atrocities to stay in power. Rival parties are banned and the leaders arrested, tortured, and gaoled without recourse to the legal system. Even in those rare cases where *habeas corpus* is part of the legal system, it is ignored. When international pressure is brought to bear on the government to release political prisoners it fabricates trumped up charges of treason, treason felony and misprision of treason, as occurred in Sierra Leone since Siaka Stevens came to power. Witnesses are suborned to give false evidence against the accused.

The constitutions in most of these countries contain provision for the protection of fundamental human rights of freedom of speech, association, religion, press. Yet the constitutions have been flouted with reckless abandon that they are now instruments of torture. As it is, valuable foreign exchange which is so essential to pay for the external costs of the goods and services that are required to lay the foundation for infrastructural development is being dissipated on arms and ammunition to keep despots in power.

Politically, unless and until democratic systems of government replace the one-party oligarches, the economic future of Africa will be bleak. That is where Africa is heading. The one-party system has failed lamentably and should be abandoned. The problem now is not that its adherents contest this necessity, they are frightened of its consequences. They have been riding a tiger and have to keep going or else the tiger would turn round to investigate what is riding it. Even President Siaka Stevens has exhausted his resilience, because his one-party is a disastrous failure, The immediate future for the people of Sierra Leone is bleak and is fraught with imponderables.

Economically, the one-party system is a major constraint on the mobility of the factors of production, equitable distribution of resources, freedom of speech, all of which are crucially essential to smooth implementation of collective self-reliance upon which the Lagos Plan of Action depends. For instance, for the people to rely on one another for collective action, there must be mutual trust and confidence. Where the people have been coerced into some artificial association by force of arms, they lack the mutual trust and confidence which are the cohesive force that unites people in free associations.

Since the African countries became independent, they have been striving strenuously to reverse the legacies of colonialism° In the economic field they have achieved remarkable resolutions in the United Nations Organization, such as the new international economic order. As usual, the developed North have not lived up to the laudable pronouncements contained therein. As a result, the Organization of African Unity have published what the African states consider, as the panacea of their economic problems from 1983-2008, known as the *Lagos Plan of Action*. The Economic Commission for Africa which provided the material for this comprehensive study, has published a caveat, that a meaningful economic development plan requires a democratic system of government. The relevant sections read as follows:

> Similarly, the socio-political milieu in which the individual exists simultaneously as a generator and consumer of wealth

has to be tuned so as to bring out of society, while at the same time offering society, the best of life. This means that at the national level the democratization of the entire social, economic and political sub-systems is a necessary feature of Africa's future.[16]

Therefore a radical change of the African social, economic and political environment is urgently called for to lay the foundation of individual and collective self-reliance and self-sustainment.[17]

(c)   Improvement of the political and social environment.

...the creation of a peaceful and serene political and social climate is a must if the ultimate goal of development is to be achieved...the lack of social, political and economic justice would nullify the very achievement of sovereignty...to ensure

(a)   the full participation of the people in all the dimensions of a genuine development;

(b)   the creation of equal opportunities for all; and

(c)   innovation from within Africa.[18]

an improved political and social climate is not merely a guarantee for political stability but a *sine qua non* for the blooming of the genius of the African people...[19]

The democratization of development is as important at the subregional and regional levels as at the national level.

At the present rate of socio-political deterioration of the continent, Africa would present a "sorry picture of 'a resigned, depleted and self-pitying continent," in the year 2008, To avert this catastrophe, "at the national level the democratization of the entire social, economic and political sub-systems is a necessary feature of Africa's future."[20] These are the prognosis of the Economic Commission for Africa. It is hardly likely that this would come about by peaceful means, given the present entrenched positions of the despots and their implacable bodyguards and leaches. Nor is the one-party system capable of bringing about a democratic system. Nothing short of revolutions of drastic dimensions would bring this about. The disciples of the almighty one-party state are loath to share power with others.   In the circumstance, these contradictions will generate the revolutionary purifying solution to our present predicaments.

When this battle has been won, then Africans will give their undivided attention to the economic development of the continent.

Chapter 15 Notes

1.   *The Trentonian*, May 11, 1961, New Jersey, USA.

2.   Hume, David *Essays: Moral, Political, and Literary*, 2 Vols., Longmans, Green and Company, London, 1898 1:252 N.3.

3.   Hegel, Friedrich G.W., *Lectures on the Philosophy of World History*, trans. by H.B. Nisbet, Cambridge University Press, Cambridge 1975, p. 177.

4.   Gobineau, Arthur de, *The Inequality of the Human Race*, trans. by Adrian Collins, Howard Fertig Inc., New York, 1967, pp. 106-7.

5.   *Encyclopedia Britannica*, Micropaedia Ready Reference and Index, Vol. IV, Chicago University Press, p. 590.

6.   Quoted by Henry Grimal, in *Decolonization: The British, French, Dutch, and Belgian Empires. 1919-1963*, trans. by Stephen de Vos, Westview Press Boulder, Colorado, USA, 1965, p. 26.

7.   Quoted by the editor of *Transnational Enterprises: Their Impact on the Third World Societies and Cultures*, in an Article by Ali Mazrui.

8.   Browne, Robert S., Article Entitled, "Africa's Economic Future: Development or Disintegration," in *World Policy Journal*, Summer 1984, New York, New York 10017, p. 796.

9.   Fanon, Franz, *The Wretched of the Earth*, Grove Press, Inc. New York, 1961, p. 164.

10.   *West Africa*, No. 3508 November 14, 1984, 53 Holborn Viaduct, London 2CIA2FD, p. 2253.

11.   Michael Tigar and Madeleine R. Levy, *Law and the Rise of Capitalism*, Monthly Review Press, New York, New York, 10011, USA, 1977, p. 23.

12.   Welfling, Mary B., Essay Entitled, Political Institutionalization, Comparative Analysis of African Party Systems, *Comparative Politics*, Series No. 01G41, Vol. 4, Sage Publications Inc., California 1973, p. 23.

13.   *Ibid.*, p. 19.

14.   *Ibid.*, p. 23.

15.   *Ibid.*, p. 24.

16. Economic Commission for Africa, *Economic Commission for Africa and Africa's Development 1983-2008. A Preliminary Perspective Study*, Addis Ababa, April 1983, p. 95.

17. *Ibid.*, p. 96.

18. *Ibid.*, p. 97.

19. *Ibid.*, p. 97.

20. *Ibid.*, p. 97.

APPENDIX I

A Letter addressed to the Commissioner
of Police by the leaders of the Sierra
Leone Peoples Party before the General
Elections of 1977.

Dear Hon. Commissioner,

From reports received after nomination day it is now clear that apart from a few districts where the Senior Police Officers concerned used their personal initiative to ensure peaceful nominations, your office failed to prevent the APC from obstructing the nomination of other candidates, particularly in the Northern Province where your senior officers stood by and allowed the APC to use the most modern weapons to gun down and prevent other candidates from filing in their nomination papers. It is even believed that some of your ISU gunmen shed their police uniforms which had no numbers and changed into APC red vests to raid and shoot other candidates from nomination.

In a number of areas: Bonthe for instance, not only were your officers made to aid and abet the APC in their wanton attacks, but they actually arrested all the SLPP and independent candidates on charges of riotous conduct to keep them away from being nominated. In this regard, as if to clear all doubts about your commitment to the APC government in which without precedent you serve as a Cabinet Minister, you allowed members of your force to form the vanguard of the outrageous and revolting triumphalism with which the APC stormed into Freetown...April, 1977 from their criminal conquest, not of an enemy, but of their own country.

What we have written so far is now a matter of the past. More important, however, is the current public knowledge that the APC having returned itself unopposed in 34 out of 85 constituencies for ordinary members without an election, have now made plans to send armed thugs and the notorious killer-wing of the ISU to rape, shoot and terrorize voters in the Southern and Eastern provinces on election day so as to manipulate for the APC a semblance of a victory at the actual pools for the remnant of the seats to be contested. The APC is desperately looking for legitimacy, which it has already forfeited by seizing four districts in the Northern Province and one in the South without election.

The details of the plan are that the thugs and gunmen who returned the APC unopposed in Kambia District, would invade Kailahun District, those from Bombali, Kenema District, the thugs of Port Loko will attack Bo District and those from Tonkolili, Kono District, Moyamba and Pujehun would be suitably dealt with by the current reigns of terror of Augustine Sandy, Harry Williams and Francis Minah.

These plans are already well known to the public, both in Freetown and in the districts concerned, and as the guardian of law and order in this country, it is your duty to stop their implementation forthwith to save this country from the further shedding by the APC of the blood of their innocent children.

Already in full view of the police stations at Masiaka Village you have allowed APC party thugs to set up road barriers at which vehicles and passengers particularly those travelling from the Southern and Eastern Provinces are search (sic), molested and robbed.

In the pre-nomination statement by the SLPP, there was a warning that there was a potential of violence in the sequence of attack and resistance and much as the inhabitants in the Southern and Eastern Provinces do not have the arms which the APC have given to the thugs and the government to the ISU, they nevertheless have a duty to defend their towns and villages, for what is more glorious than that men should die to protect the lives of their wives and children, and the sanctity of the shrines of their fathers...

Signed: S. Jusu Sheriff
            Dr. H.M. Conteh
            Alhaj M.S. Mustapha

(Source: *The People*, published by Julius Cole, May 5, 1977, Freetown, Sierra Leone).

APPENDIX II

A Letter by Sheikh Batu Daramy,
published in *West Africa*, May 24, 1982.

Dear Sir:

THE ROAD TO SERFDOM

...That the one-party system can be democratic is the wildest contradiction any one can conceive. What is democracy? It was defined in most constitutions granted to the former British colonies on the eve of independence. It consisted of freedoms of speech, assembly, association, movement, religion.

The one-party stifles opposition and is the stepping stone to despotism. In the words of Harold Laski (Grammar of Politics), some people would rather see their mothers stabbed than to forego power. Once they become president, the one-party ensures that no one else shall aspire to this post, on pain of being charged with treason and executed summarily. To avoid this eventuality, the United States Constitution provides at Article XXII Sec. 1 that "no person shall be elected to the post of the President more than twice..."

The colonial system was the best example of a one-party state, because Whitehall in London for instance, dictated what should or should not happen in the colonies. The opposition of the British subjects counted for naught. Any attempt to challenge the authority of Whitehall was interpreted in some cases as sedition. For example, I.T.A. Wallace Johnson and Nnamdi Azikiwe (Sierra Leone and Nigeria respectively) were convicted of sedition for writing an article in the *African Morning Post* of May 15, 1936, entitled "Has the African a God?" They maintained that the European's God is deceit, etc. In Court, Zik defied the British Government, that "The fight for liberty has just begun in Africa". (Reproduced by Dr. Peter Omari in

Kwame Nkrumah). So that in the heat of the Great Depression, when Great Britain was fortifying her stranglehold on the colonies at the Ottawa Conference of 1932 and could therefore brook no nonsense from colonial subjects, stalwart Africans were challenging the British Government's right to "bestride the narrow world, while we petty men" (peeped around) "to find ourselves dishonorable graves." (Shakespeare).

The one-party system is the very antithesis of freedom. In my native Sierra Leone, under the APC One-Party Constitution, everyone is compelled to become a member of that party. Some of us would have to be skinned alive in our SLPP garbs than be forced into any other party. But the dismal irony in Sierra Leone is that the APC Government detained some of us including me, for periods of up to four years because we civil servants were alleged to have meddled in politics. President Siaka Stevens when leader of the Opposition, castigated civil servants who took part in politics. Yet his One-Party Constitution makes it conditional under Section 139 (1) and (2) for promotion to the top echelon of the civil service, e.g., Financial Secretary, Secretary to the Cabinet, Establishment Secretary, Development Secretary, Solicitor General, for the aspirants to belong to the APC. This glaring contradiction and ridiculous *volte face* would appear to be a necessary ingredient of one-party democracy.

In Sierra Leone, since the APC came to power in 1968, we have witnessed the worst form of government imaginable. The one-party which they introduced in 1978 has only intensified an already despotic oligarchy. The one-party government has been wallowing from miasma to miasma. Even the most stalwart APC one-party supporters are completely disillusioned. The one-party constitution merely legalized government by selections, euphemistically called, elections--a disgraceful travesty of everything that we fought for and achieved on independence. The first general selections held in Sierra Leone since the one-party constitutional fraud has been a disgraceful dismal failure and so the general selections have, I am told, been cancelled.

Even in the heyday of British imperialism, we criticized the British one-party control over us, as orchestrated from the Colonial Office in

London. Can any one dare criticize President Siaka Stevens' one-party fraud today? How can there be progress without criticism?

Sheikh Batu Daramy
Maryland, USA

POSTSCRIPT

On the eve of publication of this book, I read some startling reports on Sierra Leone in Africa Confidential and the London Observer, two prestigious British newspapers. In view of their supreme importance to the constitutional development of Sierra Leone, I have included them as postscript.

The one-party system of government in Sierra Leone, has concentrated power in the hands of a clique of the All Peoples Congress Party, the party which has been in power for the past 17 years. This has led to "economic and political degeneracy", which *Africa Confidential* of 28th November, 1984, also describes as "institutionalized corruption." It has plagued this potentially wealthy nation since the opposition All Peoples Congress Party came to power in 1968 and began to pervert established constitutional and judicial practices. *Africa Confidential* summarised the impending revolution thus:

> Certainly all the ingredients of a populist coup are present: an atrophied, corrupt one-party system, a concentration of vast wealth in the hands of a few, a widespread popular resentment...increasing prices and shortages of food, declining incomes for the impoverished majority of the population, and a president whose life expectancy is short.

The *London Observer* of 27th January, 1985, reported (two months later), in a feature article entitled, "Row shakes diamond state rulers", by Richard Hall, that "it is reported that earlier this month Stevens called in the head of the Army, Major-General J. S. Momoh, and invited him to take over the reins. This idea flopped when senior officers refused to endorse it." For the first time in the history of post-colonial Africa, the head of state has invited the army to take over the reins of government. And yet Siaka Stevens indicted us of treason, treason felony, and misprision of treason for alleged incitement of Brigadier David Lansana to "take over" the government of Sierra Leone. President Siaka Stevens is inciting the army to take over the government and therefore, he is committing treason, for which he ought to be indicted. In God's good time the army will certainly take over without being prodded by a desperate government.

Already the International Bank for Reconstruction and Development, the International Monetary Fund, the International Development Agency, Food and Agricultural Organization, "have no confidence in President Stevens' ability to preside over any significant economic rehabilitation," according to *Africa Confidential.*

After the 1977 General 'Selections,' the APC Government declared that

> The results of the Referendum, nationwide, reaffirm the long-expressed desire of the majority of the population to have a cohesive political system which will harness all possible resources to put the country firmly on the road to uninterrupted development. (See p. 235)

In 1978, the One-party Constitution was enacted by parliament. In 1984, Sierra Leone is on the brink of economic disaster, not "uninterrupted development" as prophesied, but "economic and political degeneracy", according to *Africa Confidential.* As a result, the APC Government has been compelled to devalue the Leone by 140% from Le.2.50 to $1, to Le.6 to $1, because, as President Siaka Stevens declared to *West Africa* of March 4th 1985, "They know we are hard-up, they know we don't have money,..." In his inaugural broadcast as Prime Minister of Sierra Leone, Siaka Stevens moaned that the Sierra Leone Peoples Party had left the kitty empty. After 17 years, Siaka Stevens is pleading with West Africa (March 4, 1985) that, "Where are we going to get $5m. now?" The Sierra Leone Peoples Party Government rejected the recommendations of Dr. Lloynes of the Bank of England, for the establishment of a monetary institute and instead established a Central Bank, with all the authority that goes with it. The author played a significant role as Deputy Financial Secretary in this exercise. The All Peoples Congress Party has divested the Bank of all authority over the monetary system, as if Lloynes was right. That is why Sierra Leone cannot pay its way.

The one-party system of government which President Stevens continues to glorify because, "we are a nation in a state of emergency-emergency for roads, for hospitals, for education...." (*West Africa*, March 4, 1985), has resulted in the worst form of dictatorship. India remains the largest democracy, even though it is fraught with emergencies, no less onerous than Sierra Leone. According to President Siaka Stevens, "Democracy means different things in different parts of the world." That may be so. But among Western academics whom we pretend to emulate, democracy has only one meaning, i.e., *partitocrazia*. (See page xliii)

We do not quarrel with David Apter's quotation of Almond and Powell, 1966 in his (Apter) book, *The Politics of Modernization*, that the 'voyage towards democracy and welfare' will be 'long and uncertain', because he has no doubts that the vessel will come to port eventually. What is contested is that the road should be strewn with avoidable thorns and brambles. In the short-run, the future for Africa is undoubtedly bleak, as David Apter writes,

> Genuinely democratic political processes cannot be achieved in the immediate future but 'in the new and modernizing nations of Asia, Africa and Latin America, the process of enlightenment and democratization will have their inevitable way'.

In fact David Apter holds as 'an article of faith', that in new states, 'the long term prognosis for democracy is hopeful.'

In the case of Sierra Leone, since the All Peoples Congress Party came to power, democratic multi-party-system which they wrested from the Sierra Leone Peoples Party, has been subordinated to the whims and caprices of the APC oligarchy, headed by President Siaka Stevens, Vice-President S.I. Koroma and then Vice-President Kamara Taylor. For example, even as recently as early 1985, the judiciary which should be the guardian of the constitution, was the subject of scathing attacks by members of the Sierra Leone Bar Association in the Conference held in May, 1985. One member

> explained a whole range of issues which threaten the dispensation of justice and the independence of the judiciary including the inconvenience meted to citizens by executive detention powers as well as the police and the courts...

West Africa of 27th May, 1985 which reported the Conference, also drew attention to

> the problem of delay in the administration of justice in an attempt to stifle causes before the courts. Various methods and tactics are employed to do this, among them, frequent adjournments...absences of the trial judge for various reasons ranging from illness, unavailability of court rooms,....

As we noted elsewhere in this Book, when the judicial system of a country becomes the bye-product of executive abuse of authority, the constitution itself would be in danger of becoming the machinery of oppression. The abuses to which the Bar Association drew attention are reminiscent of the alleged perversion of the Appeal Court Judges to reject our appeals during the treason trial in 1971 and for which President Siaka Stevens arrested Dr. Sarif Easmon and detained him in Pademba Road Prison.

THE DAY OF RECKONING

The day of reckoning in relation to the one-party constitution of the Sierra Leone Peoples Congress party has come to a head. The APC revolution has consumed its best stewards, such as, Dr. Mohamed Fornah who was the APC medical colonel of their guerrilla brigade in Guinea; Ibrahim Taqui the architect of the downfall of the SLPP; Brigadier John Bangura who was inveigled from his post as Charge d'Affaires in the Sierra Leone Embassy in Washington, D.C. to go and train the guerrilla army in Guinea; and ostracised other stalwarts of the APC, such as Fofanah, S.A.T. Koroma, and the one-party constitutional lawyers.

Following the death of the Second Vice-President, Kamara Taylor, only one member of the troica remains to lament the end of the APC

oligarchy, Vice-President S.I. Koroma. He is so dedicated to the Pa, that, as
reported in West Africa of April 29, 1985.

> during recent district conventions throughout the country he
> insisted in his speeches that the president must continue in
> office until his death.

Despite this conspicuous loyalty, Siaka Stevens decided that 'in this dog-eat-
dog world of today', as he was quoted by West Africa of August 12, 1985,
Brigadier Joseph Saidu Momoh and not S.I. Koroma should succeed him as
President. The reason given by Eddie Momoh in West Africa of 19th
August, 1985 was that

> Stevens could not appoint Koroma because quite apart from
> the political sycophancy, he could no longer trust him and
> feared above all, that Koroma could even put him before a
> commission of inquiry to account for his 17 unbroken years of
> stewardship of Sierra Leone as long as this would promote
> Koroma's own standing with the masses.

As Eddie Momoh quite rightly explained, that,

> Stevens had realised that, with the increasing depressed state
> of the nation and the equally increasing lack of faith in the
> country's leadership, the appointment of Koroma, or Minah-or
> any of the leading politicians for that matter-would be a
> provocation which might tumble the entire APC
> oligarchy....The leading politicians were also themselves split
> and could not decide who was best suited to succeed the
> president.

The description given of the "economic and political degeneracy" and
"institutionalised corruption" of the APC in paragraph two, supra, have
become so intolerable, that West Africa of August 12, 1985 reported that
Vice-President S.I. Koroma of all people, "complained about political
harassment and intimidation." It was also reported that S.I. Koroma was
"shouted down by several of his colleagues" and reminded of how the APC
used to harass, intimidate, and shout down the SLPP Opposition. It is in this
context of mounting indiscipline that Sierra Leoneans wholeheartedly
support Siaka Stevens' nomination of Brigadier General Momoh to redeem
Sierra Leone from what former Attorney General Abu Bakarr Kamara,

according to West Africa of August 26 of 1985, said was the "political sycophancy and indiscipline (which) were the two 'canker worms' affecting the country." And so the revolution continues to devour its architects, as "Koroma broke down and wept." This is reminiscent of Mark Antony's arrival after the assassination of Julius Caesar, and he cried:

> O mighty Caesar! dost thou lie so low? Are all thy conquests, glories, triumphs, spoils. Shrunk to this little measure? Fare thee well.

Julius Caesar - William Shakespeare

Even late comers like Dr. Abdulai Conteh, are now compelled to confess, as reported in West Africa of July 8, 1985, that "There comes a time in one's life when one should speak the truth." It is too late in the day to repent. The harm has been done. President Siaka Stevens should have been told the truth from day one, that is, on May 28th, 1968, that the one-party system cannot work. It is founded on false premises that all men think alike and are of one political ideology.

Africa is in the throes of political instability due in the main, to the desire on the part of a handful of oligarchs to impose their will on others. This may be achieved in the short-run by force of arms, as the APC realises to its sorrow. The one-party system is a system of contradictions which contain seeds of its destruction. Having concentrated power in the hands of one man, the rest of the executive jockey for positions, as top executive party members of the APC are now confessing. The contradictions in the one-party system militate against smooth succession which a multi-party system guarantees. Executive presidency which the APC one-party constitution created has become a Frankenstein monster which even S.I. Koroma is now afraid of.

In a democratic multi-party parliamentary system, the prime minister is *primus inter pares*. He owes his position to his singular leadership qualities as voted by a majority of the executive members of the party, and not because he can harness a band of thugs into a security unit. Aspirants to leadership must prove beyond all reasonable doubt, that they are qualified to lead a group of people who are democratically elected by the people. When they have exhausted their leadership potential as decided at the polls, they bow out gracefully, and seek fresh mandate from the electorate. This is what life should have taught Siaka Stevens that, a multi-party democratic system is the solution to Africa's constitutional problems. Executive presidency makes a ruler insatiably destructive. Until and unless African leaders accept this political theory the bush fires will always be burning.

THE BEGINNING OF THE END

On the 28th of November, 1985, Dr. Siaka Stevens who had been Executive President of Sierra Leone for seventeen years, handed over the reins of government to General Joseph Saidu Momoh. By his declarations and actions, General Joseph Momoh, set in train, a process of reconciliation with dissident forces that his predecessor had created. He invited Sierra Leoneans on exile to return home; e.g., Sir Banja Tejansie, former Governor General; Dr. John Karefa-Smart (M.D.); Maigore Kallon; were invited to attend the Independence Celebrations in 1988.

Freedom of the press which was ruthlessly suppressed by Siaka Stevens, was once again restored. No longer are Sierra Leoneans haunted by the Secret Police, a phenomenon of Siaka Stevens' style of government.

When the soldiers handed over the government to Siaka Stevens in 1968, he intensified the Party's propaganda to discredit the SLPP, that "the kitty is empty." Yet to demonstrate his astute economic management skill of the country, Siaka Stevens spent over $200 million in hosting the OAU in 1980, an exercise that Sierra Leone could ill afford, because it was the equivalent of the country's annual national revenue. Shortly thereafter, the nation was on the brink of bankruptcy and workers began **clamouring** for jobs and protesting the high cost of living.

In characteristic style, he advised them that "where a cow is tied there shall it eat grass". In the process of helping themselves to the grass, civil servants misappropriated over $30 million of public funds, according to President Siaka Stevens. That was the notorious Vouchegate Scandal, which was accompanied thereafter, by public unrest, because of shortages of essential commodities and rising unemployment. Again President Siaka Stevens' palliative was that when the grass is finished, the workers should go and "dreg," that is, they should fend for themselves and the devil takes the hindmost.

Once again, the flood gates of corruption were opened and civil servants helped themselves to $40 million of government funds, the infamous 'Squander Gate Scandal'. This figure was also given by President Siaka Stevens. The economy deteriorated so badly that, three years after assumption as head of state, General Saidu Momoh declared that the economy was in 'shambles', as the Million Gate Scandal set in.

Mr. Siaka Stevens said that he inherited an empty kitty, which he converted into shambles, resulting in a corrupt nation. Thus ended a reign of terror that took away the lives of countless scores of the youth of Sierra Leone, demoralised the populace, and left the economy in ruin.

INDEX

A

Adophy, M.O., 147
Africa Confidential, 158, 171-72, 175, 178, 291
Africa Publication, 209
Africa, 243-44
Akar, John, 168-70
Amnesty International, 143-44, 176, 209
Apter, David, 293
Army
    Disaffection in the, 38-39
    Incitement of the, 38
    First Military Government (The National Reformation Council), 191-93
    Second Military Government (Anti-Corruption Revolutionary Council), 96
    Indiscipline in the, 173
Arraignment, 121
Association for the Restoration and Maintenance of Democracy in Sierra Leone, 232
Awolowo, Obafemi, 12
Azikiwe, Nnamdi (former President of the Republic of Nigeria), 12

B

Bail, 121
Bangura, John, 93-94, 97, 143-44, 153, 244
Bankole-Thompson, R.J., 147
Bash-Taqui, M.O., 145
Betts, Akibo, 176, 259, 262-63
Betts, Justice Singer C.W., 115
Blake, Charles, 118, 122

Boston, Sir Henry Light-foot, 32, 71-82
Bridges, Justice Philip, 134, 136, 138
Brigade, old and new, 174
Bright, Dr. H.C. Bankole, 243
Brockway, Lord Fenner, 80, 140
Buck, N.A.P., 147, 181
Bureh, Kandeh, 122, 179-80, 185

C

Cabral, Amilcar, iii
Carter, Gwendolyn M., 13
Cartwright, John, 30, 77, 78, 80
Certificate of Compliance, 159
Chieftaincy, Paramount, 8, 48, 56, 58, 61, 78-79, 86, 166, 218
Citizens for a Better Sierra Leone, 232
Coalition government, 153
Cole, Justice Marcus, 147
Cole, M.G.M., 253
Collier, Gershon, v, 3, 29
Congo Brazzaville, 31
Constitution of Sierra Leone 1971 Act, 165-70
    Fears of executive presidency, 171
    Repeal of Appeal to Judicial Committee of the Privy Council, 166
    Resignations from the All Peoples Congress Party, 172
    1971, 157
    1978, 229-246
Conteh, (Warrant Officer), 95
Conteh, Dr. H.M., 201
Conteh, William, 233
Corruption, 276, 291
Creoles, 3, 29, 171-72

W

We Yone, 229
Welfling, Dr. Mary B., 277
West Africa, viii, 202, 205, 210,
    261-62
Williams, Chancellor, 11
Wonde, 112
Wright, Cyril Rogers, v, vi, 4, 32,
    129-30

Z

Zeigler, Jean, 273

AFRICAN STUDIES

1. Karla Poewe, The Namibian Herero: A History of Their Psychosocial Disintegration and Survival

2. Sara Joan Talis (ed. and trans.), Oral Histories of Three Secondary School Students in Tanzania

3. Randolph Stakeman, The Cultural Politics of Religious Change: A Study of the Sanoyea Kpelle in Liberia

4. Ayyoub-Awaga Bushara Gafour, My Father the Spirit-Priest: Religion and Social Organization in the Amaa Tribe (Southwestern Sudan)

5. Rosalind I. J. Hackett (ed.), New Religious Movements in Nigeria

6. Irving Hexham, Texts on Zulu Religion: Traditional Zulu Ideas About God

7. Alexandre Kimenyi, Kinyarwanda and Kirundi Names: A Semio-linguistic Analysis of Bantu Onomastics

8. G. C. Oosthuizen, (et al), Afro-Christian Religion and Healing in Southern Africa

9. Karla Poewe, Religion, Kinship, and Economy in Luapula, Zambia

10. Mario Azevedo (ed.), Cameroon and Chad in Historical and Contemporary Perspectives

11. John E. Eberegbulam Njoku, Traditionalism Versus Modernism at Death: Allegorical Tales of Africa

12. David Hirschmann, Changing Attitudes of Black South Africans Toward the United States

13. Panos Bardis, South Africa and the Marxist Movement: A Study in Double Standards

14. John E. Eberegbulam Njoku, The Igbos of Nigeria: Ancient Rites, Changes and Survival

15. W. Alade Fawole, Military Interventions in Nigerian Politics, 1966-1985: Toward Alternative Explanations

16. Kenoye Kelvin Eke, Nigeria's Foreign Policy Under Two Military Governments, 1966-1979: An Analysis of the Gowan and Muhammed/Obasanjo Regimes

17. Herbert Ekwe-Ekwe, The Biafra War: Nigeria and the Aftermath

18. I. D. Talbott, Agricultural Innovation in Colonial Africa: Kenya and the Great Depression

29. G. C. Oosthuizen and Irving Hexham (eds.), Afro-Christian Religion at the Grassroots in Southern Africa

20. Bessie House-Midamba, Class Development and Gender Inequality in Kenya, 1963-1990